Rich Dad

My poor dad often said, "What you know is important." My rich dad said, "If you want to be rich, <u>who</u> you know is more important than <u>what</u> you know."

Rich Dad explained further saying, "Business and investing are team sports." The average investor or small-business person loses financially because they do not have a team. Instead of a team, they act as individuals who are trampled by very smart teams.

That is why the Rich Dad's Advisors book series was created. Rich Dad's Advisors will offer guidance to help you know who to look for and what kind of questions to ask so you can gather your own great team of advisors.

Other Bestselling Books
by Robert T. Kiyosaki with Sharon L. Lechter

Rich Dad Poor Dad
What The Rich Teach Their Kids About Money -
That The Poor And Middle Class Do Not!

Rich Dad's CASHFLOW Quadrant
Rich Dad's Guide To Financial Freedom

Rich Dad's Guide to Investing
What The Rich Invest In, That The
Poor and Middle Class Do Not!

Rich Dad's Rich Kid Smart Kid
Give Your Child A Financial Head Start

Rich Dad's Retire Young Retire Rich
How To Get Rich Quickly And Stay Rich Forever

Rich Dad's Prophecy
Why The Biggest Stock Market Crash In History Is Still Coming...
And How You Can Prepare Yourself And Profit From It!

Rich Dad's Success Stories
Real Life Success Stories from Real Life People
Who Followed the Rich Dad Lessons

Rich Dad's Guide To Becoming Rich
Without Cutting Up Your Credit Cards
Turn "Bad Debt" into "Good Debt"

Rich Dad's Who Took My Money?
Why Slow Investors Lose and Fast Money Wins!

Rich Dad Poor Dad for Teens
The Secrets About Money -
That You Don't Learn in School!

Rich Dad's Escape from the Rat Race
How to Become a Rich Kid by Following Rich Dad's Advice

Other Bestselling Books by
Rich Dad's Advisors

Protecting Your #1 Asset
Creating Fortunes from Your Ideas
An Intellectual Property Handbook
by Michael Lechter, Esq.

SalesDogs®
You do not have to be an attack dog to be successful in sales
by Blair Singer, Sales Communication Specialist

Own Your Own Corporation
Why the rich own their own companies and
everyone else works for them
by Garrett Sutton, Esq.

How to Buy and Sell a Business
How You Can Win in the Business Quadrant
by Garrett Sutton, Esq.

The ABC's of Building a Business Team That Wins
The invisible Code of Honor that takes ordinary people
and turns them into a championship team
by Blair Singer, Sales Communication Specialist

The ABC's of Real Estate Investing
The secrets of finding hidden
profits most investors miss
by Ken McElroy

The ABC's of Getting Out of Debt
Trade your bad debt for good debt
and your bad credit for good credit
by Garrett Sutton, Esq.

OPM

OTHER PEOPLE'S MONEY

How to attract Other People's
Money for your investments - the
ultimate leverage

Michael A. Lechter, ESQ.

WARNER
BUSINESS
BOOKS™

NEW YORK   BOSTON

Published by Warner Books in association with CASHFLOW® Technologies, Inc., and BI Capital Inc.

CASHFLOW, Rich Dad, Rich Dad's Advisors, Rich Dad's Seminars, Journey to Financial Freedom, the BI Triangle, and CASHFLOW Quadrant (ESBI Symbol) are registered trademarks of CASHFLOW® Technologies, Inc. Rich Kid Smart Kid, Rich Dad Australia, Rich Dad's Coaching, are trademarks of CASHFLOW® Technologies, Inc.

 are registered trademarks of CASHFLOW® Technologies, Inc.

Visit our Web site at www.richdad.com and www.mlechter.com

"From Ideas to Assets" is a service mark and trademark of Michael A. Lechter. "Building Forts and Fighting Pirates" is a registered trademark of Michael A. Lechter.

Warner Business Books
Warner Books

Time Warner Book Group, 1271 Avenue of the Americas, New York, NY 10020.
Visit our Web site at: www.twbookmark.com.

The Warner Business Books logo is a trademark of Warner Books.

Printed in the United States of America

First Edition: April 2005
10 9 8 7 6 5 4 3 2 1

Library of Congress Cataloging-in-Publication Data

Lechter, Michael A.
    OPM : other people's money : how to attract other people's money for your investments—the ultimate leverage / Michael A. Lechter.—1st ed.
        p.   cm.—(Rich dad's advisors)
    Includes bibliographical references and index.
    ISBN 0-446-69185-2 (alk. paper)
    1. Business enterprises—Finance.   2. Intellectual property.   3. Venture capital.   4. Business enterprises—Finance—Law and legislation—United States.   I. Title : Other people's money.   II. Rich dad's advisors series.

    HG4026.L387   2005
    658.15'224—dc22

                                                            2004029439

Acknowledgments

This book was a long time in coming. But for the support and assistance of a number of people, it would not have come at all: my lovely wife, Sharon Lechter, who kept me on task; my friend, colleague, and former client, Bob Bosserman, who graciously shared his expertise and experiences on the process of raising capital from friends, family, Angels, and venture capitalists; my friend and colleague Bob Weidenbaum, who not only lent me his eyes, but also provided materials for the chapters on financial institutions and grants; and my friends and colleagues at Square Sanders & Dempsey L.L.P., and in particular, Chris Johnson and Greg Hall, securities and corporate finance attorneys par excellence, who figure so prominently in the chapter on securities law.

I also acknowledge my good friend Robert Kiyosaki for the foreword to this book, and the folks at Warner Books for their patience with my crazy schedule.

Contents

Foreword

In training his son and me to become leaders, my rich dad would often say, "Raising capital is a fundamental skill of a leader." When I was a young boy, this statement did not make much sense. As I got older, however, I began to realize the wisdom in his words.

Remember, cash flow is the foundation on which any successful business is built. The ability to raise the capital—money or its equivalent—necessary for starting and growing a business is an essential element for the success of that business. A successful business owner must have a strategy to make sure that he or she has access to the resources that his or her business needs when it needs them.

You can have a great product or service, be very successful in the marketplace, and still not have a successful business. I know about this from firsthand experience. My wallet company introduced a product that was phenomenally successful in the marketplace. Before we knew it, orders for the product far exceeded our manufacturing capacity. We did not have the resources to meet demand. Having more business than you can handle sounds like a great situation to be in, but this was a problem for us. Unfortunately, we had decided not to patent the product—I had thought getting a patent was too expensive—and while we were out looking for resources, the competition stole our market share. We had failed to lay the foundation and plan a strategy for getting the resources that we needed in a time frame to be successful. Of course, I always learn from my mistakes.

Unfortunately, many businesses that fail, fail due to a lack of enough money. Many, if not most, business owners underestimate how much money or capital they will need to start and grow their company to the point where it can fund itself.

In this book, Michael Lechter points out that you do not have to start with money to make money, and that you can make money—acquire an asset, turn an idea into a fortune, or build a business—using OTHER People's Money (OPM) and Other People's Resources (OPR).

I know from firsthand experience that this is true. You don't need to spend your own money to build a business.

CASHFLOW Technologies, Inc. (CTI)—the Rich Dad organization—is a perfect example. Sharon Lechter, my wife, Kim, and I built CTI using very little of our own money. We were also able to avoid giving away the company in order to raise capital. Michael Lechter was our advisor. We looked for opportunities to create intellectual property. Then we took that intellectual property, made sure that it was properly protected (like I said, I always learn from my mistakes), and leveraged the intellectual property into marketplace credibility and strategic partnerships. In sum, we applied strategies that Michael discusses in this book to build CTI using primarily other people's resources—OPR. In the book Michael tells a story about "IMA, LLC," a business built from scratch around an idea for a new kitchen appliance. I've never been a short-order cook, and I know nothing about kitchen appliances, but I really identify with Ivan, the inventor of the kitchen appliance, who started with nothing but an idea (and no money) and ended up a principal of a thriving business. I see a great many parallels between IMA's strategy for success and that of the Rich Dad organization.

Of course, the OPR approach is only one of the approaches to building a business that Michael covers in the book. Sometimes a business just plain has to raise money. When you look at presidents of major universities, one of their primary duties is to raise money from alumni and corporate sponsors. Religious leaders are constantly finding ways to raise money for the construction of bigger buildings or other church projects. A charity's success or failure is often dependent upon the ability of the leader to raise money from donors. Those folks have it easy. An entrepreneur raising money for a business must also be concerned about the price of that money. One of an entrepreneur's primary jobs is to raise money from private investors, the stock market, and from customers. However, the trick is to do it without giving away the company in return. The discussions of developing a strategy for fund-raising and the timing of fund-raising efforts are a must read for anyone starting or building a business.

This is more than a book about simply raising money. It is really about a fundamental skill of successful leaders. Michael Lechter has done an excellent job of pointing out not only the many different ways of raising money, but also how to raise and use other people's money legally without giving away the store. Whether you are a business, political, charitable, religious, or educational leader, your ability to raise OPM is essential to your success. That is why I am thrilled to have this most important book join the Rich Dad Advisor series.

Robert Kiyosaki

Introduction

How many times have you heard someone say that "it takes money to make money"? That's not entirely true. While cash flow is the foundation of every successful business, it does not mean that you have to start with money to make money—or that you have to use your own.

The fact of the matter is that you can make money—acquire an asset, turn an idea into a fortune, or build a business—using *Other* People's Money (OPM) and Other People's Resources . . . (OPR).

Are we saying that you can just hold out your hand and OPM will magically appear? No, of course not. But if you have a good idea or business concept and are willing to do your homework and build a proper foundation in preparation for your quest for financing, OPM—in one or more of its many forms—is often available.

Will you have to give up control of your business if you use OPM? No, you will not. And there are a number of different types and sources of OPM. By strategically choosing the appropriate types of OPM, and strategically timing fund-raising efforts, you can build your business but minimize loss of control.

This book will detail and discuss the different types and forms of OPM as well as how to find it, the consequences of using it, the legal aspects and potential pitfalls, and the advantages and disadvantages. And perhaps most important: when and how to use OPM without giving away the store.

If you've ever felt limited by your own wherewithal, this book will empower you. It will help you overcome one of the greatest obstacles you think you have: finding a way to fund your business or ideas.

In *Protecting Your #1 Asset*, my earlier contribution to the Rich Dad's Advisors series, we discussed how to turn an idea into an asset: how to lay the foundation for building a business around an idea or leveraging the idea into a fortune. The present book was written to banish the myth that it takes money to make money. As we will discuss, a million-dollar idea *always* —using OPM when and where it's needed—has a shot at delivering a million-dollar return.

As you read this book, you may find a few instances where material seems to be covered more than once in different contexts. Although I tried to be selective about repeating material, I have attempted to accommodate those people who might want to refer to particular sections and chapters out of context. You will also come across numerous references to securities laws. While it would never occur to most people, most passive (nonmanagement) investments in businesses come under the securities law. We touch on some of the requirements and the limitations on your activities imposed by securities law. I hope that after reading this book, you will be able to identify most significant securities law issues—which you can refer to a securities lawyer for resolution. However, the specifics of the securities law are beyond the scope of this book.

The fact is that I attempted to provide a reader-friendly discussion of the securities law in the initial draft of this book. Unfortunately, that version of the manuscript weighed in at more than six hundred pages—a bit much for most people. And any securities issues would still best be referred to a competent attorney. So we took the more detailed discussion of the securities law out of this book.

Chapter 1

What Is OPM?
What Is OPR?

Getting Out of the Rat Race and Navigating the CASHFLOW Quadrant Using OPM

How do you get out of the rat race? The Rich Dad answer is to put your money to work for you instead of you working for money. You do that by investing in or creating income-producing assets. When the monthly income from those assets—passive income—exceeds your monthly expenses, you're financially free. You have made it out of the rat race.

Now, you have choices. You can continue to work at your job (or a different job) because you want to, not because you have to. Or if you choose, you can quit your job without changing your lifestyle.

Rich Dad talks about three basic types of assets: real estate, paper assets (e.g., stocks and bonds), and businesses. There is also a fourth type of asset: intellectual property, the intangible asset that results from creativity, innovation, know-how, good relationships, and reputation. Most of the time, intellectual property is part and parcel of a business and is considered part of the business asset. However, there are occasions when the intellectual property is itself an asset even without an associated business.

People go about building or acquiring assets in different ways—based, at least in part, on their past experiences and what they have been taught about money. *Rich Dad's CASHFLOW Quadrant* describes four general categories of people with respect to the world of money: the E, employee; the S, self-employed or small business owner; the B, big business owner; and the I, investor.

- The E (employee) relies on earned income from his or her job, believing that he or she is most secure by letting his or her employer "take the risks."
- The S (self-employed or small business owner) owns a business, but the business relies primarily on the time, efforts, and attention of that individual. There is typically no team of advisors and little, if any, leverage of the individual's time and expertise.
- The B (big business) leverages (a) the owner's expertise (and that of the business's team of advisors), (b) other intellectual property, and (c) resources through systems and legal relationships. In this way, the big business, in effect, uses Other People's Time and effort (OPT)— e.g., that of the business's employees and/or strategic "co-venturers."

- The I (investor) takes a more passive role and puts his or her money to work to generate more money (typically passive or portfolio income) and will often leverage his or her money (e.g., using "good debt").

Co-Venture

We use the term "co-venture" to cover not only actual business entities, such as partnerships, corporations, limited liability companies, limited partnerships, and the like, but also virtual business entities created through contractual relationships, such as licenses and profit-sharing arrangements, or through informal strategic business alliances. "Co-venturers" are the participants in the "co-venture."

There is nothing intrinsically good or evil with any of the four categories. There are, at least from my perspective, certain advantages to the S category over the E, and the B and I categories over the E and S, but it really is a matter of choice.

Of course, many people fall within more than one category. For example, people invest income earned as employees in paper assets, such as the stock market, or rental properties all the time. Other people work as employees during the day and build a part-time, home-based, or Web-based business during off-hours. In any event, an individual can develop and accumulate his or her own wealth to use, to acquire, or to build income-producing assets.

It takes the average person time to accumulate wealth. People tend to view the resources that they have to invest as limited to what they have been able to save. However, *you are not limited by your own resources*. You can use Other People's Money (OPM) and Other People's Resources (OPR), which is actually a form of OPM. Instead of expending money to grow your business, you let someone else build it *for you* with his or her resources and/or money.

Generally, use of OPM and OPR is found on the right side of the CASH-FLOW Quadrant. However, an individual can use OPM to navigate through the CASHFLOW Quadrant—to move from the E to the S, B, and/or I quadrant. Likewise, a business entity can use OPM and OPR to move from the S to the B and/or I quadrant, to grow, to take advantage of opportunities, and to become rich.

Expanding Beyond Your Own Resources: OPM and OPR

The basic concept of OPM is simple: You (as an individual or business entity) acquire or build income-producing assets—your business—by using money from sources other than your own.

Are you aware of people using OPM? Of course you are, although you may think of the use of OPM by another name.

Have *you* ever used OPM? You may not realize it, but the chances are good that you have.

Have you ever been in the position where you wanted to purchase a piece of rental property but could not just write a check for the purchase price? Did the fact that you couldn't pay cash mean that the property was out of your reach? No. You would typically go to the bank and get a loan. Getting a loan in order to acquire a rental property is a classical use of OPM. The bank that loaned you the money is the source of OPM. (What if you couldn't qualify for a loan? Throughout this book, we will discuss any number of other forms of OPM that you can use instead of getting a loan or in addition to getting a loan.)

The concept of using OPM applies to more than just real estate. Let's say you have an idea and want to build a business around it but don't have the money to go forward. Or you have a number of ideas and a number of opportunities, but you don't have enough money for all of them. Does the fact that you don't have the money mean that the business opportunity is out of your reach? Do you necessarily have to choose between opportunities? Not at all. OPM makes going forward possible. You use Other People's Money or Other People's Resources to build the business and pursue the opportunities. How do you do that? That's what this book is all about.

Forms and Sources of OPM

OPM can take a number of different forms and come from many different types of sources. In general, OPM is either direct or indirect (i.e., OPR) and tends to be categorized in terms of the particular consideration (payback) that you have to give in return for the OPM. The basic categories of OPM are "debt," "equity," and what I refer to in general terms as "in-kind."

The more conventional approaches to using OPM to start up or build a business involve raising money and are sometimes referred to as "capital formation" or "raising capital." They typically involve taking some form of loan (debt) or selling an ownership interest (equity) in your business.

Certain sources of OPM tend to come immediately to mind: high-net-worth individual investors (e.g., "Angels"), financial institutions and funds (e.g., investment banks, commercial banks, savings and loan associations, insurance companies, pension funds, credit unions, venture capital firms), and equity offerings (e.g., ownership interest offered for sale to investors), such as private placements and public offerings. However, there are other sources of OPM that may not be so apparent. These include credit card companies (your personal account or that of your business entity), your friends and family, co-venturers (e.g., vendors that provide favorable credit/ payment terms), customers (through advance payments), and government lending programs or grants.

SOURCES OF CAPITAL

- Income from other sources
- Enterprise cash flow
- Sale / Rental / Licensing of assets
  (physical and/or intellectual property)
- Accumulated funds / savings
- Gifts
- Grants (from government, foundations, etc)
- Loans
- Sale of equity in business

Co-venture - acquire virtual resources

Other People's Money, however, can also be provided indirectly—called "in-kind." Instead of providing money directly, other people provide specific services or resources that you would otherwise have to pay for. In other words, you are using Other People's Resources—OPR. Strategic use of OPR can often be the easiest way to get started and the fastest route for a business to get to the "big time."

OPR—INDIRECT OPM

Other People's Money (OPM) and Other People's Resources (OPR) are flip sides of the same coin. With OPM, you build your business by using money from other people. With OPR, you build your business by using resources paid for by other people—indirectly using the OPM that went to develop or acquire the resource.

You can think of the relationship between OPM and OPR like this (let's ignore the issue of "payback" for now): If someone provides you the money so that you can buy a ticket to the movies, that is use of OPM. If that someone actually pays for your ticket or buys the ticket and then provides it to you so that you can go to the movies, that is use of OPR (the ticket is the resource). Using either OPM or OPR gets you into the movie. And, in either case, you get the use of the other person's money to do so.

Use of OPR typically involves some form of co-venture—for example, a contractual relationship, formation of a joint venture, or a strategic alliance. By "co-venturing," you can acquire virtual resources, virtual employees, virtual manufacturing capacity, virtual distribution channels, and so on. You get the benefit of the virtual resources without having to spend the time, effort, and money to develop them yourself.

We will discuss how you can build a business with OPR later.

The Benefits of Using OPM

OPM LETS YOU DO THINGS YOU WOULD OTHERWISE NOT BE ABLE TO DO

Using OPM opens the door to opportunities for you. It permits you to participate in "deals" that would otherwise be beyond your resources. It allows you to start up the business of your dreams even though you do not have the means. It permits you to make choices that you otherwise could not make. It permits you to be able to afford opportunities instead of saying "I can't afford it." In other words, it lets you play in the game.

OPM BUYS YOU TIME—IT LETS YOU DO THINGS BEFORE YOU WOULD OTHERWISE BE ABLE TO DO THEM

Have you ever heard the term "window of opportunity"? There are many times when you take advantage of an opportunity only if you can move quickly enough. Using OPM can sometimes let you move quickly enough to take advantage of opportunities that you would otherwise miss. For example, let's say that you find a potential rental property that is worth $2 million, but the seller is asking only $1 million for it. You know that the "window of opportunity" is short—as soon as the word gets out, someone else will gobble up the property.

Let's assume that you don't have $1 million in your checking account. Realistically, what are your options? Think about it. How long would it take you to save $1 million? Even if you had a million dollars in certain fixed assets, how long would it take you to sell those assets to get the money? If you are like most people, it will take you a while—and probably longer than it would take for someone else to come along and purchase the property. Now ask yourself these questions: How long would it take you to borrow $1 million? How long would it take you to find someone to go in with you on the property (a co-venturer)? Using OPM gives you a realistic shot at being able to purchase the property before the window of opportunity shuts.

The same type of situation occurs all the time in other types of businesses. Perhaps you have an opportunity for a huge contract to supply goods to a third party. The problem is that you cannot afford to manufacture the goods because you have virtually nothing in the way of liquid assets. Your business may miss that window of opportunity if you have to rely on your own resources alone.

OPM LETS YOU LEVERAGE YOUR RESOURCES—AND DO MORE WITH WHAT YOU HAVE

When you acquire or build an asset using certain forms of OPM, you can get the full benefit of the appreciation in value of the asset, even though it was acquired or built using OPM. In fact, OPM and OPR can accelerate the appreciation in the asset. Again, a classic example of this is when you take a loan to purchase a rental property. Let's say that you put up 25 percent of the purchase price and borrow the rest from the bank. If the value of that rental property appreciates, you get 100 percent of the appreciation, even though your actual cash outlay was only 25 percent of the purchase price.

The same is true when you take a loan to build a business. If the value of the business increases, even though it was built with OPM, you get the full benefit of the appreciation.

Another example is when you use OPR to build a business. If the value of the business (e.g., the goodwill associated with the business and its trademarks) increases, even though the increased value was entirely due to the use of OPR, you can get the full benefit of the appreciation. We will discuss how this is done in Chapter 3.

OPM CAN LET YOU SPREAD THE RISK AND OBLIGATIONS

Some opportunities may present a bigger bite than you want to chew. Some opportunities present huge potential returns but also present real risks of failure. Not every venture is successful. There may be a vacancy problem with rental properties. Your new product might not sell as well as, or as quickly as, you anticipate. Maybe the size of the rental payments on the office space that the business will have to lease scares you. Even though you may be able to self-fund the venture, you may not want to risk the entire amount. You can often spread that risk by bringing in co-venturers.

The Cost of OPM

OPM is an immensely powerful tool for building your business. Great benefits can be achieved. But just like any other tool, there is typically a price for using it. The specific benefits and costs differ depending upon the particular type and source of OPM that you use. For example, you might have to pay interest or give up either a partial ownership interest in your business or some of the profits that you would otherwise make. If you use your own funds, you would not have that cost (but you would not get the benefits of using Other People's Money).

There are a number of aspects to the price you pay for using OPM. There are both short-term costs and long-term costs. The price can be monetary or nonmonetary—such as additional obligations and responsibilities or giving up a modicum of independence or control of the business. Generally, the more risk perceived by the investor, the greater the percentage of the rewards and more say-so in the control of the business the investor will expect. The trick is to choose the right form(s) of OPM for your particular circumstances and make sure that the costs are acceptable.

You also need to plan ahead and recognize that early fund-raising activities can affect your ability to raise additional funds when you need them to grow your business in the future. Strategizing when to use OPM is as important as considerations of the benefits and costs of using OPM. If you don't plan correctly, you can end up giving away the store.

The benefits from using OPM are very often well worth paying the price. In some cases, you can think of the cost as an entry fee to let you play the game. Even though you might have to give up a portion of your business or profits, even a small percentage of a large number can be much greater than 100 percent of a small number. Because of leveraging, this is particularly true if the only reason you were able to take advantage of an opportunity was by using OPM. Remember, 100 percent of a venture that doesn't go forward is zero.

Alternative Approaches to Dealing with Capital Needs

What are your options when you discover that the costs of an opportunity are beyond your resources?

- One option is to simply forgo (at least temporarily) the opportunity.
- Another option is to try to accumulate the necessary resources yourself (e.g., sell or rent assets and save the money) and hope that the opportunity will still be there if and when you finally accumulate the funds.
- The third option—and the subject of this book—is to use Other People's Money and Other People's Resources.

With this third option, you seek an "infusion of resources" from an out-side source. That infusion can be in a number of different forms. It can be a direct contribution of money or an indirect contribution of money (OPR). The OPM can be in the form of credit or a loan (debt) or in payment for an ownership interest (equity) in the business. Or, when you use OPR, you ob-tain access to the specific resources that you need to go forward (through a strategic co-venture) in return for some other consideration, such as a share of profits or bartered services.

As noted above, each form of OPM has its distinct advantages and dis-advantages. Basically, the issues relate to (a) availability, the criteria that you must meet in order to attract the OPM, and (b) the cost of the OPM. The different forms of OPM and OPR are not mutually exclusive. You can choose different combinations (at the same time or sequentially) of forms of OPM depending upon the circumstances.

There is a strategy for determining whether to use your own money or OPM, and for determining how much and the most appropriate form or combination of forms of OPM to seek (debt, sale of equity, and/or co-venture). The pros and cons of the different forms of OPM, and strategies for choosing among them, will be discussed in detail in later sections of this book.

Pitfalls to Be Avoided

There are also potential hazards for the unwary (or cheap or lazy) in the process of raising capital. Most significant, people often get into trouble by failing to properly document transactions and/or by inadvertently violating the federal and/or state laws governing securities.

WRITTEN AGREEMENTS

It is always important to have clear written agreements to prevent misunderstandings in the future. This is particularly true when dealing with family and friends. If an investment is not properly documented—if there is no comprehensive written agreement—it is very easy for legitimate misunderstandings to occur. Over and above that, it is an unfortunate fact of life that memories tend to be selective—some people remember what they want to remember.

Folks who don't bother with written agreements tend to get to know litigation attorneys very well, and, as a result, the savings from being cheap are lost.

THE SECURITIES LAWS CAN BITE YOU

A vast array of both federal and state statutes and regulations deal with the sale of securities. These laws are far from intuitive. It is all too easy to unknowingly violate those laws, particularly when you are dealing with friends and family. What is a security? As often as not, people don't even realize that they are dealing with a "security." Few people realize it, but most passive investments in businesses (as opposed to those that involve active roles in business management) are considered securities. For example, it would not occur to most people that when they send an e-mail asking their cousin George for money to help fund their business, they are probably asking him to invest in a security.

The consequences of failing to comply with the securities laws can be severe—and then some. Penalties can include payment of substantial fines. The "then some" may even include prison sentences. At a minimum, you would be vulnerable to the potentially significant claims of "aggrieved" investors. You may well be required to pay equity investors back their investment as well as other losses that they may have incurred. And more than that, if there is a securities law violation, having a limited liability business entity may not shield your personal assets, and liabilities for securities law violations are not dischargeable in bankruptcy.

When do you need to worry about the securities laws? What types of transactions fall under the securities laws? And if your transaction is under those laws, what is required of you? We will discuss these issues in more detail later in this book, and we will try to put the use of OPM and OPR in perspective by looking at a few alternative scenarios in the next few chapters.

Chapter 2

Using Traditional OPM to Start a Business

Types of Business Entities

Before we get into the meat of using OPM, we need to set the stage by covering some background material. One piece of that background material is business entities. A business can be organized in a number of different forms (types of business entity). The form of your business can have a major impact on your ability to obtain access to OPM and OPR. For example, a savvy investor will not put money into your business if making the investment will place all of the investor's assets at risk. A savvy investor is looking for a certain

Cast of Characters

Let's define some terms.

We will refer to the entities that own the business as the "principals," "owners," or "equity participants" in the business.

The entities that *initially* form the business will be referred to as the "founders."

> Individuals who are actively seeking to raise capital for an enterprise will sometimes be referred to as "promoters."
>
> Entities that make contributions to the business after it has been formed will be referred to as "investors," "co-venturers," or "lenders." We will refer to monetary investments by anyone who does not actively participate in the management of the company as "outside money."

growth (return on investment) and benefits from your business, and expects to be able to exit ("harvest" the investment and return) in a certain manner within a particular time frame. The form of business organization that you choose can affect the potential liability of the participants in the business, the potential for growth and benefits, and the availability of certain "exit" strategies.

One of the subjects we will also cover is the prospect of an investor taking an "equity" (ownership) interest in your business. The terminology used to refer to an equity interest differs depending upon the form of business organization involved. A quick review of the different types of business entities is probably in order.

Some types of business entities have a life of their own—as far as liability goes, they are treated by the law as a separate entity from the individual owners. These types of business are referred to, in general, as "statutory entities" (because there is a statute that permits them to be created) or "limited liability entities" (because the owners are not necessarily liable for the acts of the business). For example, a corporation, a limited liability company (LLC), and a limited partnership (LP) are types of statutory entities. There are specific formalities that must be followed in order to create and maintain a limited liability entity.

On the other hand, some business entities are "informal." They are just "there" based on the fact that you are doing business. As far as the law is concerned, these entities are just the alter ego of the owner(s). Examples are sole proprietorships and general partnerships.

SOLE PROPRIETORSHIP

Anytime you, as a single individual, own a business without going through the specific formalities required to create a statutory entity, the business is (by default) a sole proprietorship.

For liability purposes as well as tax purposes, the business is the alter ego of the sole proprietor. As a general proposition, a proprietor (owner) is personally responsible for the debts and obligations of the business as well as for the actions of employees. If the owner of the sole proprietorship sells someone an interest of less than 100 percent of the business, the business becomes a partnership (unless specific steps are taken to create a limited liability entity).

GENERAL PARTNERSHIP

When you share the profits and losses of a business with one or more other individuals (or other entities), unless you have formally created a statutory entity, the business is (by default) a general partnership.

For liability purposes, a business is considered the alter ego of *each* of the partners. Any general partner can bind the business to an agreement, and each partner is liable for the acts of the others. A general partner's liability is not limited to that partner's percentage of ownership. In more legalistic terms, each general partner is "jointly and severally" liable for the debts and obligations of the partnership. This means that each partner could be held personally liable for the entire amount of the partnership debt and obligations, and all of their personal assets are at risk.

While not required by law, partners typically enter into a written "partnership agreement" to define the internal rules under which the partnership will operate and allocation of profits and losses. In the absence of a partnership agreement, each partner has an equal say in management, and profits and losses are typically divided equally among the partners.

Equity interests in a partnership are typically referred to in terms of percentages of ownership or "units" corresponding to a percentage of ownership. There usually isn't any sort of certificate or "instrument" (other than perhaps the partnership agreement) representing ownership interests.

CORPORATION

A corporation is a legal entity that you can create under the laws of a particular jurisdiction (usually under state law in the United States). The corporate entity is defined by certain documents—Articles of Incorporation (also referred to as a Charter in some jurisdictions) that are filed with the designated state agency to "give birth to" the new corporate entity and "by-laws" that define the internal rules under which the corporation operates.

There Are Different Kinds of Stock

Let's say your business is a corporation and you have decided to raise money through selling stock—equity ownership shares—in your business to your investor in return for that ownership. As with most subjects we are covering, there are choices to be made. You can offer different types of stock in your company. There are two primary categories: common stock and preferred stock.

Common Stock

When people talk about stock, they are most likely talking about common stock. Common stock represents ownership in a company and a right to a portion of profits from that company. Typically, owners of common stock get one vote per share of common stock they own to elect the board of directors members, who in turn oversee the management and operations of the company.

Profits of the company are sometimes paid out in the form of dividends to the common stock holders. However, these dividends usually occur only when the company is profitable, and the "when, if, and how much" related to the dividends are determined by the board of directors. Dividends on common stock are not guaranteed.

Owners of common stock get the benefits of increases in value as the company grows. And likewise, the value of their ownership decreases if the company is unsuccessful. So ownership in common stock may provide the greatest upside potential to your investors, but it may also provide the greatest risk of loss if your business does not succeed. The common stock owners are typically the "last in line" when a business fails. The creditors (including attorneys, accountants, and employees), bondholders, and preferred stock holders are paid first and the common stock holders are entitled only to what is left.

Even though common stock generally gives you one vote per share of stock, there are other types of common stock. You might issue different "classes" of common stock. For example, you find that you need additional funding to complete your second phase of growth. You have an investor who is ready to invest but has no interest in voting rights. Rather than issuing your normal common stock, you can issue a Class B of Common Stock, which will have no voting rights attached to them. Or you can decide to invest additional money into stock and issue a Class C of Common Stock that has ten votes per share. What would that look like?

Class A—one vote per share
Class B—no votes per share
Class C—ten votes per share

Why would you want to do this? As the founder of the company, you may want to maintain control over the business. Typically, you would issue to the public the class of shares with the fewest number of votes attached to them. In contrast, you would want to reserve the class of shares with the highest number of votes per share for yourself or close team.

While this may sound perfectly reasonable and sensible from your (founder's) perspective, remember that your investors may question why they are investing dollars for less voting rights than other investors. Savvy investors may be more interested in preferred stock instead of different classes of common stock.

Preferred Stock

Preferred stock is the second most common type of stock. While it gives the investor ownership in the company, preferred stock generally does not come with the same voting rights of the common stock. However, the label of "preferred" stock is due to the various attributes of the stock that set it apart from common stock. Some of those attributes are:

- Preferred stock pays a fixed dividend (except when the company cannot afford to pay the dividend, .and in that case, there are typically relief provisions).

- Preferred stock holders have a greater claim (higher priority) than common stock holders on the company assets.
- Preferred stock holders receive their dividends first.

There are also different types of preferred stock which may provide you greater flexibility in attracting investors:

- Participating preferred stock. The dividend payments for this stock will typically be greater if the business turns a larger profit than anticipated.
- Convertible preferred stock. These shares have the right to be converted into common stock.
- Cumulative preferred stock. These shares will "accumulate" the dividends due the stockholder when a periodic dividend payment is missed due to financial problems.
- Noncumulative preferred stock. These shares will not "accumulate" the dividends due the stockholder if one dividend payment is missed.
- Callable preferred stock. These shares may give the management the option to purchase the preferred shares back from the shareholders at any time for any reason and usually at a premium.

In reviewing the different types of preferred stock, it may look more like debt than equity ownership. However, it may be advantageous to have preferred stock in lieu of debt so that you can manage your debt to equity ratio. If your business needs bank financing for equipment or other business operations, the bank may closely watch your debt to equity ratio to justify its loans to you. Banks usually prefer to see as low a debt to equity ratio as possible—which means the investors are investing in the business through ownership and share the risk and possible reward as the business grows.

There are other stock options and rights that are available for use in attracting investors, but common and preferred stock are the most typical and attract the highest amount of Other People's Money. Options (the right to purchase X number of shares in your company at

> some point in the future) produce only a fraction of the investment that selling the underlying stock generates.
>
> A carefully planned combination of common and preferred stock should provide you with the equity financing you need, provide the investors the investment opportunity and return on that investment they require, and the operational control necessary for growing your business.

A corporation is managed by a board of directors, which is headed by the chairman of the board and various officers, usually including a chief executive officer (CEO) and/or president, a secretary, and a treasurer.

Equity interests in a corporation are referred to as "stock" or "shares." There are typically written certificates (instruments) representing the interests. Not surprisingly, the owners of incorporation are referred to as "shareholders" or "stockholders." The shareholders are liable only to the extent of their contribution to business. In other words, if the corporation has a liability, the stockholders' investment in the corporation is at risk, but not the stockholders' other assets.

In the United States, the tax laws have created two species of corporations: the C corporation and the S corporation. A C corporation is taxed as an entity separate and apart from its shareholders. An S corporation is, for tax purposes, treated as an extension of the shareholders in which profits and losses "flow through" (are allocated) to the shareholders according to percentage ownership. There are, however, certain limitations on the classes of stock and number and types of shareholders permitted in an S corporation (no more than seventy-five shareholders, no nonresident aliens, and, as a general rule, only natural persons, except for certain trusts).

LIMITED PARTNERSHIP (LP)
Like a corporation, a limited partnership is a legal entity that you would create under the laws of a particular jurisdiction (typically under state law in the United States).

The limited partnership is defined by certain documents—specifically, a

Certificate of Limited Partnership that is filed with a designated state agency to "give birth to" the new business entity and limited partnership agreement, which defines the internal rules under which the corporation operates.

The limited partnership has one or more "general partners" and one or more "limited partners." The general partners are responsible for managing the partnership. The limited partners are essentially passive investors. Limited partners can have certain very limited veto and/or approval rights over certain actions, but any substantial right to be actively involved with the management or operation of the partnership will convert their status to a general partner.

General partners are, as in a general partnership, jointly and severally liable with respect to debts of the partnership. The limited partners are liable only to the extent of their partnership interest in the business. In other words, if the limited partnership has a liability, all of the general partners' assets are at risk. But other than the limited partners' investment in the business, the limited partners' assets are isolated from liability.

Often, in practice, limited partnerships have a single corporate general partner. By employing a corporation as general partner, only the assets of the corporation (and not those of the individual shareholders in the corporation) are at risk for liability of the limited partnership.

A limited partnership is, for tax purposes, treated as an extension of the shareholders, and profits and losses "flow through" (are allocated) to the shareholders according to the partnership agreement.

Equity interests in a limited partnership are typically referred to in terms of percentages of ownership or "units" corresponding to a percentage of ownership. There usually isn't any sort of certificate or "instrument" (other than perhaps the partnership agreement) representing ownership interests.

LIMITED LIABILITY COMPANY (LLC)

A limited liability company, like a corporation, is a form of business entity that you would create under the laws of a particular jurisdiction (e.g., in a U.S. state). The LLC is owned by "members" and is run by one or more "managers."

The entity is created by filing a document referred to as Articles of Organization with an appropriate agency and entering into an "operating agreement" between the members.

The LLC provides limited liability protection to its members in the same way that a corporation provides limited liability protection to its shareholders; members are liable only to the extent of their contribution to LLC.

For tax purposes, the LLC, like the S corporation, provides flow-through of profits and loss to the members. However, while the S corporation is limited to apportioning the profit and loss in accordance with percentage ownership, the LLC is more flexible. Profit and loss can be allocated (separate and apart from management responsibilities) by the operating agreement. The LLC also has the advantage of not being subject to the limitations on numbers and types of owners that are imposed on S corporations. In comparison to a limited partnership, an LLC provides the same flow-through tax treatment, without imposing a limitation on the extent to which the participants can exert management control without losing the benefit of limited liability.

Equity interests in an LLC are typically referred to in terms of percentages of ownership or "units" corresponding to a percentage of ownership. There usually isn't any sort of certificate or "instrument" (other than perhaps the operating agreement) representing ownership interests.

For more details, see the Rich Dad's Advisors book *Own Your Own Corporation,* by Garrett Sutton, Esq. (Warner Books, 2001).

Investments in a Business Can Take Many Forms

A business is typically formed by one or more entities—individuals or other businesses—that each make a contribution to (or an investment in) the business. Those contributions (investments) can be in the form of money or in any number of other forms. In fact, the contributions to the business can relate to any of the elements necessary for its success. Examples of the different types of nonmonetary contributions that may lead to success include resources, leadership, and intellectual property, such as ideas, noteworthy skills, know-how, expertise, reputation and credibility, or connections and the like. If you are a principal of a business, the contributions to the business by the other principals is OPM or OPR as far as you are concerned.

Initial contributions by principals are typically made in return for, at least in part, an equity interest (otherwise, they would not be principals).

The nature of an "equity interest" depends upon the type of business entity involved.

Subsequent contributions by principals and contributions by investors and co-venturers are usually categorized by the particular consideration (type of payback) that you have agreed to in return for the contribution. For example, OPM can be in the form of a loan (debt); in payment for an ownership interest (equity); or in return for a portion of your profits or bartered services.

Relative Value of Contributions

One of the issues that always seem to arise when more than one entity makes a contribution to a business is the relative value of the contributions. What percentage ownership of your business should an equity investor get in return for a contribution? The answer depends on the valuation of your business.

There are standard techniques for valuation of an existing business. There are times when those valuation techniques will be applicable to non-monetary contributions to a start-up business. However, most of the time with start-up businesses, the issue of relative value of contributions is simply a matter of the "credibility" of the contributors and their negotiation skills.

Cash flow or capital is clearly the foundation of a successful business, and there are those who will tell you that there is a special golden rule applicable to business: He who has the gold, rules.

That is not necessarily so. When the business and/or nonmonetary contributors are "credible," they are on a more than equal footing with the money contributors in negotiating the relative values of the contributions.

Money is completely fungible. Aside from the cost of the money (the "consideration" given for the use of the money—e.g., interest, or percentage of the company), money from one source is identical to money from another. Certain other types of contributions, on the other hand, are unique—they are not fungible. These include ideas and other intellectual property, the quality of time and effort put into the business, integrity, reputation, relationships, and management skills. Contributions of these types should not be undervalued.

There are many privately held companies that will not permit someone to participate merely on the basis of contributing money: They must bring something else to the table—such as a needed skill, reputation (to enhance the credibility of the business), or a network of contacts—in order to participate. There are also many franchisers who will not grant a franchise to someone who is merely a passive investor (puts up the money and hires someone else to run the franchise business). Their experience has shown that the business tends to be more successful when the franchisee actively works in the business.

Using Conventional OPM to Start a Business

We will discuss the different forms of OPM and various sources of OPM later. In the meantime, let's look at a few examples illustrating the everyday use of OPM to start a business. These are examples of conventional approaches to OPM—taking some form of loan (debt) and selling an ownership interest (equity) in your business. While we are at it, we will also begin to explore the differences between "debt" and "equity" OPM and revisit the issue of valuation.

EXAMPLE 1: DEBT

Let's start with an example that most everyone is familiar with: taking a mortgage to acquire real estate that you will operate as a rental property. This is an example of acquiring an asset using debt—one form of Other People's Money. You "contribute" a down payment equal to a certain percentage—say, 20 percent of the purchase price of real estate—and take a loan (the mortgage) for the remainder. In other words, you put 20 percent down and the bank funds the rest. The cost of the loan (the OPM) is the interest that you pay to the bank.

From the bank's perspective, return on investment is essentially fixed—that is, the interest that you pay over the life of the loan. Beyond the mortgage payments, the bank has no claim to any profits or appreciation. However, as will be discussed, the bank's risk is also limited.

As long as the net income (gross income less operating expenses) produced by the property exceeds the payments on the loan (known as "debt service"), it is generating positive cash flow and you are ahead of the game. The loan is "good debt." (There may also be tax benefits to factor into the equation, but we will not get into those here.) In addition, while you put up only 20 percent of the purchase price, you leveraged the investment to get full ownership, as well as 100 percent of the profits and 100 percent of any appreciation. In other words, you get 100 percent of the "upside"—the benefits.

However, you also assume 100 percent of the risk. While there are ways to mitigate and limit your risk, as a general proposition you are required to pay back the loan whether or not your property produces income at the expected level and whether or not it appreciates. The bank will not forgive the loan just because your tenant disappears into the night or because the bottom falls out of the real estate market and the value of the property drops to below what you paid for it. The bank could care less if the demagogue political party (I'll let you guess which party I'm talking about) is able to take over the government, raise taxes, ruin the economy, and cause the next Great Depression. The bank certainly will not accept the risk for declining property values. Historically, real estate has appreciated, but the assumption of future appreciation could generate unwelcome surprises in a downturn market.

Limiting Your Risk

• Entity selection. Risk of loss from a venture can sometimes be limited to the amount of the cash investment or value of the property by owning the property through the right form of limited liability business entity or by obtaining a "nonrecourse" loan. ("Nonrecourse" means that the lender feels confident that the property used as collateral for the loan is adequate security, and you are not held personally liable for the loan.) For more information on limited liability business entities, see *Own Your Own Corporation*, by Garrett Sutton, Esq. (Warner Books, 2001), one of the Rich Dad's Advisors series books.

• Profit on the buy. Most successful real estate investors know that a potential property will generate positive cash flow *before* they close on the purchase. *If* the property is generating positive cash flow each and every month, fluctuations in the value of the real estate market will not impact you unless you choose to sell.

• Education. The more you educate yourself about the power of OPM, the better choices you will make and the less risk there will be.

EXAMPLE 2: EQUITY + DEBT

Let's take another example—this time an "equity deal." Assume that you have entered into a contract to purchase the same property and are presently surprised to find out that the property is worth much more than you are paying for it. You are paying only $100,000, but it appraises at $120,000. The bank, however, playing the role of conservative lender, tells you that it is willing to lend only 75 percent of the purchase price of the property. Unfortunately, all the cash that you could come up with from your own resources (having just paid your quarterly tax bill) was 10 percent, or $10,000. Does that mean that you will not be able to do the deal? No, my skeptical reader! By virtue of the purchase contract, you still have the "exclusive" right (the purchase contract) to buy a property worth $120,000 for $100,000. That is worth something.

Now, in the role of moderate negotiator, you can go to one of your friends and propose that you go in together to buy the property: You will contribute that exclusive right to buy the property (the purchase contract) and 10 percent ($10,000) of the purchase price. Your friend will put up (contribute) the remainder of the necessary cash (the 15 percent, equaling $15,000). Both of you will sign on to the mortgage (which is expected to be paid out of rental income from the property), and each of you will own some agreed-upon percentage of the property—and the resulting profits. (We are assuming for the purpose of this example that the bank does not object to the arrangement. In the real world, it might be an issue.) In our example, let's assume that the property is to be owned, and profits shared 50 percent to your friend and 50 percent to you.

> This simple "agreement" serves the purpose of illustrating an "equity deal." In the real world, however, unless there was a written agreement specifically detailing your rights and obligations and those of your friend, you would be asking for trouble. For example, who would be responsible for making repairs? What if one of you didn't have the money? Who would be responsible for collecting rent and accounting? Would there be compensation for time spent? What happens if one of you wants to sell the property and the other doesn't? What happens if for some reason (e.g., vacancies) the income from the property does not cover the mortgage payments, and one of you does not have the money to cover the shortfall? (You would probably be jointly and severally liable.)

In essence, you (now playing the role of triumphant businessperson) have created an enterprise—a business—based on the contract. You assigned a value of 5 percent of the purchase price ($5,000) to the contract and sold your friend a 50 percent ownership interest (equity) in that business for $15,000. From your perspective, you have used Other People's Money (your friend's contribution of 15 percent of the purchase price, in addition to the bank loan) in order to acquire the property. In this case, the cost to you of the OPM was 50 percent ownership in the property (and one-half of the interest paid on the loan). Your friend will get 50 percent of the profits and 50 percent of any appre-

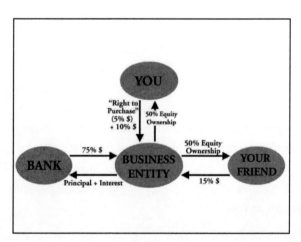

ciation. On the other hand, you were able to implement a deal that you would not have otherwise been able to do. Said another way: You paid your entry fee, so now you can play the game. And in addition to putting in only part of the cash, you have also spread the risk.

Business Entity

In Example 1 (using debt to acquire real estate), from a legal perspective when you make the property available for rental, you create a business entity—a sole proprietorship (or, if you have proper legal counsel, some form of limited liability company). In Example 2 (Equity & Debt), you initially "owned" an asset (the contract) in your individual capacity and have brought in a "partner." You have, in effect, turned a sole proprietorship into a partnership.

Neither a sole proprietorship nor a partnership is an ideal type of business entity from a risk perspective. In fact, we strongly advise against using a sole proprietorship or general partnership. Some form of limited liability entity (e.g., corporation, LP, or LLC) would be more appropriate. This, however, is not the subject of this book.

For more information on limited liability business entities, see *Own Your Own Corporation*, by Garrett Sutton, Esq. (Warner Books, 2001), one of the books in the Rich Dad's Advisors series.

Valuation

The second example illustrates one of the most difficult problems that must be faced when selling equity in an enterprise for outside money: the issue of "valuation." How much of the business do you give up for that outside money? If you can establish the value of the enterprise, the computation is a straight ratio (contribution divided by the value of the enterprise). But what is the value of the enterprise? What is the value of the contribution?

Establishing the value of a business or a nonmonetary contribution is typically easier said than done. It is difficult enough to establish the value of a business's hard assets (property, equipment, etc.). Most businesses, however, have some form of intangible asset (e.g., contractual rights or intellectual property) in addition to hard assets. What value do you assign to those assets?

Further, what value do you assign to intangible contributions? What if your friend happens to be the best handyman in the world? That intangible may not make it any easier to value his contribution.

What is the value of the enterprise in our example? Is it the value of the property? Should it be the purchase price of $100,000 or the appraised value of $120,000? In the example, you sold your friend a 50 percent interest in the enterprise for his $15,000. If 50 percent of the business is sold for $15,000, that means that the value of 100 percent of your business is $30,000 (and, of course, the value of your 50 percent is established at $15,000). You contributed $10,000 in hard cash plus the contract for your 50 percent of the business. That means you assigned only a $5,000 value to the right to buy the property. Why $5,000? What is the justification for that valuation? Why not assign a value of $20,000 (the difference between the appraised value of the property and the purchase price) to the contract (i.e., sell your friend a 33 percent interest for his $15,000)? Perhaps the $5,000 value assigned to the contract was, as is often the case with start-up businesses, the product of negotiation.

Maybe $5,000 was the best you could do. Perhaps you could only convince your friend to allocate a $5,000 value to the contract, and because of timing, it was the only way you could do the deal. Or maybe you didn't think through the value of what you were bringing to the table. We will look at that more closely later.

"Raising money," in the form of loans and equity investments to start a business, is a classical use of conventional forms of OPM. In the examples we just reviewed, the businesses involved real estate. The principles illustrated, however, are not limited to real estate businesses. They apply equally well to other types of business (although institutional loans may be more difficult to obtain for "non-asset-based" businesses). In the examples, your contribution was, at least in part, money—your share of the down payment. Can you start a business even if you don't have *any* money? The answer is yes—as long as you are not greedy and have a sufficiently valuable nonmonetary contribution that you can make to the business.

You can build a business without using your own money, or resorting to raising money per se. We will take a closer look at how to do that in the next chapter.

Chapter 3

You Don't Need Money to Start and Build a Business

In the preceding chapter, we reviewed examples of classical approaches to "raising money" to start a business. You started a business by using OPM in the form of loans or money contributed in return for equity in the business. Loans and equity investments are conventional forms of OPM.

However, contributions to a business—from you or from others—can be in any number of forms in addition to money. The contributions to the business can relate to any of the elements necessary for its success. For example, a contribution can be in the form of intellectual property, an intangible right or relationship, such as a contractual right (e.g., the right to purchase property as in the example in the preceding chapter), "sweat equity" (providing time and effort without drawing a "salary" or at a reduced "salary"), resources (facilities, distribution, R&D, management), credibility (credit, reputation), or access to sources of capital (network).

Cash In on the Intellectual Property Assets Hiding in Your Business

Do you have intellectual property? Of course, you do. Intellectual property is the intangible assets that result from creativity, innovation, know-how, and good relationships with others. Every successful business has intellectual property assets, whether the owner knows it or not.

Intellectual property includes more than just "technology stuff." Of course, it includes technology-related invention, know-how, expertise, data, and information. But it also includes those same things regarding business subjects, such as management and operations, databases, marketing, and sales.

Intellectual property also includes the things that give (or can give) your business its identity to the outside world—all the things that can differentiate your business from your competitors. Your reputation and the goodwill you have built up with the people that you deal with, and the trademarks and trade dress that symbolize that reputation and goodwill, are all part of your intellectual property.

And we should not forget the written materials and artwork relating to or created for the business—works of authorship and artistic expression. These, too, are part of your intellectual property.

Trade secrets, utility patents, design patents, copyrights, mask works, and trademark registration are the legal tools used to protect intellectual property assets.

Anytime you solve a problem, you have created a potential intellectual property asset. Think about it. If you encounter a problem in connection with your business, it is likely that your competitors will encounter that same problem. If you have found a better solution than your competitors have—perhaps the optimum solution—obtaining the exclusive rights to use that solution can give you an advantage over your competitors. If your solution is significantly better than theirs, the advantage can be significant. Competitive advantage can be parlayed into business opportunity and cash.

How do you identify your intellectual property assets? You identify everything about your business that gives you an advantage over your competitors. Ask yourself this question: Why do my customers come to me instead of going to my competitors? Dissect your business systems, products, services, and communications (e.g., customer and/or supplier relations) and analyze each component and feature to determine whether it contributes to the competitive advantage and whether there is anything about it that is perceived as "unique," "better," or "distinctive." By "unique," we mean that your competitors don't have it or provide it. Something is "distinctive" if it differentiates your business from the competition and brings your business to mind. As previously noted, "better"

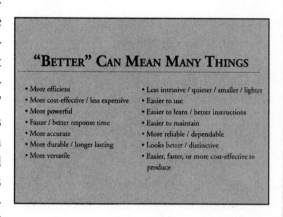

"Better" Can Mean Many Things

- More efficient
- More cost-effective / less expensive
- More powerful
- Faster / better response time
- More accurate
- More durable / longer lasting
- More versatile
- Less intrusive / quieter / smaller / lighter
- Easier to use
- Easier to learn / better instructions
- Easier to maintain
- More reliable / dependable
- Looks better / distinctive
- Easier, faster, or more cost-effective to produce

can mean many things. Determine precisely what it is about that component or feature that makes it unique, better, or distinctive.

Once you have identified the specific source of your competitive advantage, you develop a strategy to secure exclusive rights by applying the legal tools.

Anything that gives you an advantage that you can successfully keep secret can be maintained as a trade secret to use appropriate agreements with your employees and anyone else given access to the information.

Devices, processes, and methods of doing business (and features of those things) that are unique or better are "inventions" and are often protectable by utility patents. To be patentable, the invention must be "novel" and not "obvious" in view of the "prior art" (e.g., what is already known by the public). "Novel" means in essence that the invention is not already in the public domain, was not made by someone else before you (unless they abandoned, suppressed, or concealed the invention), and is not already patented. "Obviousness" is judged from the objective perspective of a hypothetical "person of ordinary skill in the art." As a practical matter, if any element of the invention is new, or even if all the individual elements of the invention are known, but nothing in the literature suggests your particular combination of elements, the invention is not obvious. If your product employs custom integrated circuits, they can be protected by mask work registrations.

Anything that is distinctive, as long as it is not utilitarian, can be turned into a protectable trademark or service mark. It may also be protected by design patents.

Your written materials, artwork, and to a certain extent software are protected by copyright.

Once you have identified and protected the intellectual property assets, they can be leveraged to sustain your competitive advantage, create credibility in the industry (and with potential investors), and add virtual mass and resources to your business through strategic alliances and/or licensing. That is how you really cash in on your intellectual property assets.

By properly identifying as much of your intellectual property as possible, you will be better able to attract OPM. Potential investors and/or co-venturers will evaluate your intellectual property and your efforts to identify and protect it when they evaluate their risk of investing with you.

For further discussion of protecting intellectual property assets, read my book *Protecting Your #1 Asset: Creating Fortunes from Your Ideas*, (Warner Books, 2001), one of the books in the Rich Dad's Advisors series.

The type of resources contributed can also take many forms. For example, a principal (or investor) could contribute the services of others, such as, for example, engineers, marketers, assemblers, clerical personnel, accountants, or attorneys; or the use of physical facilities and equipment, such as, for example, manufacturing equipment or office space; or provide access to distribution channels. Sometimes the investor's involvement is itself a contribution, providing leadership and/or giving the business credibility.

The consideration (payback) given to contributors can also take a wide variety of forms. Classically, money is provided in return for a promise to pay it back (typically) with interest (a loan) or in return for an ownership interest (equity). However, you are by no means limited to those choices of contribution or consideration.

OPM does not have to be in the form of a direct contribution of money—that's where OPR comes in. Using OPR typically expands the range of viable possibilities with respect to the type of consideration given in return for the contribution. You don't have to be able to qualify for a loan. You don't necessarily have to sell ownership interests in your business. You are limited only by your imagination and your ability to negotiate. For example, if you approach it properly, you can often get the benefit of resources or services in return for a portion of the profits made from the use of those resources or services or in return for bartered services.

In other words, you can build a business using very little of your own money or, for that matter, without resorting to raising money. You do this by making nonmonetary contributions and using the equivalent from others—OPR. Let's take a look at a hypothetical illustrating how it's done.

Example: Building a Business with OPR

IVAN'S IDEA

Ivan was a short-order cook working in a diner. One particular problem had plagued him for years: removing grease, fat, and oils from food (particularly bacon and other fried foods) quickly, without changing the appearance (squashing) of the food. One day when he was playing around at home, he came up with an idea for a new kitchen appliance that would solve the problem. He decided to start a business to manufacture and sell the appliance.

Legal Perspective

Has Ivan actually started a "business" at this point? Let's assume for purposes of discussion that he has. Unless certain legal formalities were observed, Ivan's business would have been a sole proprietorship. A sole proprietorship is the alter ego of the owner. However, if we assume, again for purposes of discussion, that he created a separate business entity, Ivan, in effect, contributed the idea—intellectual property—to the business for a 100 percent interest in the business.

MAKING THE PROTOTYPE

Ivan didn't have the know-how or the equipment to actually make a prototype or the money to engage someone to do so. So Ivan went to his friend Manny. Manny had once been a mechanic and an appliance repairman. He knew how to make a prototype of the appliance Ivan created. Ivan convinced Manny to make a prototype out of spare parts in return for "5 percent"—meaning that Manny will take a 5 percent interest in the business. Ivan and Manny, in effect, formed a partnership. Ivan contributed intellectual property—the idea—for which he got a 95 percent interest. Manny also contributed intellectual property (the know-how to make the prototype) as well as the use of facilities and services (actually making the prototype) for a 5 percent interest. (Alternatively, you could say that Ivan sold Manny a 5 percent interest in the business in return for his contribution of making the prototype.)

Legal Perspective: Doing It Right

Ivan's arrangement with Manny was, as is often the case in real life, very informal. There was no written agreement. This is a potential for problems in a number of areas:

- Confidentiality. Ideally, Ivan would have had a confidentiality agreement in place with Manny before he disclosed the idea for the

appliance. In the absence of such an agreement, Manny could legitimately use the idea of Ivan's appliance and disclose it to others.

• Ownership of intellectual property created by Manny. What
happens if Manny discovers the crucial element of the appliance, or
significantly improves the idea, during the process of making the prototype? At the very least, he would become a co-inventor of the appliance and, possibly, the sole inventor of the improvement. In the
absence of an agreement, Manny would acquire intellectual property
rights, and Ivan could be left holding the bag.

• Potential misunderstandings as to the arrangement. Without a
written agreement, it is all too easy for legitimate misunderstandings,
or for memories to become clouded. For example, "5 percent of any
money that Ivan makes from the appliance" is very different from a "5
percent equity interest in the business." (Sample agreements relating
to confidentiality and the ownership of intellectual property rights are
included in the Intellectual Property Tools kit available through my
Web site *www.mlechter.com.*)

COMETH THE ANGEL

Neither Ivan nor Manny had the facilities to manufacture the appliance. At
that point, they could have sought to raise money to develop a manufacturing capability. However, they chose an alternative approach. They went to
Manny's employer, Angelo, to see if he was interested in "purchasing the
rights to the appliance." Angelo had started and sold two successful businesses before starting his present business and was well known in the community as a successful and savvy entrepreneur.

Ivan demonstrated the appliance to Angelo using the prototype. Angelo was impressed. He saw great potential for the appliance. However, he
recognized that he didn't have the right type of facilities to manufacture
the appliance cost-effectively in production quantities and, in any event,
didn't have the excess capacity. While he thought that the market for the
appliance might be huge—fast food restaurants as well as many house-
holds—he also recognized that he really didn't know that market or have

distribution channels into it. Nevertheless, he felt that the opportunity was worth investigating.

Legal Perspective: Doing It Right

• Confidentiality. Ideally, Ivan and Manny would have had a confidentiality agreement in place with Angelo before they demonstrated the appliance. In the absence of such an agreement, Manny could legitimately use the idea of Ivan's appliance and disclose it to others.

• Preservation of patent rights. As a general proposition, public use of an invention, an offer to sell product incorporating the invention, or commercial exploitation of the invention (e.g., use of the invention in the normal course of business) has consequences with respect to patent rights. In the United States and the NAFTA countries, a one-year "grace period" begins with the first public use, commercialization or offer for sale of the invention, and at the end of that year you are barred from filing for a patent. In most other countries, there is no such grace period; any public use prior to the effective patent filing date bars patent protection. (Those countries require what is referred to as "absolute novelty.") For more information on patent protection, see my book *Protecting Your #1 Asset: Creating Fortunes from Your Ideas* (Warner Books, 2001), in the Rich Dad's Advisors series.

Ivan and Manny demonstrated the prototype to Angelo to convince him to invest in the invention, not to buy product incorporating the invention. That being the case, as long as the demonstration was private (as opposed to being in public), it should not present a problem to patentability. However, in the event that a patent was obtained, and there was infringement litigation, the infringer could try to characterize the demonstration as an offer for sale. That tactic can be prevented by having Angelo sign a confidentiality agreement that acknowledges that no product was being offered for sale. This type of agreement is sometimes also used when field-testing a product (alpha test and beta test). (Sample confidentiality and alpha/beta test agreements are included in the Intellectual Property Tools kit available through my Web site *www.mlechter.com.*)

DUE DILIGENCE

With Ivan's and Manny's permission, Angelo began doing some research. Before he made a decision to invest, he wanted to know (a) whether or not there were any similar appliances on the market, (b) more about the market—the size and nature of the market and who the players were in that industry (to identify potential competitors and co-venturers), and (c) whether or not there were any patents or published patent applications.

Ivan and Manny were lucky to have approached someone like Angelo. Most potential investors would not take the time to do an initial investigation. Ivan and Manny would have been much better served to have done the investigation themselves and presented the results to Angelo when they did the demonstration. If Angelo was a typical sophisticated investor, and Ivan and Manny came to him without having done their homework, the project might never have gotten off the ground.

Angelo started by going "online" and performing a general Internet search on the appliance. He entered keywords describing the appliance and the problem that it solved into a series of search engines and studied the results. Angelo liked to repeat the search using a number of different search sites, since differ-

---

Investigation Using the Internet

There are numerous search engines available on the Internet:

www.allsearchengines.com	www.metacrawler.com
www.37.com	www.yahoo.com
www.google.com	www.alltheweb.com
www.dogpile.com	www.galaxy.com
www.altavista.com	www.jayde.com
www.lycos.com	www.msn.com
www.mamma.com	www.ask.com
www.search.com	

ent search engines often provided different results. Angelo found a number of references to the problem solved by the appliance—unhealthful grease and oils retained in food—but no appliances in the market that targeted that problem.

He also performed searches on the fast food industry and the marketplace for kitchen appliances and confirmed that the potential market for the appliance was indeed huge. He identified half a dozen sizable companies that made appliances that were sold to the same market and that were manufactured using processes and materials similar to those that would be used to manufacture Ivan's appliance—potential competitors or co-venturers.

Angelo then did a patent search. He could never remember the URL for the patent office site (www.USPTO.gov), so he accessed it through a link on a site that he could remember—www.MLechter.com. As he did with the general Internet search, Angelo searched the patent and published application databases using keywords describing the appliance and the problem that it solved. He found no patents or published applications on point, but he was able to identify another "industry player" from the assignee (owner) information provided as part of the patent data.

> ### Publicly Available Patent Search Databases
>
> U.S. Patent and Trademark Office—www.USPTO.gov
>
> European patent office—http://ep.espacenet.com
>
> Canadian patent office—http://patents1.ic.gc.ca.
>
> World Intellectual Property Organization (WIPO)—www.wipo.int/ipdl/en/index.jsp
>
> Australia—www.ipaustralia.gov.au/
>
> Japan—www.ipdl.jpo.go.jp/homepg_e.ipdl

Then he searched the patent and published application databases (using the "assignee name" field) for patents held by the industry player companies that he had identified earlier. The industry players held numerous patents, but none on point.

BUILDING THE LEGAL FOUNDATION

Angelo met with Ivan and Manny. He told them that he had finished his preliminary investigation and was interested in doing something with them but that the appliance was not an appropriate product for his present company. It did not fit into his product line and could not be made cost-effectively on his production line. He suggested that the three of them form a new company, a limited liability corporation (LLC).

He explained that he did not think it made sense for the new company to try to manufacture and sell the product itself. They were much better off licensing the invention to one of the powers in the kitchen appliance industry—one of the "big boys." They would, in effect, use the big boy's resources to take the appliance to market. He figured that 10 percent of sales through the big boy's resources would be a whole lot more than the total sales that they could generate if they tried to go forward on their own. However, before they approached any potential co-venturer, they needed to protect their intellectual property rights. A patent application on the appliance needed to be filed.

Angelo proposed that he would contribute the costs of (a) forming the business entity (which he estimated to be between $500 and $1,000), (b) obtaining patent protection (which he estimated to be between $15,000 and $20,000 over the course of eighteen months), and (c) registering a trademark (which he estimated to be between $1,000 and $2,000 over the course of eighteen months). He would also handle approaching potential licensees and negotiating licenses. He would cover any costs involved. In return, he asked for 30 percent of the new company. Ivan and Manny agreed.

Relative Value of Contributions

How did Angelo come up with a 30 percent ownership interest? One of the issues that always seem to arise is the relative value of contributions to a business. When an equity investor puts money into a company, what percentage ownership of the company will the investor get in return for the money? There are standard techniques for valuation of an existing business. There are times when those valuation techniques will be applicable to nonmonetary contributions to a start-up business. However, most of the time with start-up businesses, the issue of relative value of contributions is often simply a matter of "credibility" of the contributors and their negotiation skills.

A new company (LLC) was formed. They named it IMA, LLC. It was owned by the three of them: 66 percent by Ivan, 30 percent by Angelo, and 4 percent by Manny. In essence, in return for his 30 percent interest, Angelo contributed the services of others—his patent attorney as well as his own services in connection with identifying and negotiating with potential licensees.

Dilution

Did you notice that Ivan's ownership interest went from 95 percent to 66 percent and Manny's went from 5 percent to 4 percent? This is a perfect example of the concept of "dilution." When someone new enters the picture and takes an equity position in the business, the newcomer's ownership interest has to come from somewhere. Very often, that means that the percentage ownership of each of the prior owners decreases on a pro rata basis. The prior owners don't necessarily give up shares. Instead, new shares are issued to cover the newcomer's position. The number of shares held by prior owners does not change. However, that number of shares corresponds to a smaller percentage of the total number of shares. Sometimes the newcomer will simply be given a number of shares based upon the value of the business and the value of the newcomer's contribution (e.g., the newcomer pays $10,000 for $10,000 worth of shares).

In other cases, the newcomer gets a specified percentage ownership of the business entity. That is the case in our example. So if the newcomer ends up with a specific percentage of the business after the dust settles, how can you determine the percentages retained by the original owners? In some cases, the original owners, in effect, renegotiate their relative percentages—and agree how much each will contribute toward the newcomer's interest. In other cases, the percentages retained by the original owners are determined on a purely mathematical basis. The easiest way to understand the process is to think in terms of shares in the company. (In a corporation, there will be actual shares. In other forms of entities, there may not be— the principals each own certain percentages of the entity. In those cases, simply assume that each 1 percent interest corresponds to one share.) The relative percentages can be calculated using the following equations:

(New Shares Issued) =

(Original Total Shares) 2 (Newcomer's Interest)/(1 − Newcomer's Interest)

(Principal's Retained Interest) =

(Principal's Original Interest)/(Original Total Shares + New Shares Issued)

Let's assume that prior to Angelo coming on board, Ivan's 95 percent interest corresponded to 95 shares and Manny's 5 percent interest corresponded to 5 shares, for a total of 100 shares. Angelo's interest will be 30 percent. Accordingly, when rounded to the closest whole number or 1 percent, as appropriate:

(New Shares Issued) = (100) 2 (0.30)/(1−.30) = 43

(Ivan's Retained Interest) = (95)/(100 + 43) = 0.66 (66%)

(Manny's Retained Interest) = (5)/(100 + 43) = 0.04 (4%)

Angelo's patent attorney met with Ivan and Manny and prepared and filed a patent application on the appliance. The application was assigned to IMA. The attorney also filed an application to register the phrase "IMA Not Greasy" as a trademark with the U.S. Patent and Trademark Office.

BUILDING CREDIBILITY

Once the patent application was filed, Angelo began to search for a licensee. He initially attempted to get potential licensees to sign a confidentiality agreement prior to any detailed discussions. None of the big boys would agree to do so.

Use of Confidentiality Agreement

When dealing with potential licensees, it is important to keep confidentiality in mind. Remember, under normal circumstances, unless there is a contractual obligation to the contrary, the potential licensees can use (and tell others) any information that you give them.

Having a patent application pending (filed but not yet granted) stakes your claim to the invention and fixes the date at which patentability is measured. However, you do not have any enforceable rights until the patent is granted. The application is kept in secret for at least eighteen months after it is filed.

It is desirable to keep the patent application itself out of the hands of potential competitors. When they know that there is a pending application on a product but do not know what features of the product will be covered by the patent, or the extent that the patent claims may go beyond the particular embodiment in the product, their design efforts are likely to be hampered, since they are not quite sure what they can and cannot do. If the patent application gets into their hands, you lose that advantage.

It is also often to your advantage to minimize the time period that the invention is known to the public but not covered by a patent grant. However, it is not critical to keep the invention secret once the application is filed. There are a variety of reasons why a business might take its product to market once the patent application is filed and not wait for the patent to actually be granted.

Depending upon the stage of development of the invention, and your business, there may be other confidential information that might be disclosed to potential licensees. This information includes, for example, detailed design information that would not be in the patent application, market studies, marketing plans, projections, sourcing information, and the like.

However, many companies, particularly the big boys, are reluctant to sign confidentiality agreements with respect to "outside submissions"—at least until they have decided that they are interested. In certain industries, the big boys, as a matter of policy, will not sign confidentiality agreements with respect to outside submissions. In fact, they will not consider an outside submission unless the submitter first signs a "nonconfidentiality" agreement acknowledging that none of the information given to them is confidential. The typical nonconfidentiality agreement is to the effect that "we will respect any patent rights you may have, but anything else you tell us is fair game."

There are actually legitimate reasons for that policy. The big boys are concerned that they will have ongoing independent research on the same subject as the outside submission. They are afraid that they will end up in litigation if they decline to do business with the outside submitter and instead continue with their independent research. In some industries—the toy industry, for example—that tended to happen a lot. That is why those companies now insist on nonconfidentiality agreements.

As a practical matter, to proceed in the face of that attitude, you assume that "anything you say can and will be used against you." You have to take a calculated risk—the risk that potential licensees will "appropriate" everything that you disclose to them—but that risk can be minimized. Information can be provided in stages. You do not disclose any information that is truly sensitive in your initial communications. In many instances, the potential licensees are sufficiently interested to take the next step, and disclosure of sensitive information is required; they are at that point willing to enter into a confidentiality agreement. If they are not, you can choose to take another calculated risk or terminate the discussions.

Angelo then decided to sanitize his presentation to remove information that he thought was important to remain confidential (there was actually very little other than the particulars of the patent application) and went forward without attempting to secure a confidentiality agreement. Even so, while Angelo was a study in persistence, his efforts were unsuccessful. A few of the potential licensees were not interested in talking to him before a patent was actually granted. Others said that they did not accept any outside submissions from anyone with whom they did not have a prior relationship. For the most part, however, Angelo was simply unable to get anyone to agree to economic terms that he felt were satisfactory. In a nutshell, IMA and its technology were not sufficiently credible to command the economic terms—royalty—that Angelo wanted.

From the potential licensees' viewpoint, the appliance was untested in the marketplace. That meant that they would be assuming the risk that the appliance would not be accepted in the marketplace. If the appliance was not accepted, the licensees stood to lose the investment that they would have to make in order to produce the appliance and bring it to market.

Angelo's assurances that the appliance would be a hit were not enough to convince the potential licensees. Angelo had a track record of success, but it was in a different field, and the potential licensees did not feel that his experience translated into their industry. His endorsement of the appliance did not carry the weight with the potential licensees that it would have in his own industry.

Angelo ultimately came to the conclusion that in order for IMA to get anywhere near the economic terms that they wanted in a license agreement, they would have to find a way to develop credibility. They would have to find a way to minimize the risk perceived by the potential licensees.

Angelo went back to Ivan and Manny and suggested that rather than accepting a "bad deal," they should do some things to become more credible—prove marketplace acceptance of the appliance. Then they would resume their efforts to license the technology to one of the big boys. They agreed that the best way for them to prove market acceptance was to actually bring the appliance to market and show that it sold. Assuming that things went well, it would also give them the opportunity to build value into their trademark, IMA Not Greasy.

Bringing the appliance to market meant that it had to be manufactured. Did that mean that they had to raise the money to develop a production capability? What do you think? The answer is no! They could rely on *Other* People's Resources—OPR. Rather than going to the expense of acquiring equipment, bringing on people to run it, and setting up production on their own (assuming that they had the expertise to do so), they outsourced the manufacturing to a job shop that already had the capability.

In this case, the manufacturing techniques used by the job shop were far from optimum—under normal circumstances, other production methods would be used that were far more efficient and cost-effective. However, the job shop manufacturing process involved essentially no up-front (e.g., tooling) costs, required little lead time for production runs, and was very flexible with respect to the number of units manufactured at one time. In addition, Angelo was particularly concerned with cash flow. He struck a deal with the job shop. He agreed to pay a significantly higher than normal price in return for "just in time" manufacturing, meaning that small production runs of the appliance could be provided with less than one week's notice, and extended payment terms (payment was due ninety days after delivery). This arrangement gave IMA the ability to match production to sales and, they hoped, gain some control over cash flow.

In essence, the job shop provided OPM in the form of credit—it advanced the cost of manufacture to IMA for ninety days. (The cost of the OPM was paying the significantly higher price for manufacturing.) Angelo hoped to limit the number of units manufactured at one time to the number of units that could be sold in a week. His intent was to make sure all the manufactured units were sold (or at least projected to be sold at a specific event) before ordering the next production run. He did not plan, at least initially, to extend any credit terms to purchasers. (The credit card company extended terms of payment to the purchaser, and IMA received payment from the credit card company within a matter of days of the purchase.) That way, he expected to have payment from purchasers of the appliance before he had to pay the job shop.

Manny worked with the job shop to finalize design and production details. They decided to initially concentrate on a "commercial" unit, rather than a home kitchen appliance. After pricing was finalized, Angelo determined that, based on market research, IMA could price the appliance at about five times its cost to them from the job shop. He also estimated that using more conventional manufacturing processes, the cost could be reduced by, at a minimum, approximately one-half.

Bringing the appliance to market also meant that it had to be presented to potential purchasers. Did that mean that IMA had to go to the expense of hiring marketing talent and a sales force? Again, the answer is no! In this case, they relied in part on their own efforts and in part on OPR. Their marketing strategy involved three primary activities: a Web site, demonstrations at trade shows, and placing demonstration units in certain fast food restaurants. For sales, they relied on direct sales at trade shows, sales through the Web site, and independent representatives (reps).

Angelo, Ivan, and Manny all recognized the value of having a credible Web site, particularly one that permitted the appliance to be ordered and paid for online. None of them, however, had any idea how to set one up. Angelo agreed to loan IMA the money to have a Web site designed and implemented. As it turned out, however, the loan was not necessary.

Angelo searched around a bit and had Ivan demonstrate the prototype to a number of potential Web site designers, to get their proposals. Ultimately, Angelo found someone who was willing to design, manage, and host a Web site for a percentage of the sales through the Web site until the Web site designer/host had been paid an agreed amount for developing the site. After that, the designer/host would receive a percentage of sales each month, up to a predetermined monthly limit, for hosting and maintenance services. In the long run, if the Web site generated the sales that they thought it would, the arrangement would cost IMA much more than if they simply paid for the design and hosting. However, the Web site, in effect, paid for itself. The Web designer/host assumed the risk of the site's success. IMA did not have to spend any money up front, and if the Web site did not generate sufficient sales, the designer/host did not get paid. Once again, IMA had used OPM and OPR.

Ivan and sometimes Manny or Angelo began attending trade shows relating to the fast food industry and kitchen appliances. To minimize expense, they initially restricted themselves to shows being held locally. Their expenses were minimal—typically less than $10 for admission and a few dollars for food—but they kept track of expenses anyway so that they could ultimately be reimbursed by IMA when the company could afford it. They were initially on a fact-finding mission. They wanted information regarding:

- Fast food chains and franchises that were likely to use the appliance, particularly where purchasing decisions for all locations were made at a central location
- How purchasing decisions were made at the chains and franchises and who made those decisions (and contact details if possible)
- How appliances and other equipment were marketed to fast food chains and franchises and who did the marketing (and contact details if possible)
- The prices being charged to the fast food chains and franchises for appliances (to verify that the contemplated prices for the IMA appliance were in line with other appliances on market)
- Manufacturer's sales representative firms
- Other firms, particularly manufacturers of other appliances that sold to the fast food chains and franchises that were likely to use the IMA appliance
- The trade shows themselves—who attended, the cost of a booth, which booths seemed to be most effective, etc.

In the meantime, Ivan worked with the Web designer/host to develop a sales presentation that could be used on the Web site. All agreed that the Web site would do double duty—it was easy enough to access the site or download a copy to a notebook computer to use as a sales tool with potential customers.

Angelo and Ivan began a road show to find "sales partners." One by one, they met with a number of the manufacturer's rep firms, a couple of the other appliance manufacturers that sold to the fast food industry. They demonstrated the appliance to each and proposed that the other organizations sell the IMA appliance on a straight commission basis. Ultimately, agreements were reached with one of the manufacturer's rep firms and one of the appliance manufacturers.

The terms of the agreements weighed heavily in favor of IMA's sales partner. In each case, IMA paid a significant (higher than typical in the market) commission on sales, sold demonstration units to the sales partners at cost, and agreed to "exclusive" relationships within specified markets. IMA agreed that it would not engage any other manufacturer's rep within a specified geographical area or enter into similar relationships with any competitor of the appliance manufacturer. Angelo was unable to get the sales partners to agree to any specific minimum sales figure (the IMA appliance was still unproven in the marketplace, and they were not willing to assume that risk).

However, the sales partners did agree to make certain minimum efforts—going to certain trade shows, making a minimum number of sales calls, etc.—and it was clear in each case that the exclusivity did not prevent direct sales by IMA, sales through the Web site, even if in a rep's exclusive territory, sales by its other sales partner, or sales through franchisors to franchisees (another prong of IMA's marketing plan). In addition, the term of the agreements was relatively short—only one year—and IMA would be able to renegotiate at that point.

In any event, the agreements met IMA's needs. IMA paid high commissions and assumed some risk that their sales partners would not perform, but was able to effectively field a significant sales force with an existing customer base without having to go to the effort (or take the time) and expense to build one on its own. Once again, IMA was able to use a resource that someone else had spent the money to develop rather than spend its own money. Once again, IMA used OPR.

Angelo and Ivan also took their road show to a dozen or so fast food franchisors. In this case, they left demonstration units with the franchisors for a thirty-day trial. All but four purchased the demonstration unit at the end of the month. Orders started coming in.

The manufacturer's rep had booths at most of the major trade shows. Arrangements were made for Ivan to attend the trade shows and put on demonstrations at the rep's booth. The rep was happy that IMA was putting in the effort to help market the appliance, and IMA was able to demonstrate at the trade shows without going to the expense of subscribing for its own booth. IMA's only expenses were related to Ivan's travel. Once more, IMA was able to use a resource someone else had paid for—OPR.

The orders kept coming in.

It quickly became apparent that someone had to coordinate the manufacturing orders to the job shop and purchase orders received. Manny was elected. When the extent of the efforts required became apparent, Ivan and Angelo decided that Manny deserved additional "sweat equity." Manny was given an additional 6 percent (by agreement, taken 3 percent each from Ivan's and Angelo's holdings).

Practical Issues with Trading Equity for Sweat

What happens if you give someone equity in return for services and he or she fails to perform? What happens if he or she quits after three months? What happens if circumstances change and it no longer makes sense for that person to provide the services? Do you get the equity back? It is important to know the answers to these questions. The only way to be sure of the answers is to agree beforehand and, preferably, commit that agreement to writing.

Typically, the right to equity does not vest until after the services have been performed for a predetermined period. For example, Manny might have been awarded a predetermined percentage of equity—say, 1 percent—at the end of each year that he performed the services up to some cumulative limit—say, 6 percent. Often when the equity is in exchange for services and that individual later decides to leave his or her employment, there may be a provision to "buy back" his or her equity.

Over the course of the next year, IMA's sales steadily increased. The profit margin was nowhere near what it should be—the costs of manufacture and distribution were much higher than would normally be the case. However, the sales proved that the appliance was viable in the marketplace. And if manufacturing and distribution costs were brought down to the norm, the business would be quite profitable.

As they were approaching the end of the first year, Angelo felt comfortable with reapproaching the big boys. This time, because their efforts during the year had proved the viability of the appliance, Angelo had the credibility he needed to negotiate a license with satisfactory terms.

GROWING PAINS

By now, Manny was stretched to the point of breaking. The volume of orders and manufacturing issues were beginning to escape him. While IMA had thus far been able to get by without employees, it had reached a point where it could no longer handle the volume of business on its own.

Did that mean that IMA had to begin hiring employees? No. It could outsource the "fulfillment" function (although in this case actual shipping was done by the manufacturing service).

A License Agreement Is Perhaps the Ultimate Use of OPR

With licensees, you are paid while your product is manufactured and distributed entirely through OPR—the resources of your licensees. Obviously, the licensees also gain something from the relationship. From the licensees' perspective, they are also using OPM or OPR—yours. They did not have to go to the effort or expense of developing (assuming that they could) the intellectual property that you are licensing to them. Presumably, they are generating income using your intellectual property and are keeping a significant portion of the income. You get only a portion of the income generated by the licensees' efforts. However, a small percentage of a large number is often considerably more than 100 percent of a small number.

EXAMINING COSTS

As you can see, a business can be built, and money made, using Other People's Money and Other People's Resources, without resorting to the classical approaches to raising money. Granting a license to the big boy, particularly an exclusive license, would provide the exit that Angelo had contemplated. But what if the principals of IMA were not ready to exit? What are other options?

Clearly, IMA could continue on as it was. While not as profitable as it could be, IMA was still making money. Ivan, Manny, and Angelo originally chose to use the job shop manufacturing process because of its flexibility (for cash flow management), because it did not require an initial outlay of cash, and because the job shop was willing to extend credit terms. They paid for those benefits with a significantly higher cost of production. Presumably, however, if IMA continued to do business, it would ultimately want to convert to less costly and more efficient manufacturing and distribution processes. The same thing was true with respect to the distribution of the product through its sales partners. IMA had initially entered into agreements that weighed heavily in favor of the sales partner. At that time, IMA did not have the credibility or wherewithal to demand better terms.

Angelo viewed the higher costs and unfavorable agreement provisions as the price of entering the game. The arrangements permitted IMA to go forward. They provided benefits that IMA needed at the time. Angelo was willing to pay for those benefits. It was a matter of cost-benefit analysis. If the point came where the benefits were no longer worth the cost, it would be time to change.

Would IMA have to use its own money to make that conversion? Of course not! It could generate the funds internally if it wanted to, but it could also use OPM or OPR. It had all sorts of choices and combinations of choices. For example, rather than paying out income to the principals, IMA could retain profits to accumulate the funds necessary to set up an efficient production facility. It could bring in money from an outside source—direct OPM—in the form of either a purchase of equity in IMA or a loan. (The outside source could be Angelo—and from IMA's, Ivan's, and Manny's perspective, money from Angelo would be OPM.) IMA also had the option to outsource the production to a more efficient vendor (or get the present vendor—the job shop—to change the process).

Once IMA no longer needed the flexibility provided by small just-in-time production runs, converting to the more cost-effective processes became a viable option. The up-front (e.g., tooling) costs had to be dealt with. Once more, those costs could be paid from internal funds or using OPM. However, once you have the credibility to attract OPM or OPR, the costs tend to take care of themselves. For example, if you are creditworthy and willing to make a commitment for a sufficiently large order, a manufacturer will sometimes advance the cost of any necessary tooling.

IMA had yet another option to both go forward and take optimum advantage of OPR—a joint venture. Let's consider a hypothetical situation where a joint venture would make sense.

ENTERING THE BIG TIME

Angelo was leery of any sort of exclusive arrangements with any particular fast food franchise or chain. He viewed the fast food franchise market as the primary market for the commercial version of the appliance and was afraid that association with any particular franchise could make it difficult to do business with the other franchises. However, Flavorful Fligles (FF), one of the large international franchises that specialized in grilled and fried foods, became particularly enamored with the IMA Not Greasy appliance. One of its franchisees had called the appliance to the attention of corporate headquarters. Intrigued by the franchisee's enthusiasm, FF corporate headquarters had the appliance tested by an independent lab. The tests more than verified IMA's claims regarding the effectiveness of the appliance. They found, in fact, that IMA's claims were actually understated.

FF corporate then field-tested the appliance at a few of the corporate-owned restaurants. The use of the appliance was an easy fit (just one more step) in FF's established procedures. It determined that even before it made any mention of the health benefits, the sales at those locations increased because of more short-interval repeat business—the consumers reported that the foods tasted better.

FF corporate planned to propose that all franchisees in the United States use the appliance. If the proposal was adopted (and it would be, unless there was strenuous objection by a significant number of franchisees), IMA could expect an immediate order for fifty thousand units. FF corporate called IMA to explore a potential volume discount. (It planned to resell the appliances to its franchisees, passing one-half of the discount to them.)

During the course of the discussions, Angelo learned about the independent lab tests on the IMA Not Greasy appliance and that the FF franchise contemplated a major national advertising campaign emphasizing the relatively healthful nature of its food as compared to that of its competition, based in large part upon its use of the IMA Not Greasy appliance.

Building the Brand

In the end, Angelo agreed to sell the appliances to the FF franchise at a substantial discount in return for the following considerations: (a) FF paid a significant portion of the price in advance—enough to pay for the up-front (e.g., tooling) costs of converting to the more efficient manufacturing processes; (b) FF provided IMA with the report from the independent lab tests and gave IMA permission (and secured permission from the independent lab) to use the test reports in its promotional materials and advertising; (c) FF would show and prominently mention the IMA Not Greasy appliance by trademark in all of its promotional materials and advertisements in the "healthful food" campaign; and (d) IMA would have adequate time to have the fifty thousand units manufactured.

Angelo approached the job shop to see if it had the capacity to handle the fifty-thousand-unit order. The job shop did not but referred Angelo to a more conventional manufacturing service that did. The manufacturing service took care of ordering parts and materials, assembly, quality control testing, and shipping to the customer. As you would expect, there was a premium paid for the services.

In any event, the order to FF was filled, the appliances were sold to the franchisees and integrated into their operations, and the advertising campaign featuring the IMA Not Greasy appliance was launched. Soon the IMA Not Greasy trademark became well known, not only within the fast food industry but also to the fast food consumer.

Leveraging IP

It quickly became apparent that it was time to bring out a consumer version of the IMA Not Greasy appliance—the demand was clear. The time was right to cash in on the consumer recognition of the IMA Not Greasy trademark.

At this point, IMA was not only credible but well regarded in the industry. Having the IMA Not Greasy trademark on a product helped sell it. It became an intellectual property asset that could be leveraged. This did not go unnoticed.

Angelo began to receive calls from the big boys asking if he was willing to reopen talks on licensing or, perhaps, sell them IMA. Being acquired by one of the big boys was a perfect exit for Angelo, but Ivan and Manny were not ready to let go of the business. They were having fun. Improvements to the original appliance, and products combining cooking (grilling or frying) and fat, oil, and grease removal functions were in the works. They wanted to have a say in the direction of a continuing business.

When all was said and done, IMA entered into a "profit-sharing agreement" (a joint venture without creating a separate entity) with HugeCo, one of the biggest of the big boys. HugeCo brought a lot to the table—but so did IMA. In essence, IMA contributed a license to use intellectual property—patents, know-how, and trademarks—to the venture. HugeCo was responsible for manufacturing and distributing the product. Certain costs, which were agreed upon beforehand, were reimbursed from the gross receipts (to IMA or HugeCo as appropriate), and what was left—the "profits"—were split between IMA and HugeCo. HugeCo's costs, reimbursed out of gross receipts, to manufacture and distribute the products were only a fraction of what IMA had been paying, and with HugeCo's marketing and distribution capability, the volume of sales increased a thousandfold. You can do the math. IMA was well ahead of the game. That, however, was not the whole story.

HugeCo Builds IMA's Business
The agreement was structured so HugeCo's activities would be leveraged to help IMA continue to grow its business.

Sales of the products by HugeCo would continue to build recognition of the IMA Not Greasy trademark. Under the agreement, HugeCo was not only permitted but *required* to use the IMA Not Greasy trademark prominently on all of the appliances, on all packaging and promotional materials, and in all advertising. Certain marketing activities and levels of advertising were also required. In that way, HugeCo's activities would make IMA's trademark even more well known, and more valuable.

The intellectual property license was limited to certain products: the original IMA Not Greasy appliance and "such other products as the parties may agree upon in the future." That permitted IMA to develop other products and sell them under the IMA Not Greasy trademark, taking full advantage— leveraging—of the consumer recognition and goodwill of the trademark. In many instances, but not necessarily all, it would make sense to bring the new products under the agreement, to take advantage of HugeCo's resources. HugeCo might not want to take on that particular product for some reason. However, when it made that decision, it had to keep in mind that IMA had the option to pursue it on its own. In those cases where HugeCo's resources were somehow not applicable to the product (the particular product was directed to a different market or required different manufacturing techniques), IMA was free to go forward on its own or with another co-venturer.

IMA also retained a say in the management of the venture. IMA not only had veto rights with respect to the products of the venture but also retained design control (although with consultation from HugeCo) and had approval rights with respect to all advertising and packaging and certain management decisions. Specific quality control standards had to be met (quality control is required in a trademark license).

Accountability was built into the agreement. The risk of the big boy simply swallowing up or riding roughshod over the little guy was minimized.

The agreement very specifically spelled out HugeCo's obligations. Everything that IMA thought was important was included in the agreement explicitly and in detail. The agreement was also for a relatively short term (five years). If HugeCo did not live up to IMA's expectations, the agreement would not be renewed. (That, of course, was a two-edged sword: IMA also had to live up to HugeCo's expectations—or HugeCo might not renew.)

Because HugeCo's activities under the agreement were leveraged to help IMA continue to grow its business during the term of the agreement, if the agreement was terminated for some reason, IMA would not be behind the eight ball. IMA would not have to start all over again and rebuild its market position. That put IMA into

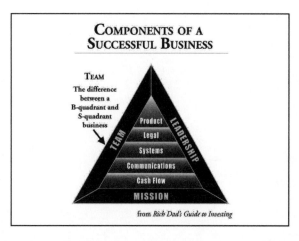

COMPONENTS OF A SUCCESSFUL BUSINESS

TEAM
The difference between a B-quadrant and S-quadrant business

TEAM

Product

LEADERSHIP

Legal

Systems

Communications

Cash Flow

MISSION

from *Rich Dad's Guide to Investing*

a position of parity with HugeCo when the time came to extend or re-negotiate.

IMA was well ahead of the game by going forward using OPR from HugeCo.

So what do you think? Can you build a business without using your own money? Can you build a business without raising money? It takes patience, foresight, and planning, but it can be done. Ivan did it. He started with an idea and no money. He put together the right team and ended up owning the majority interest in a thriving business.

In this example, the business was built primarily through the use of Other People's Resources. In the next few chapters, will will take a closer look at more conventional approaches to using OPM to start up or build a business: raising money.

Chapter 4

Your Money or OPM? Debt, Equity, or OPR?

We have discussed a number of different approaches to dealing with capital needs. Each approach has its distinct advantages and disadvantages. The particular approach that's best for you really depends on your specific circumstances. You can use the different approaches to meeting capital needs, and the different forms of OPM and OPR in combination, at the same time or sequentially, depending upon the circumstances. There is a strategy involved. Do you use your own money or OPM? When should you look for OPM? How much money should you raise? What is the most appropriate form or combination of forms of OPM (debt, sale of equity, and/or co-venture) to seek? What is the best source of OPM?

Let's take a look at the pros and cons of the different approaches to capital needs, and the different forms of OPM, and begin to consider different strategies for meeting capital needs.

Different Approaches to Dealing with Capital Needs

Assume that you have come up with the idea for a new product or business. It could be high-tech, low-tech, or "no-tech" for the purposes of our discussion, it does not matter. The market is huge. You are convinced that you have the greatest thing since sliced bread and have decided to take on the project of developing and marketing the product and building the business.

Let's also assume that you have come to a point where the costs of the next steps in the project are beyond your personal resources. This could be right at the beginning—at "start-up"—or after you already have a successful business but need the money to expand. For example:

- You may still be at the idea stage and need to prove to yourself and/or potential investors that your idea will work; or
- You may be sure that the idea will work but now need to lay a legal foundation to protect that idea (e.g., file patent applications) and/or build a prototype and do further testing; or
- You may have built a prototype but now need additional engineering and tooling or facilities to develop a production version of the product and/or bring it to market; or
- You may have a product on the market or a business that is up and running, but now need to expand in order to meet the orders that are coming in or to enter a new market; or
- Your business is up and running and you may have a product on the market but now need to work on releasing the next-generation improvement of the product.

What are your options when you discover that the costs of the next steps in the project are beyond your resources? We touched on this briefly earlier. You could simply shelve the project. You could self-fund. Or you could go forward using Other People's Money or Resources.

SHELVE THE PROJECT
You could delay or abandon the project. You simply forgo the opportunity "for the time being." If a delay is part of a plan, and you return to the project after you accomplish something else that is more important or makes it easier to proceed, delay can be a viable strategy.

Unfortunately, "for the time being" often means forever. You never get around to pursuing the project, the window of opportunity closes, or someone else (maybe a competitor) comes out with the product during the hiatus. This tends to be the course that most people take.

Of all the options, doing nothing, letting inertia take its course, is the least trouble. It is also the least rewarding. There are few guarantees in life, but one thing is relatively certain: If you don't try, it won't happen.

SELF-FUND

You can wait until you personally accumulate the necessary resources to go forward with the project. If you have other sources of income, or already have positive cash flow from your business, you may be able to save enough money to go forward.

What sort of things can you do to raise money outside of your normal course of business? You could exploit (sell, rent, or license) assets to raise money. For example, you may be able to generate income by providing consulting services, leasing out unused space or equipment, or licensing others to use an intellectual property asset.

There is one significant advantage to self-funding. Your own money is typically the least expensive form of capital (at least in terms of hard cost). You would not have to pay for the use of OPM; you would not have to be concerned with sharing ownership or control of the business or pay interest on a loan.

> ### *Licensing Intellectual Property vs. Competitive Advantage*
>
> Can you license others to use your intellectual property without giving up a competitive advantage? Yes, you can—as long as you either pick the right intellectual property asset or limit the scope of the license. We will get to this issue in Chapter 14.

Another advantage of self-funding is that since there is no transaction with investors, you do not have to be concerned with inadvertently violating the securities law. On the other hand, even a large public corporation has to account to its investors for the usage of their cash reserves.

Unfortunately, you might never be able to accumulate sufficient resources, or if you did, it may be too late—you may well have missed your window of opportunity. You may also be missing an opportunity to leverage your money. And, of course, you may continue to be limited by your own resources in the future, which may mean that other windows of opportunity are missed.

RAISE MONEY—CONVENTIONAL DIRECT OPM

You can seek an "infusion of capital"—money—from an outside source. Typically, this is in the form of a loan (debt) or sale of an equity (ownership) interest in your business or a combination of both.

The question is whether the OPM is available and if so, at what price. Do you qualify for a loan at reasonable interest rates? Are equity investors available? Do you meet their investment criteria? Will they accept a reasonable (in your view) percentage of ownership for their contribution? A lot will depend on the stage of development of your business at the time you are seeking to raise the money and the particular sources of OPM you are approaching. For example, when you are a start-up with an unproven idea, it is typically considerably more difficult to obtain financing from professional investors than when you have a successful business that you need to expand. We will discuss these issues again later.

You must also be careful to comply with the applicable securities laws in the United States, both federal and state. Securities laws apply in many instances that you would not expect, and they can place limitations on the way that you find potential sources of OPM and can regulate the form and content of your communications with them. We will also discuss securities law in a later chapter.

OPR

You can use OPR—obtain access to the specific resources that you need to go forward (through a strategic co-venture)—in return for some consideration. The nature of that consideration is limited only by your creativity and your ability to negotiate. Typical examples are payment of a fee (preferably with delayed payment to facilitate cash flow), a share of profits, and bartered services.

OPR is often available even when conventional OPM is not. There are a multitude of sources of OPR. You are usually not faced with the stringent, relatively inflexible investment criteria of professional investors and financial institutions. In addition, the use of OPR typically does not trigger many of the more onerous provisions of the securities law.

OPR is particularly applicable when the resources that you need involve a high capital expenditure (e.g., expensive equipment), a high level of special expertise, a high volume of throughput (that you don't have by yourself) in order to be cost-effective, or relationships with third parties (e.g., distribution channels) that would take time to establish.

However, using OPR is not always appropriate or your best choice. Under some circumstances, the cost of using OPR over the long run can be much greater than developing or acquiring the resources yourself. And, of course, there are occasionally things that you really just have to do yourself.

A COMBINATION OF APPROACHES

As previously mentioned, you are not limited to using only a single approach to filling your capital needs. You can use each of the different approaches to its best effect. For example, if the project can be broken into sequential stages, you may opt to go forward as far as you can with your own resources before seeking to bring in OPM. This tends to accomplish two things. It will tend to make you more credible with potential investors and build the value of your business. This is likely to make OPM, when you do seek it, easier to obtain and less expensive.

Similarly, if the project can be broken into autonomous aspects or pieces, you can deal with each piece individually. You might shelve (hopefully temporarily) certain aspects of the project, self-fund other aspects, and seek OPM for yet others. For example, let's assume that you have come up with an idea for a new way to do business—let's say an inventory control system—that is applicable to a number of different fields. Let's also assume that you are in the office supply business, so that is your immediate concern. However, there are also huge markets for that type of system in the pharmaceutical and automotive industries, albeit with somewhat different features than the system used for office supplies. You could treat each of those industries separately and use a different strategy for each one.

The office supply industry is where your core expertise lies, and you expect activities in that area to generate the greatest appreciation in the value of your business. You might choose to self-fund, or take a loan to fund, the development of the system for the office supply industry. You could then retain the exclusive rights to sustain a competitive advantage, or you could license others in that industry—e.g., outside of your market area—to use it.

On the other hand, since you don't know the pharmaceutical industry, it would be more difficult and expensive for you to develop the pharmaceutical industry version of the product. So you might use a form of OPM to take advantage of another business's expertise to develop a product for the pharmaceutical industry—you grant a license to a pharmaceutical house. You can then use the licensing income to help fund your own development efforts. In fact, you may be able to negotiate a "grant-back" of a license to the pharmaceutical house's implementation of your idea so that you would be able to take advantage of your licensee's development efforts.

The automotive industry is notoriously difficult to enter. Accordingly, you might hold off on activity in the automotive industry until you have developed additional credibility. Or perhaps your acquaintance Otto has expertise in the auto industry and wants to participate as a co-venturer. You, however, do not want to dilute your ownership interest with respect to the office supply industry. In this case, you might create a completely new and separate entity (e.g., a subsidiary), license the new entity to use the technology in the automotive industry, and sell an equity interest in the new entity to Otto.

There is a strategy for determining whether to use your own money or OPM, and for determining how much, and the most appropriate form or combination of forms of OPM (debt, sale of equity, and/or co-venture). This will be discussed in detail later.

Is OPM Available on Reasonable Terms?

Under some circumstances, OPM may not be available at all, or its price may be too high. You may not be able to find a suitable source that will consider investing in your business. You never get a chance to tell your story. You can't get Mr. or Ms. OPM to read your proposal. We will discuss the details of getting access to sources of OPM in a later chapter.

On the other hand, you may sometimes get the opportunity to make your presentation but are unable to convince the potential source of OPM to invest. Generally, this occurs for one or more of a number of interrelated reasons:

• You simply don't meet the criteria of the OPM source. Perhaps the OPM source has a set of criteria that it follows, and after hearing your presentation, the OPM source realizes that you don't fall within it. For example, some venture capitalists may only fund projects where the investment is at least a million dollars and you need only $100,000 to get your project going. Or perhaps you need a million dollars, but the local OPM source to whom you are presenting has decided to "diversify" and limit any single investment to $250,000. Or perhaps the OPM source invests only in technology and you are proposing to fund a durable goods business. Or perhaps the source doesn't fund new product at all, but only mergers and acquisitions. *Frankly, this should not happen very often.* You should know the OPM source's investment criteria beforehand and tailor your presentation accordingly. If you know that you do not meet the investment criteria, you should not waste your time or the potential investor's.

• You are not able to demonstrate that your business is likely to "succeed." In other words, you are not able to demonstrate that your business meets (or will meet) the OPM source's investment criteria. The opportunity, as you present it to the potential investor, may not meet the criteria on its face. Or the opportunity, as you present it, may meet the criteria, but the potential investor is not convinced because you are not sufficiently "credible." We will discuss this further in the next chapter.

• You lose in a competition with other opportunities available to the source of OPM. There are lots of opportunities for investment. Professional investors such as venture capitalists, in particular, often see dozens, if not hundreds, of potential investments in a given month. What can you do about this?

You can concentrate your efforts on finding "amateur" investors who do not see so large a "deal flow." You can find professional investors who resonate with the opportunity your business presents. Professional investors often specialize in particular technical fields or markets. If you can find a professional investor who specializes in the field of your business, you can sometimes narrow the playing field.

You also need to do your homework. Make yourself as credible as possible.

• The valuation of your business by the OPM source, and, in particular, the value of your contribution to the business are too low. The valuation of your business at the time you seek equity investors tends to control the percentage ownership that the investors expect to get for their money. If the investors place a value on your business as it exists at the time of the potential investment below what you believe to be fair, they will typically ask for too high a percentage of ownership. Valuation also plays a hand in an institutional lender's decision to give a loan.

• The OPM source drives too hard a bargain. There will be times when, for whatever reason, you simply are not able to negotiate an agreement. A lot depends upon your negotiation skills (or those of your advisors). Perhaps the expectations of one or another of the parties are unrealistic. Or the OPM source perceives that you have a weakness or need and tries to exploit it. Or a lender perceives a loan to your business as risky and demands an unacceptably high interest rate. Realistically, in those situations, your choices are to self-fund to the extent that you are able, delay as you work to become more credible, and/or use OPR.

VALUATION, CREDIBILITY, AND LOANS

The availability of OPM from institutional lenders is often a function of the valuation of your business. Institutional lenders will typically not make a loan to a business entity unless they are confident that they will get paid back.

If the amount of the loan is a small percentage of the valuation of your business, and there is clearly adequate cash flow, the lender may feel comfortable making an unsecured loan. In many cases, however, the institutional lender will not make the loan unless it is secured with adequate collateral. Valuation is the central issue when a lender determines whether there is adequate collateral to secure a loan. Many institutional lenders, however, do not consider the entire value of a business when determining the adequacy of collateral. They tend to look only at what I refer to as the "demonstrable" assets of the business—tangible assets, such as real property and equipment, "certified" intellectual property, such as patent grants and trademark registrations, and, in some cases, certain contracts that will generate a "guaranteed" cash flow.

The interest rate on a loan tends to be a function of your credibility. The higher the risk of nonpayment perceived by the lender, the higher the interest rate. In the United States, a good credit risk will typically pay an interest rate within a few points of the prime rate. On the other hand, a bad credit risk will pay considerably higher rates. If you have "junk credit," you will pay junk bond interest rates.

VALUATION, CREDIBILITY, AND EQUITY INVESTORS

What percentage ownership of your business will an equity investor expect to get in return for a contribution? The answer depends on the perceived value of your business. The valuation of your business often depends upon your credibility. As previously mentioned, there are standard techniques for establishing the value of a business. However, in many instances, either those techniques cannot be applied or the application provides speculative results, meaning the results are based upon projections. How credible are your projections?

The ultimate valuation of your business is typically the product of negotiation between you and the potential investors. The results of negotiation will depend upon your credibility and your negotiation skills.

Let's say that one of your vendors, George, is willing to pay $100,000 for a 20 percent ownership interest in your business. George's offer means that he is assigning a *pre*-investment value of $400,000 to your business. Based on your projections, however, the business is worth $900,000 before the investment, and it's your position that George should get only a 10 percent interest for his $100,000. Unless there is movement from your respective positions, or a

Calculation of Valuation

How does an offer of $100,000 for a 20 percent interest translate into a $400,000 pre-investment valuation? It's simple mathematics.

If $100,000 is equal to 20 percent of the value of the business after the investment ($100,000 = 0.2 \times$ Value), then the value is equal to $100,000 divided by 20 percent (i.e., $500,000) (Value = $100,000/0.2 = $500,000).

Since George's contribution is $100,000, and the *post*-investment value is $500,000, for purposes of the investment, George placed a value of $400,000 on the business *prior* to his contribution ($500,000 − $100,000 = $400,000).

compromise, the investment will not happen. Are you credible enough to convince George to accept your projections?

As we will discuss, valuation of your business also plays a significant role in the timing of efforts to raise money.

Your Money or OPM?

If you have a choice between self-funding and using OPM, which should you choose? The answer depends upon the circumstances. For example, you may not be able to self-fund, or OPM may not be available to you on reasonable terms.

One of the primary benefits of using OPM is that it can open the door to opportunities for you. It permits you to participate in "deals" that would otherwise be beyond your resources. It can also permit you to move quickly enough to take advantage of windows of opportunity. As we stated earlier, it lets you play in the game. If your resources are not sufficient to let you take advantage of the opportunity, the choice between self-funding and using OPM is made for you.

On the other hand, depending upon the circumstances, the classical forms of OPM may not be available to you at a reasonable price. For example, you might not qualify for a loan at reasonable interest rates, and equity investors, if available at all, might insist on too large a percentage of ownership for their contribution. Realistically, in those situations, your choices are to self-fund to the extent that you are able, delay until you become more credible, and/or use OPR.

Let's assume, however, for the purposes of discussion that you can self-fund if you are so inclined and that the classical forms of OPM are available to you. In other words, you are in a position to choose between self-funding and using OPM.

There may be circumstances, depending upon your risk tolerance and your ability to attract investors, when you want to minimize your cash investment and leverage your resources to the fullest extent possible. There may be other things that you want to do with your money, other opportunities that you want to pursue. And, remember, with certain forms of OPM, you can get the full benefit of the appreciation in value of the asset, even though it was acquired or built using OPM.

There may be times when the valuation placed with your business by a potential equity investor is so favorable that using the OPM is too good to pass up. If you have determined that the value of your business is $100,000 and George insists on paying $100,000 for a 10 percent interest, how would you respond? (As a note of caution: Actually, you would want to make sure George understood all the facts before you took his money; the last thing that you need is an investor who comes to think that he was misled.)

There may be other circumstances where your risk tolerance is exceeded—the opportunity presents a bigger bite than you want to chew. Even though you may be able to self-fund the venture, you may not want to risk the entire amount. So you bring in co-venturers to spread the risk.

In a typical case, a cost-benefit analysis of using the OPM is in order. Is the post-OPM value of your ownership interest greater than the value of your pre-OPM ownership interest? (Remember, a small percentage of a large number can be much greater than a large percentage of a small number.) If so, is it sufficiently greater to compensate for any nonmonetary aspects of the price of the OPM?

Let's try to put this in perspective with some examples. (By the way, we will ignore any tax considerations in these examples.) Let's assume that you need to purchase equipment to increase your production capacity in order to meet customer demand for your product. The equipment costs $100,000. Let's assume, at least initially, that you have $100,000 in cash on hand. You could purchase equipment outright, but you want to explore your other options.

DEBT

One option is to borrow the money. Let's say you could borrow the $100,000 at 10 percent interest to be paid back in monthly installments of $1,852.58 over six years. (We will assume that 10 percent is the market rate and that the terms of the loan are otherwise standard.) What is the cost of the loan? Over the course of the loan, you pay $33,386.13 in interest—that is the finite cost of the OPM. The short-term cost is the monthly payments until the loan has been repaid. There is no long-term cost—once the loan is repaid with interest, there is no further cost. Under the circumstances in our example, it is unlikely that the loan will place any constraints on your control of the business.

Compared to equity investments, loans typically place minimal limitations on your management and control of the business. However, you lose a measure of flexibility with respect to cash flow management—you need to make sure that you have sufficient cash flow to service the debt (make the monthly payments).

There can also be additional restrictions on your management. If the loan is secured by collateral, there will likely be restrictions on what you can do with that collateral—for example, the collateral is tied up because you cannot sell it and are typically not able to use it as collateral for other loans unless somehow it is an appreciating piece of collateral, such as real estate. In some cases, especially where the loan represents a significant percentage of the value of your business, you are required to keep your cash flow above a certain level or the ratio of your business's debt to equity below a certain level. Beyond limitations of that sort, lenders (at least institutional lenders) typically leave the control of your business to you.

Does taking the loan make economic sense? (Remember, our assumptions remove any issues regarding the interest rate and terms of the loan and your ability to go forward without a loan.) The answer to that question depends on the anticipated cash flow and appreciation (increases in value) of your business.

Let's consider cash flow. If there is a significant risk that your cash flow will not support the monthly loan payments, assuming that you were able to get the loan in the first place, it probably does not make sense. On the other hand, you are ahead of the game if the equipment (a) permits you to immediately increase your monthly net income by more than the $1,852.58 loan payment or (b) assuming monthly cash flow is not an issue, increases your net income over the six-year term of the loan by more than the cumulative interest ($33,386.13). In those cases, the loan is good debt. If you have other productive uses for your cash, taking a loan probably makes sense. Of course, if you have nothing better to do with your cash, then purchasing the equipment outright would save you the $33,386.13 interest expense.

Now let's look at appreciation—increases in the value of your business.

Assume that, for some reason, the value of the equipment increases after your purchase (e.g., because of increased demand, and scarcity of the equipment). Or, more realistically, your business appreciates because of increased "goodwill." For example, your relationship with your customers improves and consumer recognition of your trademarks increases once you begin using the equipment. This results in an increase in the value of the goodwill asset of your business. In either case, you get the full benefit of that appreciation, even though the equipment was purchased with borrowed funds. If significant appreciation is anticipated, the loan permits you to leverage your money. So if you have other productive uses for your cash, taking a loan probably makes sense. Of course, if you self-fund, you will still get full benefit of the appreciation. If you have nothing better to do with your cash, then purchasing the equipment outright would save you the interest expense.

On the other hand, if the equipment did not result in an increase in net income and/or appreciation greater than the interest paid, the cost of the loan (interest) would be more than the benefit achieved. In that circumstance, taking the loan in lieu of self-funding or some other form of OPM probably would *not* make sense. Again, we are assuming that you have the cash on hand and do not need to use it for something else.

Other factors to consider are "spreading risk" and the effect of outstanding debt on your ability to later attract equity investors if you need them.

While there are ways to mitigate and limit your risk, as a general proposition you are required to pay back the loan whether or not an expected increase in income actually results from increasing your production capacity. You are not relieved from your obligation to repay the loan just because your market projections were wrong, or you lose your biggest customer, or you find yourself faced with a fierce new competitor that drives down your prices. You still assume 100 percent of the risk.

Outstanding debt can also be a huge impediment to attracting "new money" to an emerging business. Potential investors typically do not want their money to pay off existing debt. They expect their contribution to fund activities that will cause the value of the business to appreciate. That is how they get their expected return on investment. Retiring debt does not usually equate to appreciation.

EQUITY

Another option is to bring in equity investors. Let's go back to our earlier example of an equity investor. George is willing to pay $100,000 for a 20 percent ownership interest in your business. For purposes of discussion, let's assume that in this case that $400,000 is a fair pre-investment valuation of your business. In other words, we are assuming in this example that you are neither making money nor losing money based solely on the valuation of your business.

What is the price of the equity investment? There are both monetary and nonmonetary costs.

The hard (monetary) cost of the OPM is 20 percent of all of the income you would otherwise receive from the business in the future. The monetary cost is not a finite number as was the case with the loan. (Remember, with a loan, once you pay off the loan and the interest, you are done.)

The intangible (nonmonetary) costs are the additional obligations and responsibilities and the loss of independence that follows from having a co-venturer with a minority ownership interest in your business. There is no short-term hard cost in the sense of having to make immediate payments to the investors. You do not have the constraints on cash flow created by the necessity of making a monthly payment on a loan. The long-term cost is a percentage of future rewards that you must share with the investors. The nature of the obligations and responsibilities incurred is typically controlled by agreement. For example, you might have a shareholders' agreement giving George a seat on the board of directors or an operating agreement requiring unanimous approval of certain actions. Unless there is an agreement to the contrary, however, you will, at a minimum, have to consider George's interests when you make business decisions in the future. On the other hand, unless there is an agreement to the contrary, you would not lose control of the business by selling a minority interest (although, even then, you may owe a fiduciary duty to George, which may affect your control over the business).

Does bringing George in as an equity investor make sense if self-funding is a viable option? You have the cash, and you don't need it to take advantage of some other opportunity. We are assuming that valuation is a neutral factor in the decision. If you are confident that your business will grow in value, and money is all George is bringing to the table, the answer is probably no. You are better off self-funding or resorting to some other form of OPM. Of course, in many instances, a co-venturer brings nonmonetary contributions to the business, such as leadership, expertise, credibility, or a network of potential future sources of OPM.

For purposes of discussion, let's assume that your only viable options are to bring in an equity investor or forgo the purchase of the equipment. In that case, does bringing George in as an equity investor make sense? Since we are assuming that the valuation is not an issue, the answer depends upon whether the purchase of the equipment results in an increase in the net income of the business in excess of 20 percent over pre-investment levels or otherwise increases the value of the business from the pre-investment valuation by more than 20 percent.

Let's explore the issue of changes in the value of the business. Absent an agreement to the contrary, changes in valuation (increases and decreases) are shared pro rata. You are sharing potential growth with your equity investors, but you are also spreading the risk of loss.

Share the Rewards

Assume that the value of your business increases. For example, the equipment purchased with the $100,000 increased in value to $150,000. Or the value of your business or a business asset such as goodwill increases by an additional $50,000 over and above the value of your new equipment because of the service that you now provide. In either case, the value of the business would be $550,000, and you would be ahead of the game. Your 100 percent interest in the pre-investment company was worth $400,000. Your 80 percent interest in the post-investment company (valued at $550,000) is worth $440,000. George's position has also improved: His $100,000 investment is now worth $110,000. (If you had self-funded or taken a loan, the entire $50,000 appreciation would have been yours.) Up to this point in time, the OPM from George has cost you $10,000—20 percent of the $50,000 appreciation.

Spread the Risk

While you are sharing income and appreciation with George, you are also spreading the risk of loss. Let's change the scenario to illustrate the point.

Assume that the equipment was made to your specifications. No sooner do you install the equipment than your archcompetitor is granted a patent that covers precisely what you are doing. You investigate and find nothing that would invalidate the patent. You investigate further and determine that there is no way to modify the equipment to get around the patent and still make an economically viable product. In a nutshell, your new equipment is now essentially worthless, and your business has just suffered a $100,000 loss.

Let's assume that after the loss, the business is worth $400,000. Your 80 percent interest (for which you contributed the equivalent of $400,000) is now worth $320,000. You have suffered an $80,000 loss. George's 20 percent interest (for which he contributed $100,000) is now worth $80,000. George has suffered a $20,000 loss. If you had self-funded or financed the purchase of the equipment with a loan, you would have suffered the entire $100,000 loss. However, since George took a 20 percent equity position in the business, he absorbs 20 percent of the loss. Up to this point in time, the OPM from good old George would have diminished your risk, and subsequently your loss, by $20,000.

OPR

A third option is not to purchase the equipment at all but instead to enter into a strategic co-venture with an entity that already has the equipment. The strategic co-venture can take any number of forms. Some of these were illustrated in the example of Ivan, Manny, and Angelo in the previous chapter.

You could create a new joint venture entity, owned in part by you and in part by the entity that owns the equipment. Or you could establish a contractual relationship without creating a new entity. The contributions of the respective participants to the venture would depend on their relative strengths and weaknesses—what they bring to the table. Your contribution to the venture would include, for example, intellectual property—the use of your product designs, trademarks, etc. Their contribution would include the use of the equipment. One or both of you would be responsible for production or distributing the product.

The price of the OPR is the consideration given to your co-venturer in return for his or her contribution. The nature of the contribution and the consideration given for the contribution are limited only by your creativity and negotiating skills. For example, receipts from sales of products made by using the equipment could be shared according to some predetermined formula. The participants can be reimbursed for certain predetermined expenses and the remainder split between them according to a predetermined formula. We will discuss this in more detail in a later chapter.

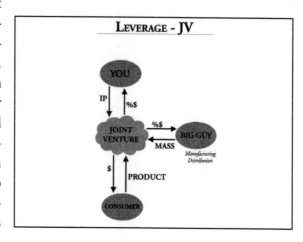

Outsourcing can be another form of OPR. You are able to get the benefit of equipment and expertise without having to expend the time, effort, and money to actually acquire or develop them up front. The issue is primarily the nature of the compensation to the service provider.

How does using OPR stack up against self-funding, taking a loan, or bringing in equity investors? The answer depends upon the specific details of the agreement between the parties. Agreements are commonly structured so that you can take full advantage of any appreciation in the value of your company—particularly through the development of goodwill. However, you typically would not own the equipment and would not participate in any increase

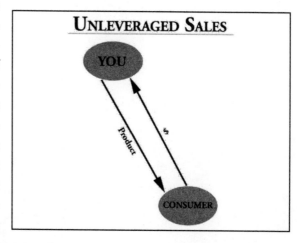

(or decrease) in the equipment value. The extent to which you share the risks and rewards with your co-venturer depends entirely upon the terms of the agreement.

Okay, let's assume that you made your choice to go with OPM and that you've chosen to raise money rather than OPR. How much money do you want to raise? We will talk about that in the next chapter.

Chapter 5

Raising Money: When and How Much?

You have decided that you need to raise money for your business. We have already discussed the difference between debt and equity money. But how much money should you raise? When is the best time to raise it?

The amount of money that you seek to raise affects a number of factors.

- The amount of money that you seek often puts boundaries on the type of sources from which it is available. The amount may be beyond the resources of certain classical sources—your family and friends. On the other hand, it may not be large enough to interest professional investors—venture capital funds. From their perspective, they have to put as much effort into a small deal as a large deal, and therefore they stick to the large deals.
- The amount of money that you ask for is also a factor in determining which form(s) of OPM you seek. Is it feasible to raise the entire amount as debt, or will you have to seek "equity money"? Can you qualify for that large of a loan? Will taking on that much additional debt be in violation of the

covenants of any previous loan? Will taking on that much additional debt make it difficult to bring in additional investors in the future?

• The amount that you are raising is also a factor in determining the manner in which you seek it. Can you get the money from a single source, or do you need to go to multiple sources? Can you raise the amount through sources with whom you are already acquainted, or do you have to "go public"?

• The amount that you are raising can also affect your obligations under the securities law.

• Perhaps most significant, the amount of "equity money" that you raise can affect your ownership and control of the business.

The timing of your fund-raising efforts is also important. Timing can affect both the availability and the price of OPM. Timing should be viewed relative to both the stage of development of your business and the condition of the market.

How Much Money Should You Raise?

The real question here is: How much money do you need?

If your reason for raising money is to acquire a specific asset—for example, a piece of equipment—you may know exactly how much money you will need. Even this can be tricky, however, because you may have to take into account additional operating costs for the equipment, such as maintenance, insurance, or additional employee expenses.

The more difficult case is when you are a start-up business and your goal is to bring the business to a point where it is self-sufficient, or to a point where it is feasible to raise additional funds at a lower cost. Then you must resort to projections. You should find the answers to the "how much" questions *in your business plan*. The same is true with respect to the expansion of an existing business. We will discuss business plans in more detail in a later chapter.

RULES OF THUMB

There are many rules of thumb with respect to how much money to raise. Some commentators will advise: "You can never have too much cash. Raise as much money as you can." Those folks assume that you either have no financial plan or are never successful in raising enough money to achieve your goals. Other commentators will tell you that a start-up should raise enough money to keep afloat for three years. Or that it should raise enough money to cover start-up expenses and a period, ranging from two to six months, of recurring expenses. That advice makes an assumption, which may or may not be accurate, with respect to the length of time it will take to establish positive cash flow. Frankly, I'm not sure that any of the rules of thumb are any good.

COMPETING CONCERNS—ADEQUACY AND COST

Basically, when you are determining how much money to raise, there are competing concerns: adequacy and cost. There should be a reason for raising money—an immediate goal. You want to be sure that you don't run out of money before you accomplish that goal—in other words, that you have adequate amounts of funds. You want to be able to deal with unforeseen contingencies and take advantage of opportunities that might arise. But at the same time, you don't want to pay a steep price for something that you don't need. This second concern is particularly important if the price for OPM is paid with equity interests in your business. You need to plan in order to avoid a cash shortage, but if you raise too much "equity money" too early, you may unnecessarily dilute the ownership of your business—give

> ### *Financing Goals*
>
> The goal of raising money could be any number of things. In the case of a start-up, the goal is typically to cover expenses until the business either becomes self-sufficient or reaches a milestone where sufficient value has been created in the business to attract additional investment.
>
> The goals of an existing business might be to acquire a particular asset, such as equipment, facilities, or another business. Or its goal could be to expand production, develop a new product or enter a new market, or expand its presence in an existing market.

away the store. We will consider the timing of fund-raising efforts in a moment.

CASH FLOW ANALYSIS—PRO FORMA FINANCIAL STATEMENTS

There's no question that you need to know how much money you need before you start on your search for OPM. When you are financing business operations, whether in the context of a start-up or an expansion, you need to have a handle on your anticipated cash flow. You need to know what your approximate expenses will be and when they will occur, how much income you can expect, and when you can expect it.

At the very least, you need to list all anticipated expenses and income. You can do that informally, but, generally, the best way to approach estimating future income and expenses is to prepare a draft business plan. You will need a well-crafted business plan in order to have any realistic hope of receiving funds from professional investors.

Your business plan should cover the two main sides of the cash flow analysis. That is, how your business will earn money and where it will spend it. More specifically, it should include pro forma financial statements (profit and loss, balance sheet, and cash flow) for the next three to five years. The process of preparing the business plan and pro forma financial statements will force you to systematically think through your business model, establish a logical progression of business goals, and identify the expenses you are likely to incur and income you are likely to receive in the course of achieving those goals. You examine your assets, the market for your product or service, and any historical data that you might have, make assumptions, which you should be sure to record, and make estimates.

If you do not have experience in making financial projections (or even if you do), you may want to enlist the aid of your advisors. If you know that you are the type of person who is challenged by the most simple budget—that is, you can't even come up with your household budget—it's definitely time to call in the reserves. Professional assistance—from an accountant experienced at preparing financial projections, for example—can make a huge difference not only in the validity of your planning but in your credibility with investors. We will touch on financial plans and projections again later.

HOW MUCH SHOULD I RAISE FOR A START-UP?

In general, a start-up will need sufficient initial capital to cover all of the expenses of setting up the business and working capital to operate the business until you have sufficient cash flow to cover expenses. But your capital needs don't end once you are in a positive cash flow situation. You might also want capital specifically earmarked for research and development, promotional and marketing expenses, and a contingency reserve.

The expenses of setting up a business vary considerably depending upon the nature of the business. They typically include such things as initial supplies and starting inventory; deposits for rent, utilities, and leased equipment; fixtures; computers, telephones, and other equipment; software licensing fees; installation costs for equipment and fixtures; tenant improvements; insurance; creation of a Web site; signage; printing; business licenses and permits; and fees to attorneys, accountants, and consultants.

The working capital should cover all of the recurring expenses and anticipated incidental expenses of your business. For example, recurring expenses usually include payroll; materials and supplies; equipment lease payments; rent or mortgage payments; utilities; telecommunications (e.g., telephone, Internet access); maintenance; transportation and delivery; loan payments; and any other expenses relating to running the business. Incidental expenses would typically include taxes; fees to attorneys, accountants, and consultants (to the extent that they are not recurring expenses); the cost of hiring employees (keeping in mind the need to hire additional staff as business expands); and the cost of additional equipment that might be required as the business grows during that period. If you do not have separate budgets for research and product development, and promotion and marketing activities, then those expenses would also be accounted for as working capital.

One thing to be aware of is that potential investors will want to know how much of the anticipated payroll expense you have allotted for yourself. Keep any compensation for yourself as low as possible—your investors will want to know that you have "skin in the game" and that you are investing your time in the venture as well as any financial investment you are making. In fact, you want to carefully analyze all "overhead" expenses that may not be required to get your business up and running. Make any and all start-up funding required essential to the success of the core business or products. The "extras" can come *after* your business is generating positive cash flow from operations.

How much of a contingency reserve should you have? The "authorities" are all over the board on this. As previously noted, sources suggest reserves of anywhere from 10 percent to 25 percent of start-up costs and working costs. Other sources suggest reserves of anywhere from two to six months of working expenses. However, contingencies can be covered just as well by a line of credit as by a cash reserve.

How do you know what your cash flow will be? That is what financial projections are all about. You (preferably with your advisors) examine your assets, the market, and any historical data that you might have. You make assumptions and estimate. As I've said, we will touch on financial plans and projections again later.

When and How Much? Sequencing and Staging

The timing of your fund-raising efforts can have a significant effect on both the availability of OPM and the price that you have to pay for it. Are you in the best position to raise money? Is the "market" in the best condition to provide it?

The valuation of your business at the time you seek equity money tends to control the cost (in terms of percentage ownership) of the money. In its early stages, the valuation of the business will tend to be less than it will be later on. One aspect of valuation is "perceived likelihood of success." The earlier you are in the development of your business, the greater the perceived risk. Investors, if available at all, will typically expect a larger percentage of ownership for a given amount of money invested.

For that reason, financings are usually planned to correlate with critical growth stages and milestones in the development of your business. Typically, you raise only enough money to get you to the next milestone. In other words, you build up the value of your business as much as you can before each successive round of financing and do not raise money until you actually need it, taking into account the lead time necessary to raise funds. The type of OPM and sources often vary from round to round.

People in the financial industry often refer to different "stages" of private financing defined by specific milestones in the growth and credibility of the business. The labels attached to the different stages and the specific milestones used to differentiate between them tend to vary within the industry. However, in general, the stages of growth are the early stage, involving seed, start-up, and first-stage financings; and the expansion stage, involving second-stage, third-stage (mezzanine), and perhaps bridge financings.

Stages of Private Financing

In the real world, no one is particularly concerned with whether you fit precisely within the boundaries of one of the stages or another when you seek to raise money. The real issue is whether the opportunity presented by your business meets the investment criteria of a particular source of OPM. However, an understanding of the stages of financing can be helpful.

Seed Financing
Milestone: Conception of idea
Use of Funds: Seed capital is used to prove the feasibility of your idea and/or business model and structure your business. This may involve forming the business entity, identifying key members of your management team and advisors, performing research to assess market potential, prototype development, patent and trademark investigations and filings, and preparing an initial business plan.
Typical Source of Funds: Seed capital is typically self-funded or provided by family and friends.

Start-up Financing
Milestone: Feasibility of idea proven, business plan prepared, business entity formed
Use of Funds: Start-up financing is used to complete product development and prove marketplace acceptance of the product. This may involve

completing development and testing of a prototype, completing the product development, market testing, and the initial marketing efforts. The funds may also be used to complete the legal foundation for the business (formation of business entity, patent and trademark filings, and agreements), assembling your management team and advisors, and refining and adjusting the business plan.

Typical Source of Funds: Start-up capital is self-funded or provided by family and friends and Angel investors. Depending upon the management team, intellectual property protection, and success in the marketplace, you may begin to meet the investment criteria of Angel and professional investors.

First-Stage Financing

Milestone: Your product or service has been successfully tested and is now commercially available.

Use of Funds: First-stage capital is used to initiate full-scale commercial production and sales of a product or rollout of services. This involves undertaking efforts to refine manufacturing and business processes to increase efficiency and reduce costs, build sales, fund marketing and promotion, establish distribution mechanisms, and achieve certain initial market penetration and sales goals. Second-level management is identified and hired, and more sophisticated business systems are put into place.

Typical Source of Funds: All of the various sources of funding are theoretically potential sources of first-stage funding. The amounts involved tend to be beyond the limits of family and friends' investments, so this level of funding is most often provided by self-funding or by Angel or professional investors. You may also qualify for a loan program offered by the Small Business Administration (SBA) to be discussed in a later chapter. The availability of the funding depends upon your ability to demonstrate that you meet the investment criteria of investors.

Second-Stage Financing
Milestone: Significant sales
Use of Funds: Second-stage capital is used as working capital for business expansion and cash flow management—for example, supporting growing accounts receivable and inventory—and to reach the point of consistent profitability. Often the business is expanded from regional to national and, perhaps, international.
Typical Source of Funds: The amounts involved tend to be beyond the limits of family and friends' investments, so this level of funding is most often provided by self-funding, Angel or professional investors, and traditional lending institutions. Again, you may want to review the programs sponsored by the SBA. The availability of the funding depends upon your ability to demonstrate that you meet the investment criteria of investors.

Line of Credit
Milestone: Cash flow is breakeven, occasional profitability.
Use of Funds: The line of credit is drawn down to provide short-term financing for cash flow management.
Typical Source of Funds: Commercial bank

Third-Stage (Mezzanine) Financing
Milestone: Increasing sales volume; profitability; potential for a major success is apparent.
Use of Funds: Third-stage funds are used for further facilities expansion, marketing, and working capital, or for the development of product improvements, new technology, or to expand your product line.
Typical Source of Funds: The amounts involved tend to be beyond the limits of family and friends' investments, so this level of funding is most often provided by self-funding, Angel or professional investors, and traditional lending institutions. The availability of the funding depends upon your ability to demonstrate that you meet the investment criteria of investors or lenders.

Bridge Financing

Milestone: Plans for liquidity financing (IPO) or exit (business acquired by another company) within the next year

Use of Funds: Bridge financing is typically short-term debt (often repaid out of the proceeds from the liquidity financing) used to permit the business to buy out founders and early investors in whole or in part. For example, this is sometimes done when founders or early investors want to reduce or liquidate their ownership before the business goes public, or after there has been a change in management and the business wants to buy out the former management.

Typical Source of Funds: Institutional lenders

After the various stages of private financings, the business reaches what I refer to as the "liquidity" (exit) stage, through which the founders and early investors "harvest" their investment. This typically involves either an initial public offering (IPO), where securities—like stock or bonds—are issued by the business and offered for sale to the public at large, or acquisition of the business by a larger entity.

There are also specific-purpose financings that are not categorized by the stage of development of your business, such as research and development financings, management/leveraged buyout financing, and acquisition financing. (I'll bet you can guess what the special purposes are.)

Research and development financings are worth special mention. While often either equity or debt financings, R&D financings are sometimes a form of joint venture, referred to as a "royalty financing." The investor contributes money to fund the R&D but receives compensation (a royalty) for each unit of the product resulting from the R&D sold rather than equity in the business. The royalty can be a fixed amount or a percentage of sales. In some cases, the payments are terminated when the cumulative payments reach a predetermined amount.

PREMATURE FINANCING—DON'T GIVE AWAY THE STORE

Irrespective of your business's stage of development at a given point in time, you need to consider anticipated increases in value when you are thinking about bringing in equity investors. This is particularly true when you are a start-up venture: Value tends to increase in spurts, and the largest percentage appreciation tends to occur during the early stages of a company's history. Timing can make a huge difference in the cost of OPM.

Let's revisit the scenario from the preceding chapter with potential investor George to illustrate this point. George is willing to pay $100,000 for a 20 percent ownership interest in your business. Assume that at the moment, your business is in fact worth $400,000. However, you are on the verge of a breakthrough that will make it worth $900,000. The breakthrough could be, for example, signing a lucrative contract, or it could be a significant milestone in the development of a new product or process.

Do you want to let George invest now, with your business valued at $400,000? If you do, he gets a 20 percent ownership interest for his $100,000. Or do you want to try to wait until after the breakthrough before you let him invest? Can you wait and still have the breakthrough without George's money? If you can wait, George will get only a 10 percent ownership interest for $100,000. You will have cut the cost of George's $100,000 in half. This sort of scenario is commonplace for an emerging business.

PARSING A FINANCING

Even if your business is not transitioning between defined stages of growth when you are raising money, you may want to break a financing out into a series of smaller financings. Let me draw an analogy. Building your business is like driving down the highway, and money is your fuel. Sources of OPM are like gas stations. You are driving down the highway in your car when you realize that you are low on fuel. You pull into the first gas station that you come to. You find, however, that the price of fuel at that gas station is extremely high. Although you can't be positive, you are relatively sure that there will be other gas stations with more reasonable prices down the road. The closer you get to your destination, the less expensive the fuel. So do you fill up with the high-priced gas? Do you pass altogether and hope that you have enough fuel to make it to the next gas station? Or do you buy just enough gas to make sure that you reach the more reasonably priced gas station closer to your destination?

In your journey down the highway of financing your business, is there a less expensive gas station down the road? In other words, can you identify specific milestones or events that would cause a significant increase in the valuation of the business? And if so, how much fuel—money—will it take to get there? If you can make it to that next gas station—or milestone—your fuel will be less expensive.

There are a number of factors to consider when parsing out a financing—that is, breaking it into smaller pieces.

• Are there sources of OPM available to fund the entire amount immediately? If the price of the money is not too egregious, you may want to go for it. Sometimes you simply have to strike while the iron is hot. If there is a shortage of "gas," you might want to go ahead and fill up. Do you remember the saying about a bird in hand versus those in the bush? If you opt to break the financing out into rounds, you should feel relatively confident that the sources of OPM will still be there when you are ready for later rounds of financing.

• Can you identify specific milestones or events that would cause a significant increase (appreciation) in the valuation of the business? What sort of events am I talking about? Examples are proof of concept, completion of a prototype of your product or technology, filing a patent application (or better yet, obtaining a patent grant), completion of product development, completion of market research, a product launch, a major contract or customers, and filling out the management team. Any of these may be a natural "breakpoint" for financing. Rounds of financing occurring after the "breakpoints" may cost you less than earlier rounds.

• Can you divide the total amount of money that you will need into a number of smaller, discrete portions that will be needed at different times? Specifically, are you able to determine how much money you need to get to the next breakpoint?

• Will asking for the smaller amounts affect the potential sources of OPM available to you? How do the smaller amounts fit with the range of investments made by your potential sources of OPM? Will the smaller amounts take you beneath the radar screen of your potential sources of OPM (venture capitalists)? Will the smaller amounts make other sources (family and friends, Angels) available to you?

- Will you have the necessary lead times to raise the funds in separate rounds of financing? Will you be able to have the money in hand when you need it? Will your ability to move your business forward be hindered by not getting the financing in on a timely basis? Can you arrange it so that when you reach a milestone, you will already have a commitment for funding of the next milestone? Or can you survive during the time it takes to raise the funds? Is it feasible to deal with this problem through a contingency fund?

- How much will the process of raising the money in separate rounds (as opposed to a single round) cost in terms of time, effort, and money (e.g., fees for professional services)? Using the road trip analogy, consider whether the savings are great enough to make it worthwhile to drive out of your way to get to the cheaper gas station—and then wait in line at the pumps for the gas. It doesn't make good use of your time and effort to drive across town to save pennies on the gallon. Will your time and effort be better spent on growing the business than on finding the money in different rounds?

- Are there securities law issues with the timing of successive rounds of financing? If sufficient time passes between rounds, breaking the financing into smaller amounts may permit you to take advantage of certain exemptions from some of the more onerous obligations imposed by the securities law.

- Is there some advantage to being associated with only one source of financing? Perhaps your source is someone or some company that has particular credibility or "fame" in your industry, and the association with your source of OPM may give you standing in the eyes of people in your industry, the media, the public, or even other sources of OPM. Or perhaps a single, larger funding may cement a relationship that will facilitate future fundings. In those cases, it may not make much sense to parse out financing to others.

The logic of this parsing analysis is applicable regardless of the size of a financing.

EXAMPLE: PARSED FINANCING FOR DEVELOPMENT OF A PRODUCT

Assume that you have decided to finance the development of a product by bringing in equity investors. Let's also assume that if you shift your resources to this project, it will cost you $8,000 a month in excess of income to meet your payroll, overhead, and other general expenses. (The investment community refers to this as the "burn rate" of your business.) You project that the development effort will cost $335,000 over the course of the next eighteen months, according to the following schedule (using a 25 percent contingency factor):

Task	Estimated Months to Complete	Labor and Overhead (@ Burn Rate of $8,000 + 25% contingency)	Estimated Cost (+25%) of Components, Materials, Expenses, and Outside Services	Task Total Expense
Proof of principle	2	$20,000	$5,000	$25,000
Prepare and file patent application	1 (concurrent with designing prototype)		$15,000	$15,000
Design and build prototype	5	$50,000	$10,000	$60,000
Test prototype	1	$10,000	$5,000	$15,000
Design production version	6	$60,000	$5,000	$65,000
Testing and finalizing production design	4	$40,000	$25,000	$65,000
Establish manufacturing process	4 (concurrent with testing design)		$80,000	$80,000
Design packaging	1 (concurrent with testing design)		$10,000	$10,000
TOTAL	18 months	$180,000	$155,000	$335,000

Let's assume for the purposes of discussion that the only prospects that you have at the moment for raising that much money are a group of acquaintances, all of whom are accredited investors under the securities law, who are willing to fund the entire project. They offered to contribute $350,000 in return for a 70 percent equity interest in your business ($5,000 for each 1 percent unit). In other words, they have placed a pre-investment valuation of only $150,000 on your business, which we will assume is a fair pre-investment valuation at this stage of the development. They justify their offer as follows:

There is a high risk that they will lose their money—you have not even proved that your idea will work. And you, on the other hand, have no "skin in the game"—none of your own hard cash will be at risk. You are not contributing the use of your personnel and facilities—their investment would be paying for that. That means that you are (or, rather, your pre-investment business is) effectively contributing only intellectual property—an unproven, unprotected idea—and your expertise.

Finally, your potential investors have identified a number of comparable (in their view) businesses that were sold for $150,000 or less.

So you have a source of OPM available to provide all of the money that you need for the project, but the money is, as they say, pretty pricey. You would literally give up control of your business. What do you do?

Going back to our road trip analogy, is there a less expensive gas station down the road? And if so, how much fuel will it take to get there? In other words, can you identify specific milestones or events that would cause a significant increase in the valuation of the business? And can you determine how much money it will take to get there? In this case, the answer is clearly yes to both questions. Each milestone in your projection is a potential breakpoint for financing. Rounds of financing occurring after the breakpoints may cost you less than earlier rounds. At the very least, you have the option of releasing any contingency reserves left over when you reached the earlier milestone.

Timing, of course, can be an issue. By the time you reach one milestone, you already need to have funding for the next milestone. Your expenses—particularly your overhead and payroll—do not necessarily stop while you scramble for funds. Going back to our road trip analogy, you do not stop using fuel just because you are stuck in a traffic jam. How do you deal with timing issues? The answer is simple: Plan ahead. You make arrangements for funding well in advance of when you need the funds. You include adequate contingency reserves.

For example, you can sometimes come to an agreement with your source of OPM to provide funding in stages. You would come to an agreement on a valuation of your business at each milestone. The investors would provide funding for you to reach the first milestone and would commit to provide further funding when you reach successive milestones. The price of the fundings would be consistent with the agreed-upon valuation of your business at the time you reach the milestone. Each round of financing would be enough to get to the next milestone in succession. If for some reason you do not reach a milestone, the source of OPM would have no commitment to provide further funding.

This type of staged approach makes the investment less risky for the investors, while at the same time making it much more certain that you will have the funds that you need when you need them. In our example, we will assume that the group of acquaintances has made it clear that the funds will be available on short notice for staged financing. (In the real world, you would not want to depend on the money being available unless you had a written commitment from the potential investors.)

You budgeted $25,000 and two months' efforts for "proof of principle"—to prove the feasibility of your idea. Once that is accomplished, you have taken one of the elements of uncertainty out of the equation. You can show that you are much more likely to succeed. There is still considerable uncertainty, but the risk is greatly diminished from the point where you had an unproven idea. That means that once you have achieved proof of principle, the value of what you bring to the table will increase measurably.

Scorecard—Going into the 1st Round

Project Status	Unproven idea
	Need proof of principle
Financing Needs:	
To completion	$ 335,000
To next milestone	$ 25,000
Valuation	$ 150,000
Ownership:	
You	100% (Value = $150,000)
Investors	0%

Round 1—Proof of Principle

Let's assume that after proof of principle, a fair valuation of the business, based on a comparison to similar ("comparable") businesses, would be $250,000. And if the proof of principle was coupled with a patent application prepared by a respected patent attorney (providing a credible third-party validation), the fair valuation of the business would be $450,000.

A Patent Application Can Be a Third-Party Validation of Proof of Principle

Under the patent law, filing a patent application is essentially the same as actually building the invention and proving that it works for its intended purpose. A patent describing an "inoperative" invention—something that does not work—would be invalid. A good patent attorney would not prepare an application on an inoperative invention. In other words, a patent application represents, among other things, a statement by the patent attorney—a third-party verification—that the invention actually does work for its intended purpose. You are able to leverage on the credibility of the patent attorney.

Do you have to perform actual physical experiments to prove that your idea works or build a physical prototype before you file a patent application? The answer is no. You can design it on paper. As long as you are able to describe the invention in enough detail to permit the average person involved in relevant industry to make and use the invention, no prior actual experimentation or physical prototype is required. This means that the patent application itself can sometimes be the proof of principle.

To learn more on the subject, read my book *Protecting Your #1 Asset: Creating Fortunes from Your Idea* (Warner Books, 2001), one of the books in the Rich Dad's Advisors series.

You need $25,000 to get to proof of principle and an additional $15,000 to have the patent application prepared. You may be able to negotiate a better valuation than $150,000 from other equity investors who have lower expectations with respect to return on their investment than the original group. However, for purposes of this example, we are assuming that the $150,000 pre–proof of principle valuation is about as good as you will be able to negotiate, and the price of equity investments will be in the ballpark of a 1 percent ownership interest for each $5,000 invested. In other words, you would give up around 5 percent ownership in your business to raise the $25,000 to take you to proof of principle and an additional 3 percent to raise $15,000 for the patent application. You may want to "buy" that much high-priced fuel to get you far enough down the road to reach the next station.

In this example, it may appear that establishing the valuation of the company at the various stages of development is cut-and-dried, based on comparison to the sale of comparable businesses. In the real world, however, valuation tends to be the result of negotiation between you and the potential investors. Information regarding the price paid for nonpublic companies is often very difficult to obtain, and it is often difficult to find a comparable public company, particularly if you are a start-up. There are no hard (historical) numbers and, at least during the early stages of development, few physical assets. The valuation is typically based, in large part, upon projections of income and cash flow (and the validity of the assumptions that were made in connection with the projections) and intangible assets, such as patents, trademarks, goodwill, and other bases for sustainable competitive advantage. The result often boils down to credibility and negotiation skills.

The fact that you are seeking to raise only $25,000 (or $40,000 if you pursue the patent application), instead of the full $335,000, may make other sources of OPM available. Maybe you could self-fund. Or you might try to obtain a loan, presumably secured by your personal assets. Of course, you need to have a high tolerance for risk: If it turns out that your idea does not work, you still have to repay the loan. On the other hand, you would get the full benefit of any appreciation in value of your business.

Perhaps you can find someone with the resources to perform the proof of principle in return for bartered services or some form of credit.

Let's assume that you decided to hold off on raising money to prepare the patent application until after you achieve proof of principle. So you sell 5 percent of your business to raise the money and prove that your idea is feasible.

What's next? Let's also assume that you did not need the 25 percent contingency reserve ($6,250) and decided to apply that money to the project rather than continue to hold it in reserve. At this point, you still need to raise $303,750 ($310,000 less $6,250) to complete development.

Do you try to raise it all now? With a fair valuation of your business at $250,000, you would still have to give up more than 50 percent ownership interest to do so: 303,750 / (250,000 + 303,750) = 55.9%; approximately $5,537 per 1% unit. Or do you—once more—break it down into pieces and raise only enough to get you to the next milestone (or through the next few)?

Scorecard—Going into the 2nd Round

Project Status	Principle proven
	Need patent application
	Need prototype
Financing Needs:	
To completion	$303,750
To next milestone	$15,000/$90,000
Valuation	$ 250,000
Ownership:	
You	95% (Value = $237,500)
Investors	5% (Value = $12,500)

Round 2—Prepare and File Patent Application

At this point, your plan calls for you to do two things concurrently. You need to protect your idea—for which you have budgeted $15,000 for preparation of a patent application—and you need to design, build, and test a prototype, for which you have budgeted $75,000. While building and testing the prototype were separately budgeted, it probably makes sense to group them for purposes of raising capital—a prototype that has been tested and shown to work is the much better milestone.

Your credibility will be enhanced once patentability has been assessed by a reputable patent counsel and a patent application has been prepared and filed. You have staked your claim to the invention and have stopped the clock with respect to the information, referred to as "prior art," against which patentability is measured. While not as good as an actual patent grant, the patent application is demonstrable evidence—third-party verification—

that your invention works and, at least to some extent, is verification that it is protectable. As a practical matter, filing a patent application makes communication with sources of OPM easier. Confidentiality becomes somewhat less of a concern. In any event, the value of your company will increase once the application is filed.

A Patent Application Isn't a Grant—but Can Be a Third-Party Validation of Probable Patentability

The filing of a patent application is not a guarantee that a patent will be granted or that the patent will have a meaningful scope of coverage. However, a reputable patent attorney will typically not file a patent application on an invention that he or she knows is not patentable. This means that the act of filing the application is a representation of sorts by the attorney—a third-party verification and validation—that the attorney thinks the invention is patentable. Again, you can leverage on the reputation of your patent attorney. There are, however, three caveats to that statement:

1. The attorney or firm must have a good reputation for you to leverage on. Some attorneys and firms have a reputation of being more concerned with cost than quality. (How was that for being polite?) The fact that an application was filed by that type of firm is, frankly, not much of a validation.
2. Many patent attorneys, if not most, will take "aggressive" positions—file an application if there is *any* chance at all that the invention is patentable.
3. The scope of protection—coverage of—a patent that ultimately issues is always in question.

Sophisticated investors typically have their own patent attorneys assess the patent application with respect to patentability and probable scope. Over the years, I have evaluated many patents on behalf of venture capitalist and sophisticated angel investors.

Some entrepreneurs will have their patent counsel prepare a formal "patentability opinion" to bolster their credibility. In cases where there is a particularly pertinent piece of prior art—for example, where the invention is an improvement on an existing product—such an opinion may be helpful in explaining the value of invention to potential investors. However, the opinion is typically based only on the particular prior art in front of the attorney and will specifically note that there may be information relevant to patentability that is not known and therefore not considered. Generally, there are so many disclaimers in a patentability opinion that you are better off just spending the money on having the application prepared and filed. A bulletproof opinion, if there is such a thing, would require so much investigation that it would probably be cost-prohibitive.

There are a number of factors that are relevant to whether or not, and how much, filing a patent application will cause the value of your business to increase. Those factors include the particular industry that your business is in and the importance of patents in that industry; the nature of your invention and substance of the application; the nature of your competitors; the sophistication of the potential investors (this can cut both ways, depending upon the nature of your invention and substance of the application); and the reputation of your patent attorney and/or his or her firm among the potential investors. As noted above, we are assuming in our example, that with a patent application prepared by a respected patent attorney, a fair valuation of the business would be $450,000.

Likewise, once you have a prototype that you can demonstrate, your credibility (and hence the value of your company) will significantly increase. We will assume that, based on the price at which comparable businesses were sold, the value of your business would be $400,000 if you had a working prototype but did not file a patent application, and $625,000 with both patent application and prototype.

> ### *The Whole Can Be Greater than the Sum of the Parts*
>
> The patent application by itself and prototype by itself caused a $200,000 and $150,000 increase in value over the value at proof of principle, respectively. Add those amounts to the $250,000 valuation of the business at the proof of principle stage and you get $600,000. So why is the value of the business $625,000 with both patent application and prototype rather than $600,000? It could be because it's my book and I get to pick the numbers. Then again, it could be that the valuation is $25,000 more than you would expect because having both physical prototype (which you can demonstrate to the potential investor) and patent application (providing third-party validation) typically has a synergistic effect on your credibility.

Let's assume that you decided to get a patent application on file before raising capital for developing and testing the prototype. There are a number of reasons why you might want to do that. In this example, filing the patent application gives rise to considerable appreciation (a $15,000 investment increases the valuation of the business by $125,000). You may want to adopt an approach to funding that would give you the full benefit of that appreciation—self-funding or getting a loan. Funding the preparation of a patent application is also particularly amenable to unconventional forms of finance, such as a bartering arrangement or "royalty financing" (e.g., the investor would get a royalty on each unit covered by the patent that is sold until he or she is paid a certain amount).

Let's assume that you decide to apply the $6,250 reserve to the cost of a patent application and your uncle agrees to loan your business (with your personal guarantee) $10,000, to be repaid with fifteen monthly payments of $733.33. The loan will cost you $1,000 in interest (as compared to a 3 percent ownership interest in your business). You rework your projections taking present status of the project and the monthly loan payments, plus a 25 percent reserve, into account, using a burn rate of $10,916 rather than the original $10,000.

Task	Estimated Months to Complete	Labor and Overhead (@ Burn Rate of $10,916)	Estimated Cost of Components, Materials, Expenses, and Outside Services	Task Total Expense
Proof of principle (completed)	0	0	0	0
Prepare and file patent application (completed)	0		0	0
Design and build prototype	5	$54,580	$10,000	$64,580
Test prototype	1	$10,916	$5,000	$15,916
Design production version	6	$65,496	$5,000	$70,496
Testing and finalizing production design	4	$43,664	$25,000	$68,664
Establish manufacturing process	4 (concurrent with testing production design)		$80,000	$80,000
Design packaging	1 (concurrent with testing production design)		$10,000	$10,000
TOTAL	16 months	$174,656	$135,000	$309,656

Scorecard—Going into the 3rd Round

Project Status	Patent application filed Need prototype
Financing Needs:	
To completion	$309,656
To next milestone	$80,496
Valuation	$450,000
Ownership:	
You	95% (Value = $427,500)
Investors	5% (Value = $22,500)

Round 3—Design and Build Prototype/Test Prototype

At this point, you set out to raise $80,496 to fund designing and building and testing a prototype. (Note the effect of the increased "burn rate" incorporating the loan payments.) Let's assume that you decide to bring in equity investors. With your business valued at $450,000 before the investment, you sell approximately 15 percent ownership interest to raise the money.

Assuming that the reserve was not needed, at the point that the prototype is built and tested, your company is valued at $625,000 and you have a reserve of approximately $20,000. Ignoring the reserve, you need another $229,160 to complete the project. If you apply the reserve, you need an additional $209,160.

Scorecard—Going into the 4th Round

Project Status	Patent application filed
	Prototype built and tested
	Need to design and test
	Production model
Financing Needs:	
To completion	$209,160
	($229,160 – $20,000)
To next milestone	$70,496
Valuation	$625,000
Ownership:	
You	80% (Value = $500,000)
Investors	20% (Value = $125,000)

Round 4—Complete the Project

Let's assume that you decide to bring in equity investors to raise the $209,160 necessary to complete the project. With your business valued at $625,000 before the investment, you sell approximately 25 percent ownership interest to raise the money: $209,160/($625,000 + $209,160) = 25%.

The Parsing Pays Off

When the dust settles, the project is completed: Your product is ready to launch. You end up owning 55 percent of the business, and your investors 45 percent.

Do you recall that your investors' initial proposal was that they would take 70 percent of your business in consideration of providing the funding? By parsing the financing and taking advantage of appreciation (diminishing the risk factor), you were able to keep an additional 25 percent of your company. Do you think that parsing the financing was worth the trouble?

Now you know how much money to ask for—and when to ask for it. The obvious next question is: Whom do you ask? That is the subject of the next chapter.

Chapter 6

Sources of OPM—Where Do You Find the Money?

You have chosen between self-funding and using OPM and between debt, equity, and OPR. Let's assume that you have decided to raise money—through either debt or equity. You have determined how much money to raise and when to raise it. You have made all of those decisions. Now it's time to actually find the money.

From which sources will you seek it? Do you start using credit cards or lines of credit (your personal account or that of your business entity)? Can you get advance payments from customers? Can you get favorable credit terms from your vendors and suppliers? Are grants available? Are government lending programs available? Can you find co-venturers that can provide the resources that you need? Do you approach "amateur" investors (such as your family, friends, and high-net-worth individuals) or professional investors such as financial institutions and venture capitalists? Do you approach investors through private placements or a public offering?

Your choices will in large part be dictated by the circumstances. The different sources of OPM tend to have different investment criteria. And, from your perspective, each type of source of OPM has advantages and disadvantages.

Let's run through some of the different sources of OPM that may be available.

Personal Credit of Principals

CREDIT CARDS (YOUR PERSONAL ACCOUNT OR THAT OF YOUR BUSINESS ENTITY)

With good credit and a number of credit cards, you can have ready access to tens of thousands of dollars. Many small businesses use credit cards to pay for everything. Some businesses use credit cards as a tool for record keeping and take advantage of the incentive programs (free airline mileage, points toward merchandise) by certain credit card companies and merchants. There is nothing wrong with this—as long as the account is paid off each month or (if by some miracle) the interest rate is extremely favorable. Others use credit cards for cash flow management.

In any event, credit cards must be used with care. The interest rates and charges can be extremely expensive—financing your business with your personal credit cards can be a very expensive proposition and typically involves significant personal risk.

COSIGNED/COLLATERALIZED LOANS

Banks and other financial institutions typically will not make a loan unless they are relatively certain that they will be repaid the principal with interest. When your business doesn't meet the lender's criteria, you may secure the loan by "cosigning" (providing a personal guarantee of repayment) and/or pledging your personal assets as collateral. In most states, if you cosign and the business misses a payment, the lender can immediately collect from you without first pursuing the business. The implications are significant if you have co-venturers. Even though they may be responsible for a proportionate share of the debt, the lender can collect the entire amount from you if you are a cosigner.

Cosigning a loan also affects your personal credit. Lenders will look at debt that you have guaranteed in determining whether you are creditworthy for a loan. In other words, if you cosign a business loan, you might *not* qualify for a mortgage on that nice new house you have been looking at.

Collateral is a form of security to the lender in case the business fails to pay back the loan. If the business defaults on the loan, the assets that are offered as collateral to secure the loan become subject to seizure.

Whether you are cosigning for a loan or offering your personal assets as security, there is a high degree of personal risk.

Friends and Family

The first place that most start-ups look for OPM is the founder's friends and relatives. OPM from family and friends is the most common form of financing for start-ups. About three-quarters of start-up capital for the nation's small businesses is either self-funded or provided from family and friends. Investments from friends and family are more than ten times the total amount of money coming from traditional venture capital sources.

The OPM can be in the form of a loan, an equity investment, or in-kind. For example, friends and family commonly contribute credibility, particularly in the form of credit, by cosigning for loans.

Friends and family OPM is typically the most accessible for small enterprises. It is difficult to generalize the investment criteria applied by friends and family. As often as not, they are investing in you as much as or more than they are investing in your business.

Friends and family will be discussed at length in a later chapter. However, there are a few points that should be kept in mind when dealing with friends and family. For instance, there are added responsibilities when your investors are friends or family. It is essential that you are absolutely candid about the investment and leave no room for misunderstandings. Your relationships are placed at risk. It is all too easy for the problems of the business to affect the family and the problems of the family to affect the business.

It is particularly important to observe all of the formalities when dealing with friends and relatives. The best way to avoid misunderstandings is to have a comprehensive written agreement. The nature of the investment and the particulars of the payout to the investor need to be absolutely clear. If they are not both clear and memorialized in writing, you are asking for trouble.

As far as the law is concerned, "friends and family" are not a special category of investor. You are not relieved from complying with the securities law just because your source of OPM is a friend or relative. The participation of your friends or relatives may prevent you from taking advantage of certain exemptions from some of the more onerous obligations imposed by the securities law. Unless the investor qualifies as an "accredited investor" (e.g., is a millionaire or has an annual income in excess of $200,000), there are requirements with respect to the information that you must provide them and the form in which the information is provided. In fact, if any of your investors are not "accredited," as a practical matter you will have to comply with the "disclosure" requirements with respect to all of your investors. In addition, unless the transaction meets certain very specific criteria for one of the exemptions, registration with the Securities and Exchange Commission (SEC) is required. Certain of those exemptions have limits on the number of investors that you can have that do not qualify as accredited. If the securities laws are not observed, there's a potential for criminal liability or, more likely, a civil lawsuit by a dissatisfied investor.

Employees

Existing and prospective employees are an often overlooked source of OPM. Since employees typically have an appreciation for the merits of your business, and a stake in its success, they can be excellent candidates for investors.

The OPM can be in the form of a loan, an equity investment, or in-kind (e.g., deferred compensation, "sweat equity").

While there are responsibilities that go along with permitting your employees to invest in your business, there are also intangible advantages. The affect that an ownership interest can have on someone's attitude and work ethic can be astounding.

Angels

"Angel" is a term used to refer to high-net-worth individual investors—rich folks—who are looking for a better return than traditional investments will give them. The term was originally used to refer to the financial backers of theatrical productions. Angel investors tend to focus on companies that have already developed a basic concept and business strategy and are in the seed or start-up stage of investment. Angel investors can provide a critical bridge between the start-up phase and the first-stage rapid-growth phase of an emerging business. They typically invest amounts greater than those provided by individual friends and relatives, but not as much as professional investors and financial institutions.

The OPM from Angels is usually in the form of a loan, an equity investment, or a combination of the two (e.g., warrants or convertible debt). Angels, however, can also make in-kind contributions—typically in the form of expertise and know-how, credibility, and contacts.

Warrants and Convertible Debt

Warrants and convertible debt are considered a combination of debt and equity because:

- A warrant is an instrument that gives the holder a right to purchase equity—that is, an ownership interest—in the future at a certain time and at a certain price. Warrants are sometimes given as part of the consideration for a loan.
- Debt is "convertible" when part of the consideration for the debt is the right to convert the debt into equity—that is, debt coupled with a warrant.

Angels typically make investment decisions based on *projected* future potential of a business. That brings your credibility—and the credibility of your projections—directly into issue.

The investment criteria applied tend to vary widely from Angel to Angel. There are no hard-and-fast rules. Historically, to the extent that data are available, Angels have tended to:

- Invest in amounts ranging anywhere from around $10,000 to $1 million. The average investment is between $10,000 and $250,000.

- Look for a 20 percent to 25 percent annual return on investment
- Expect to hold their investment for five to seven years
- Limit their investments to businesses located in their home state or region

There are a wide variety of Angels. Some are extremely sophisticated and can bring much more than just money to the table. They can bring you expertise and credibility. Others are simply people with money to invest. Some Angels will insist on taking an active role in the management of your business. Others will expect to be purely passive investors. Make sure that you do your homework to find the right Angel.

You'll typically need a sound business plan and great persistence to obtain Angel funding, though there are many Angel networks that permit you to present your business to a group of potential Angels.

Make sure that you have a written agreement. Sophisticated Angels will insist upon one. However, the less sophisticated your Angel, the more important to have a written agreement to avoid misunderstandings.

You must also be careful to observe the securities laws when dealing with Angels. The securities law can place limitations on the way that you find potential Angels, and it can regulate the form and content of your communications with them. As a general proposition, unless you have registered with the SEC or qualify for certain specific exemptions, you are not allowed to make "general solicitations" for investments. In other words, no cold calls, mass mailings, or broadcast e-mails. You are limited to contacting people with whom you already have some form of relationship or who come to you through an introduction.

ANGEL NETWORKS

You don't need to approach individual Angels one at a time. They sometimes fly in flocks. As professionally managed venture capital pools have become more and more institutionalized, and the minimum size of investments by venture capital funds has increased, Angel investors have organized to fill the void. Groups of Angels with common investment goals have been formed. These Angel networks often have Web sites and otherwise advertise their existence with contact information. Most Angel groups have periodic breakfast or dinner meetings where two or three aspiring capital-raisers make presentations to the members of the Angel group.

The organization and structure of the Angel networks run the gamut. Some are informal organizations. Others have well-defined legal structures. Some have part-time volunteer management. Others have full-time management. Most, however, have some form of standardized investment review processes. Most also have a Web site. Some are simply a system (typically with some form of screening) to give entrepreneurs seeking capital a venue to present their business to a group of individual investors acting on their own. Others provide a manager-led pool of funds. At a minimum, Angel networks give you the opportunity to make efficient use of your time and effort.

Co-venturers

Co-venturers, through their dealings with you, often gain an appreciation for the merits of your business and sometimes have a stake in its success. This tends to make them an ideal source of conventional loans and equity investments. A co-venturer can make an excellent Angel with respect to loans and equity investment. However, they may also provide OPM in unconventional forms.

Vendors and suppliers may provide OPM in the form of favorable credit or payment terms.

Your customers, distributors, and resellers may also provide OPM in the form of advance payments and purchase of inventory in advance of expected need.

Joint ventures are one of the primary vehicles for getting access to OPR. Joint venturers and licensees may also provide OPM in the form of advances on royalties and advance payments. Depending upon the nature of the joint venture, the joint venturer may also purchase inventory from you in advance of actual need.

Factors

Factoring is a tool that can be used for cash flow management when you have large outstanding accounts receivable. In essence, you sell your open invoices (accounts receivable) to someone called a "factor." The factor will pay you the face value of the invoice less a discount (fee). In other words, it costs you the "discount" to get immediate cash for your accounts receivable.

The discount—the price you pay for the advance of funds—is typically a percentage of the face value of the invoice. The factors establish that percentage as a function of the creditworthiness and payment history of your customers and the payment cycle (length of time it takes the customer to pay after receiving the invoice). The percentages typically range from 2 percent to 6 percent for each thirty-day period it takes your customer to pay the invoice from the time the factor purchases the invoice.

Factoring is available even to start-up businesses. Your personal or business credit rating is not really important to the factoring company. The credit rating of your customer will determine the availability of factoring and the factor rate.

We will come back to factoring later in the book.

Institutional Lenders

Financial institutions are organizations that are in the business of collecting funds from the public and placing the funds in financial assets, such as deposits, loans, and bonds. Institutional lenders are financial institutions that give loans. Most institutional lenders use creditworthiness—past performance and the availability of collateral for security—as the primary criterion for deciding whether or not to lend money to a business. There are many flavors of institutional lenders.

Commercial banks. Commercial banks are what most people think of when they hear the term "bank." Banks are financial institutions chartered by a state or federal government. Banks characteristically receive "demand deposits" (deposited funds are put into accounts that can be drawn upon on demand, such as a conventional savings account) and "time deposits" (deposited funds are put into accounts that can be drawn upon only with advance notice or after a fixed term, such as a certificate of deposit). The bank honors instruments drawn on the accounts (e.g., checks) and pays interest on the accounts. Banks also collect checks, drafts, and notes, discount notes, certify depositors' checks, and issue drafts and cashier's checks. Most significant from our perspective, banks also make loans and invest in securities. "Consumer" banks specialize in personal loans.

Savings and loan associations. Savings and loan associations, sometimes called S&Ls, are financial institutions chartered by a state or federal government that take deposits from individuals, fund mortgages, and pay dividends but are required by law to make a certain percentage of their loans as home mortgages.

Credit Unions. Credit unions are nonprofit financial institutions created for the purpose of providing financial services, such as saving and lending, to their members. A credit union is owned and operated entirely by its members. To join a credit union, a person must ordinarily be employed by or belong to a sponsoring organization, such as a large company or a professional or trade association.

Commercial Finance Companies. Commercial finance companies are asset-based lenders (give loans secured by assets) that tend to be more aggressive (less risk-averse) than banks. They typically process loans more quickly than banks, but they tend to charge higher rates (commensurate with the risk). Some commercial finance companies are willing to use receivables and inventories as collateral.

Specialized foundations. There are foundations (typically nonprofit) that have been created to facilitate the growth of certain industries or development of certain technologies or research, or to provide aid to certain ethnic or socioeconomic groups. If you or your business fits within their area of interest, they can be a source of funding, typically in the form of either a loan or a grant. We will discuss grants in a later chapter, and we will also come back to loans from financial institutions.

Other Financial Institutions

Other financial institutions represent indirect sources of funds to businesses. For the most part, they are financial intermediaries or invest in businesses through financial intermediaries.

Investment banks. Investment banks are not what most people think of as banks at all. They do not provide normal banking services to the general public. They act more in the role of a financial intermediary, underwriting (finding investors to buy) securities issued by corporations and municipalities, functioning as a broker/dealer, and advising with respect to corporate finance and mergers and acquisitions.

Merchant banks. Merchant banks are essentially investment bankers with an international flavor. They tend to deal mostly in international finance and long-term loans to companies. Like investment bankers, merchant banks will act as intermediaries underwriting securities. However, merchant banks frequently also act as investors in their own right.

Institutional investors. Various organizations, such as pension funds, mutual funds, trusts, endowment funds, and insurance companies, are commonly referred to as "institutional investors." However, institutional investors of this type are not a direct source of funds to an emerging business. Instead, the institutional investors invest in venture capital funds and public offerings. They are the folks that the underwriters go to when there is an initial public offering of securities.

Lease Financing

Lease financing is in essence the OPR version of a loan. The "lender" (leasor) buys and owns equipment and then "rents" it to you at a flat monthly rate for a specified number of months. (The leasor's ownership of the equipment is the ultimate security interest.) At the end of the lease, you have the option to purchase the equipment for its fair market value or a fixed or predetermined amount, continue leasing, lease new equipment, or return it.

Leasing can also finance the soft costs often associated with equipment purchases, such as installation and training services. The leasor pays for installation and training and adjusts the monthly rental fee accordingly. Lease financing can be more expensive than bank finances, but in most instances, it's more easily obtained. The range of funds available is unlimited.

In some cases, sale/lease-back transactions can be used to obtain cash from your existing assets. You sell the assets (equipment) to a third party, who then leases back the equipment to you for a monthly rental fee.

Professional Investors—Venture Capitalists

Professional investors (venture capitalists) tend to invest in businesses that represent the opportunity for a high rate of return within a relatively short period—businesses that need substantial sums of money to grow very large very quickly and that serve very large markets. In return for the investment, they generally expect a substantial portion of the business's equity and/or profits.

Venture capital funds typically make investments in the range of $500,000 to $5 million. Investments in excess of $5 million usually involve a syndicate of more than one venture capital fund (to spread the risk). With rare exceptions, venture capital funds are not interested in funding less than $500,000. It costs them just as much time and money for due diligence in making a $50,000 investment as it does for $500,000. Individual venture capitalists (whom I refer to as "professional Angels") make investments in the range of $50,000 to $500,000.

In general, the investment criteria applied by venture capitalists vary considerably from firm to firm. Many restrict their investments to businesses within a particular industry sector, or businesses located within a specific geographic area, or businesses that are at a specific stage of development. In any case, the criteria for investment are relatively stringent. In general, in order to attract venture capital, you will have to be able to show that your business is capable of providing at least certain minimum returns on the investment (often referred to as the "hurdle rate") while at the same time holding downside risk to a minimum. In those cases, you will have to demonstrate not only a likelihood of success but that you play in a big-enough game (your market is large enough) to generate the threshold returns on investment. In other words, you generally have to show that your business is ready for the big time—that it is capable of explosive growth (e.g., reach gross revenues in the tens of millions of dollars in three years), has a sufficiently large market for your product (e.g., $50 million to $100 million or more revenues), and that there is a viable liquidity point/exit for the investors within a relatively short period of time (e.g., five to seven years).

Significantly, venture capitalists, like Angels, make investment decisions based on *projected* future potential of a business. One of the major issues is your credibility and the credibility of your projections.

Venture capitalists can also make "in-kind" contributions—typically in the form of expertise and know-how, credibility, and contacts. In fact, when venture capitalists invest in a business, they insist on taking an active role in management. Most of the time this involves giving the venture capitalist a seat on the board of directors of your company. However, in some instances, the venture capitalist may insist that you bring certain people into your management team as a condition of the investment.

We will discuss venture capital in more detail later on.

Government Agencies

Funding is available in various forms from various government agencies. For example, the Small Business Administration (SBA) has established direct loan, loan guarantee, and grant programs to aid small business. The Small Business Innovation Research (SBIR) program can provide a grant to a small business to engage in research and development "that has the potential for commercialization." Grants are also available from the U.S. Department of Commerce, U.S. Department of Education, and National Science Foundation.

The SBA is also an indirect source of funding through the Small Business Investment Companies (SBIC) and New Markets Venture Capital (NMVC) (economic development in low-income areas) programs. Private equity funds (e.g., venture capital funds) that invest in small businesses and otherwise meet the SBIC or NMVC requirements can receive matching funds from the SBA. Presently, for every $10 million in private equity in the fund, SBIC licensees are eligible to receive up to a $20-million SBA commitment (2:1 public-private leverage).

We will discuss the many and varied types of government loan and grant programs in a later chapter.

Grants

Grant money may be available from not only government sources, as mentioned above, but from private foundations as well. Grant funding can be obtained for a variety of different purposes, but you have to know where the grant money is and how to obtain it. This is the subject of Chapter 15.

"Offerings"

We are actually taking a little bit of literary license here. The term "offering" does not really refer to a source of OPM. An offering is a mechanism for getting access to sources of OPM. You are offering to sell an "investment" to an investor—the source of OPM. That investment could be an equity interest in your business, or some "instrument" representing debt, such as a promissory note or a bond.

Most people think of an offering as an offer to sell investments to a relatively large group of prospective investors—so that instead of having one or two "big" investors, you have a relatively large number of "small" investors. However, if you think about it, *anytime* you are offering to sell an equity interest in your business, you are making an "equity offering." And if you are selling a debt instrument ("note," bond, or the like) by your business, it is a "debt offering." That is certainly the way that the securities law views the term.

This is an area where you have to be particularly careful to comply with the securities law in the United States, both federal and state. We will discuss when the securities law applies later. However, unless you have consulted an experienced securities attorney and received his or her blessing, you should assume that any "offering" to anyone who does not actively participate in the management of the business involves securities. And that means that the disclosure provisions of the law must be observed, and unless the transaction falls within very specific exemptions, registration is required.

PRIVATE OFFERINGS AND PUBLIC OFFERINGS

An offering can be private or public. With a few exceptions, the exemptions to the registration requirement require an offering to qualify as private. Does "private" mean that you have to offer the investment in secret? No. In fact, there can be no secrets, at least from the potential investors. And you are restricted to offering the investment only to specific "qualified" potential investors with whom you have a "pre-existing relationship" at the time of the offering. In this context, "qualified" means either "sophisticated" (has sufficient business and industry know-how to understand the issues) or "accredited" (e.g., is a millionaire or has an annual income in excess of $200,000). We will talk more about what those terms mean later. And guess what? If an offering is not private, then it's public. With a few exceptions, any public offering must be registered with the Securities and Exchange Commission.

In many instances, the securities law also regulates the form and content of your communications with potential investors. In order to qualify for many of the exemptions, you are required to provide certain information to all nonaccredited investors at a reasonable time prior to sale. (As a practical matter, if *any* of your investors are not accredited, you will have to provide that information to all of your investors.) The disclosure materials are often called "offering memorandums" or "private placement memorandums" (PPM). We will cover the subject of disclosure requirements later.

Keep in mind that if the securities laws are not observed, there's a potential for criminal liability or, more likely, a civil lawsuit by a dissatisfied investor. You may be required to pay investors back their investment as well as other losses that they may have incurred.

Generally, when people think of public offerings, they think of large-scale sale of securities to the public, perhaps even on one of the stock exchanges. Many entrepreneurs and investors think of an initial public offering (IPO) as the pot of gold at the end of the rainbow—the ultimate liquidity/exit event. They may or may not be right. We will talk about that later.

Okay—we've been through a whole list of types of potential sources for OPM. So how do you find them? And how do you find them without running afoul of the securities law? That is the subject of the next chapter.

Chapter 7

How Do You Get to the Money? Getting Access to Funding Sources

How do you identify potential funding sources? For the moment, let's ignore friends and family. I suspect you have their contact information, although sometimes even friends and family become scarce when they think you want their money. At this point, let's concentrate on Angels, professional investors, and financial institutions.

There are numerous directories of funding sources available. Most are available in any good city library. Examples include *Pratt's Guide to Venture Capital Sources* (Securities Data Publishing), *The Directory of Venture Capital & Private Equity Firms*, (Grey House Publishing), and the membership directory for the National Venture Capital Association (NVCA), a U.S. venture capital industry trade association. All are updated annually.

Frankly, in today's electronic age, it's an easy task to identify potential sources of OPM. The Internet is an amazingly effective tool. Most venture capital firms, Angel networks, and financial institutions have Web sites. And the Web sites spell out investment criteria that are applied and often give excellent pointers on the information that should be included in your business plan and presentations.

There are also numerous Web sites that provide long lists of funding sources. Some provide links to funding source Web sites; others are databases and provide posting or matching services. They make your business plans available to, or present your business plan to, potential investors. Let me give you a word of caution, however, on the posting and matching services. If you post data with a service indicating that you are seeking capital, and the matching service does not adequately prequalify everyone who is given access to your posting, you may find yourself in violation of the securities law. That can be a huge problem.

Funding Source Web Sites

Most venture capital firms and Angel networks have web sites. And there are numerous Web sites that provide long lists of funding sources. (A link to these funding sources is provided at www.mlecter.com.) Here are some.

www.nvca.org/	National Venture Capital Association
http://acenet.csusb.edu	SBA-sponsored, SEC-approved, matching service
www.sba.gov/INV/index.html	Small Business Investment Companies (SBIC) program by state
www.angelcapitalassociation.org/ directory.cfm	Angel Capital Association (directory)
www.inc.com/articles/2001/09/ 23461.html	Directory of Angel-investor networks
www.ventureforums.org	Venture groups, venture clubs, and venture capitalist organizations by state
www.venturea.com/clubs2.htm	Angel and VC network forums
www.entrepreneur.com/listings/ vc100/1,5946,,00.html	Entrepreneur.com's list of 100 venture capital firms
www.netpreneur.org/funding/ Resources/Angel_Funding.html	Links to Angel networks, online services

members.aol.com/allenweb/angels.html	Angel sites and Angel network contact numbers
www.startupreport.com/	Start-up Report posting service
www.northstareconomics.com/angel_investing.htm	Links to Angel networks in Midwest
www.allianceofangels.com/sta.res.asp	Links to Angel networks, online services in Northwest
www.arizonaangels.com/index.htm	Angels in Arizona
www.angelatlanta.com/	Atlanta, Georgia, Angel network
www.houstonangelnetwork.org/	Houston, Texas, Angel network
www.localfund.net/niic/	Northeast Indiana Angel network
www.niacc.cc.ia.us/pappajohn/angel1.html	North Iowa Business Angel network
www.c-cap.net/about.html	Ohio Angel network
www.venture-forum.org/default.html	Pennsylvania Angel network
www.greatvalleyalliance.com/programs/paan.html	Great Valley Pennsylvania Angel network
www.kellysearch.com/gb-product-102023.html	Funding sources by country
www.cbsc.org/alberta/search/display.cfm?Code=6082&coll=AB_PROVBIS_E	Calgary, Alberta, Angel network
www.vef.org	Vancouver, British Columbia Angel network
www.mediacorp.com/e-media_news/business_news/venture_capital_list.asp	Venture capital related companies
www.chinasite.com/Business/VentureCapital.html	Information and links to venture capital sources in China
www.isis-innovation.com/about/ian.pdf	Oxford University matching service
www.techinvest.org/about-techinv.asp	Northwest England Angel network
www.bestmatch.co.uk/gateway/about/default.asp	U.K. Angels
www.technologyscotland.org/wholepicture/financing_angels.html	Scotland Angels
www.eban.org/index.htm	European Angel network
http://angels.ne.jp/en	Japanese Angel forums
www.vnet.co.th/ban/index.shtml	Southeast Asia Angel network

There are numerous fee-based, online databases and matching services as well. The nature of fee-based services available runs across the board. Some simply post your business plan, making it available online to subscribing investors. Others provide coaching and advice on preparing your business plan and presentations. Some will send your business plan to selected potential investors. Yet others will help you prepare your business plan and make the presentation to potential investors.

Some services are able to open doors for you—and lend you their credibility. Their recommendation can get you an audience with potential sources of OPM that you could otherwise never reach. Those guys, however, are *very* selective. They have to be in order to retain their credibility with the potential investors. Their services can be very expensive.

You need to know precisely what you will get for your money and how much money you will have to pay. Read the fine print! Some of the services charge up-front fees, some charge "success fees," and others charge both. The success fees can be a fixed amount or a percentage (typically 2 percent or 3 percent but sometimes as much as 5 percent or 6 percent) of the funds raised.

It is difficult to generalize about the efficacy of such services and whether or not they are worth the cost. The big question is whether they are really giving you needed credibility and truly opening doors for you, or just passing information around. Suffice it to say that there is a wealth of information available for free. And many of the funding sources have their own Web sites or are affiliated with networks with Web sites and are not at all difficult to find. You are often able to get as good an access to the same potential funding sources as the fee-based services by going directly to the potential sources or to networks with which the funding sources are affiliated.

Here's the bottom line: It's not at all difficult to identify potential sources of OPM and their investment criteria. Will your business fit their criteria? Let's assume that it does. Then the question is whether you can get the funding source to look at you closely enough to peak its interest.

With the exception of financial institutions, the more institutionalized an investor is, the more difficult it is to get an audience. Professional investors, in particular, have a limited amount of time and resources to devote to selecting particular potential investments to consider. For example, for a venture capital fund to make two or three investments, it might look at two thousand business plans over the course of a year, actually consider twenty of those, and perform due diligence on ten. The odds of getting in front of an Angel network are considerably better. But while it tends to vary from group to group and from season to season, you are still typically looking at about 5 or 10 to 1 odds. And this assumes you meet the network's investment profile.

As we will discuss, there is a good way to ensure that your business plan will be given due consideration. That is for the potential investor to either know you or know of you. In other words, in addition to possibly being a professional investor or Angel, the potential investor is also a "friend" (or family). Failing that, your next best shot is if you are introduced to the investor by someone he or she views as credible. It also helps if you have a reputation of success in your own right.

I suppose there are things that you could do to bring an Angel into your family, but we will not get into those in this book. We will talk about what you can do to make it more likely that you will number potential Angels and venture capitalists among your friends.

Beware of Making General Solicitations— Securities Law Alert

We've talked about funding sources having Web sites that are accessible to the public that advertise for potential businesses to invest in. You can apply for funding over the Internet or at least get the ball rolling. We've also talked about online posting and matching services, where your business plan is made accessible or sent to potential investors that subscribe to the service.

Why not just put up a Web site, tell the world about your business, and ask them to contact you if they would like to invest? There is a very simple reason: the securities law.

Most people don't realize it, but most passive investments (as opposed to those that involve active roles in business management) in businesses are considered securities. The securities law can place limitations on the way that you find potential sources of OPM, and it can regulate the form and content of your communications with them.

As we noted earlier, unless you have registered with the SEC or qualify for certain exemptions, you are not allowed to advertise or make "general so-licitations" for investors. You are limited to offering the opportunity to invest to people with whom you already have some form of relationship. A Web site is considered to be a general solicitation or advertisement. So are mass mail-ings, broadcast e-mails, and cold calls.

You can use a Web site to raise capital for a business, but there are very specific rules that must be observed, or you quickly find yourself in violation of the securities law. You typically have to restrict access to the investment in-formation—through, for example, passwords—to *qualified* investors. The criteria for being a "qualified" investor depend on the circumstances. For ex-ample, to be qualified, sometimes the potential investor must have a certain net worth and/or income level or reside in a specific state. Sometimes he or she has to be someone with whom you have an existing relationship.

So investors can make a general solicitation to the public for invest-ments—but for the most part, a general solicitation for investors can put you in jail!

Association and Networking—Getting Access to Qualified Potential Investors

You need to be able to place your offer in front of enough qualified investors to raise the money that you are seeking. But what if you don't know enough qualified investors? How can you get the word out and still comply with the ban on advertising and general solicitation? What can you do to legitimately expand the list of qualified investors to which you can offer the opportunity to invest in your business? What can you do to bring potential qualified in-vestors—Angels and professional investors—into your circle of friends? A harried investor is most likely to consider your business for an investment if he or she knows and respects you.

Do you remember the example of Ivan and Manny in Chapter 3? Their Angel was Manny's employer, Angelo. The example was an extreme case. Ivan and Manny were particularly unsophisticated. They had not done their homework. Do you think that Ivan and Manny would have gotten anywhere with Angel Angelo if he did not already have a relationship with Manny? I certainly don't.

Am I saying that you should go to work for potential Angels? No, I'm not saying that at all. You bring them into your circle of friends and acquaintances. So how do you do that? The answer, in two words, is "association" and "networking." You "associate" with the right people (co-venturers, board members, advisors, employees) and "network" through your individual efforts, the efforts of those with whom your business "associates," and, perhaps, the efforts of brokers.

Most people already have a network of contacts when they start a business. You build that network of contacts as you go through life. Many of those "contacts" are potential sources of funding or can provide you access to sources of funding.

Let's assume that you are the average Joe (or Joan) and consider in general terms whom you know. The list would be something like the following:

- Your family
- Friends in general
- Friends from school
- Friends from organizations—the local car club, your place of worship, or even the moms in your kid's Girl Scout troop
- Neighbors (present and past)
- Acquaintances that you make through activities (present and past)
- Acquaintances that you make through your work—co-venturers, employers, employees, coworkers, vendors/suppliers, customers
- People who provide you with professional services—doctors, dentists, attorneys, accountants
- Social acquaintances—the guys and gals from the country club or even the local watering hole

How many of these are, or can lead to, potential sources of funding? And if that is not enough (and many times it is not), you consciously develop a plan to associate with the right people (co-venturers, board members, advisors, employees) and to network into introductions with potential qualified investors.

One aspect of "association" is just another way of saying pick the right "partners," advisors, and employees. Another is to pick the right professional and charitable associations (organizations) in which to network.

Let's look at the networking aspects of association first. Joining, or more accurately, becoming active in, the right organizations can get you access to all the right people. The organizations can be professional, business development (e.g., Chamber of Commerce), charitable, or religious. In selecting your organizations, look at both their membership and their activities (particularly activities in which you participate). Sometimes merely being involved in an organization will give you credibility. Sometimes being involved in certain activities and being associated with the other people involved in those activities or that you meet through those activities will give you credibility.

All other things being equal, you should choose to become involved in organizations that will give you the opportunity to meet and work with the "right people." Who are the right people? The answer to that question depends upon your specific needs at a given time, but in general, the right people are potential mentors, advisors, investors, co-venturers, and other entities that could help you along the way.

The trick is to become visible to the membership of the organization. You want to get involved in activities that will not only introduce you to the "powers-that-be" and members of the organization but also provide you with a vehicle to become acquainted, and perhaps even build a rapport, with "powers" and "people of stature" outside of the organization to which you might not otherwise have access.

For example, becoming the program chair, the person who organizes the program/speakers, for an event gives you the opportunity to become acquainted with potential speakers. Many times, as program chair, you would have the ability to choose the particular people who participate in the program. These are often people of stature in your industry or in the community. They tend to be well established, highly placed, and perhaps even famous. They tend to be the people and businesses with which you want to be acquainted for your own fund-raising or other business purposes.

The same thing goes for fund-raising for charitable organizations. Raising money for a credible charity can sometimes open doors for you that, quite frankly, under other circumstances would be slammed in your face. Historically, many large corporations have been very generous to worthy charities. In many cases, when a charitable institution begins efforts to find funding for the current year, the first to be approached are the donors from the previous year. If you are involved with obtaining contributions from corporate donors, you are often literally given a list of whom to call. In many cases, particularly if you are new to the fund-raising effort, you will have the opportunity to work with someone of stature who can help open doors.

Understand, the activities that we are discussing merely open the door. It is up to you to make what you can of the opportunities.

As we discussed earlier, the contributions of the various principals of, or co-venturers in, a business (or for that matter, employees of the business) can take many different forms. One form is providing a network of contacts with qualified potential investors. When choosing your co-venturers and employees, their ability to provide access to OPM can certainly be a consideration. Obviously, there are other, typically overriding considerations in choosing co-venturers and employees—little things like integrity, competence, ability, and reputation.

The same thing is true with respect to choosing your advisors—professional service providers, such as attorneys and accountants, and technical and business advisors. When you choose your advisors, one consideration should be their ability to provide access to OPM. One of the best sources of introductions to qualified potential investors is often your attorneys and accountants.

Businesses can sometimes gain access to sources of funding by putting the right outside people on their board, or more accurately, getting the right outside people to accept seats on the board. Many board of director seats are offered to individuals outside the company for their expertise, business acumen, relevant experience, and credibility that they bring to the venture. The guidance provided by those outside directors is often invaluable. Beyond that, having the right people on your board can be one of the most significant factors in making your business credible both in your industry (to potential customers) and to potential investors. And most important to our present discussion, the outside board members, if not themselves qualified potential investors, often have their own network of contacts that can provide access to funding sources.

Some organizations, in years past, actually offered "trophy" positions on their boards that had little or no duties or responsibilities, strictly for the purpose of getting access to OPM. The trophy positions were often offered to (and taken by) wealthy individuals with few qualifications other than the fact that they were qualified potential investors and had many wealthy friends that were qualified potential investors as well. Of course, when funding was required, the first people approached were those occupying the trophy positions on the board and then their friends and contacts.

In the old days, it was not uncommon for outside board members to receive little or no monetary compensation for their service. In fact, compensation for being on the board was sometimes in the form of the opportunity to invest in the company! The board member might be given a warrant (option) to purchase shares in the business at some later date at the business's present valuation (e.g., the present price of the shares). Assuming that the business was successful (and thus the value of the business increased), "present valuation" could be very favorable for the board member/investor. Even so, it was not that difficult to find people willing to accept board of director positions. Being on the board of a company tended to give the individuals status, and, for the more astute, the opportunity to observe the business before committing to making an investment. On the other hand, at least at that time, there was little downside to taking the board position; as long as the individual board member did not "self-deal" and applied reasonable business judgment, there was little exposure to liability.

Those days are gone. The law, or at least the application of the law, has changed. Exposure to significant potential liabilities comes with taking a seat on the board of directors of a company. Certainly, trophy seats on a business's board of directors are a thing of the past. There are still individuals outside of the company who are willing to bring their considerable expertise, business acumen, relevant experience, and network of contacts to a seat on the board, but the cost to a company is now significant. Because of the increased exposure, outside board members insist on the comprehensive directors and officers liability insurance, which can cost a pretty penny, and significant compensation is often expected.

Today a more viable strategic tool for, among other things, raising OPM is to establish an "advisory board" in addition to your actual board of directors. The advisory board is made up of businesspeople and professionals with relevant experience who can provide you guidance in your business—act as your mentors. The advisory board, however, is not responsible for managing your business and incurs no liability for the actions of your management.

Many people who would be reluctant to take an actual seat on your board might be willing to participate in an advisory board. Having the right people on an advisory board can provide your business essentially the same types of benefits as having them on the actual board of directors, albeit to a somewhat lesser degree. Associating your business with the advisory board members can make your business more credible both in the industry and with funding sources. And as with the outside board members, the advisory board members, if not themselves qualified potential investors, have their own network of contacts that can provide access to qualified potential investors and other funding sources.

Advisory board members often are not paid for those services. Why would a successful businessperson or professional want to be on your advisory board? There are actually a number of reasons. Sometimes the advisory board member is a retired executive who is looking for something "fun" to do that will take him or her out of the house. Sometimes the advisory board member is just "giving back" to the business community. Acting as a mentor for an emerging company is a form of community service and can be very rewarding. Often it is a form of networking for the advisory board member as well. He or she gets to meet and do business with, and observe and perhaps learn from, other accomplished people. In some instances, it may be a form of client development or marketing, particularly when the advisory board member is a professional service provider (attorney, accountant, consultant) or a potential or actual vendor to, or customer of, your company or others on the advisory board. And, of course, some may consider the advisory board position as providing an inside track on a potential investment, co-venturer, or strategic alliance.

A word of caution: You need to be credible in order to attract the right type of people to your advisory board. You should not form the advisory board (or at least not fill the board) prematurely, or you can actually lose credibility and be unable to attract the people that you want in the future. We will discuss how to build credibility in a moment.

How can you meet potential members of your advisory board? There are few rules. As long as you are not in the process of offering securities (investments in your business) or about to make an offering of securities, there is nothing in the law that would prevent you from making cold calls or sending out a mass mailing to everyone you can think of with suitable credentials asking them to sit on your advisory board. It must be clear, however, that you are not making the request as a mere pretext for offering to sell securities. How effective a cold call or mass mailing would be is another question. Assuming that you could get an audience, you would have to tell an amazingly compelling story in order to attract the type of people that you want.

Association and Networking—an Example

Let's consider a good example of how to associate and network.

JT had been living on the West Coast, employed by one of the "big guy" corporations—let's call it OutListen Inc. He operated a sophisticated grinding machine used in the manufacturing process for one of OutListen's products. The grinding machines did an excellent job but had a tendency toward catastrophic breakdown if they were not properly maintained and serviced. JT came to know the grinding equipment inside and out. He also learned how to (and how not to) maintain and service the equipment in a way that was most efficient and effective for his employer.

JT heard that OutListen was having a difficult time getting its grinding equipment properly serviced at one of its other manufacturing plants in the Southwest. He began to realize that his expertise with respect to the equipment could be very valuable.

JT was not involved in any purchasing decisions for his employer, but he had become acquainted with George, the manufacturer's rep for the grinding equipment. George's territory covered not only the West Coast but also the Southwest. In talking to George, JT learned that the Southwest was a hotbed of activity in industries using grinding equipment. OutListen was only one of a number of other companies that had manufacturing plants in the area. While these companies were in different industries, all of the plants used similar grinding equipment. According to George, the plants were having the same difficulty getting the equipment serviced properly. Both JT and George recognized an opportunity. They decided to start up a business to serve grinding equipment in the Southwest. JT would contribute his expertise, and George would contribute the necessary initial funding and his contacts.

JT's boss was sorry to see him go but was supportive. He put JT in touch with his counterpart at the Southwest plant and paved the way for a contract to service the grinding equipment in the plant once JT had his new venture up and running. George and JT founded the new venture. They called it GQF (Good Quick Fix) Services. George and JT shared management responsibilities. George fronted the initial funds needed to get the business going. Other than his shared management responsibilities, however, George would not put any time into GQF—he continued in his business as manufacturer's rep for the equipment manufacturer. George and JT both assumed that George's continued representation of the machine manufacturer would put him in a position to send service work to the new venture. JT, on the other hand, was to work full-time in connection with GQF. JT was to receive a commission (20 percent of profits from "customers serviced"). Initially, George would also get 20 percent of profits, which they referred to as a "commission." Their understanding, however, was that once George got his initial contribution back, his commission would stop, although JT's would continue. Any excess profits would then be split between the two of them.

The business was soon up and running. Over the course of its first two years, GQF exceeded expectations in many ways. The business was certainly lucrative. Certain things, however, did not go as expected.

The good news was that the contract with OutListen came through, resulting in as much work as JT could handle and then some. During the two-year period, GQF gainfully employed, equipped, and trained a dozen service providers. The great news was that OutListen planned to expand its Southwest facilities in stages over each of the next few years and wanted GQF to service the new equipment after it was installed.

The bad news was that George fell upon hard times. Both JT and George assumed that George would be able to provide an entrée to the other manufacturers in the area using grinding equipment. For a variety of reasons, that did not happen.

JT knew that the other manufacturers in the area could really benefit from his services. The market was clearly there. He also knew that in order for him to take advantage of that market and still be able to service OutListen after the expansion, he would have to expand. JT projected that GQF would have to at least double its service force over the period of the next year or so. It was an expensive proposition to train the new personnel. The training involved, for the most part, tagging along on service calls and observing—non-revenue-producing activities. Things would be tight, but with a little planning, GQF should be able to save enough from revenues to fund the training, assuming, of course, that JT could get George to agree to reinvest those profits.

JT also had a number of ideas for improvements to and accessories for the grinding machines that he serviced. Those were still literally on the drawing board, and it would be at least a couple of years before he could produce them. At that point, he would have to get additional funding to proceed, but that was years off.

JT's immediate goals were twofold. He wanted to meet the decision makers at the manufacturing facilities using the grinding equipment that GQF serviced. He also wanted the benefit of their advice—to learn more about their business to see how well GQF's services fit their needs and whether there were things that he should be doing differently. But JT was also planning ahead. He wanted to expand his list of potential investors against the time in the future when he actually needed additional funding.

The way in which JT planned to fulfill both his immediate goals and his long-term plan was to create an advisory board. However, he recognized that to do it right, it would have to be done in steps. Here is what he did:

He identified the companies in the area that used the highest number of grinding machines, and the largest suppliers of the materials used with the grinding machines. He identified the companies through Internet research and, to a lesser extent, with information from George. He sent a letter to the CEO (or manager of the local facility) of each of those companies and to each member of certain professional/trade societies (that tended to indicate that they worked with grinding machines) who was employed by those companies and invited them to join a grinding machine user group that GQF was forming where they could compare notes and discuss common problems. He sent out fifty or sixty letters. He received a response to approximately half of the letters. He generally had ten or twelve guests at the monthly meetings, half of whom were regulars, half varying from meeting to meeting. A few of the attendees had potential as advisory board members and/or qualified investors.

JT held the user group meetings at the GQF office. He made sure that the attendees passed a prominent display of GQF marketing materials on the way to the conference room where the meetings were held. He also had meetings with his employees to discuss how they could best present themselves to the attendees: "All right, folks, I don't care if the meetings start at 7:30 in the morning, I want you all in the office. I want the coffee and doughnuts set up in the conference room before any of our guests arrive. You will all be neatly dressed—dress to impress. Field personnel, make sure your uniforms are cleaned and pressed. Remember, those uniforms are one of our trademarks. Let's make sure our guests see them. I want smiles on your faces and friendly 'Good mornings'! We need to be sure to make a good impression."

JT, in his role as founder/chairman of the user group, sponsored various seminars and social events. He always invited the CEO/decision makers from the various companies on his original list in addition to the active participants in the user group meetings (with the exception of one who specifically indicated that he was not interested). Even though the CEO/decision makers infrequently attended the functions, they were being exposed to GQF and JT, and JT was building GQF's credibility.

JT met with his attorney and then with his accountant. He also had similar conversations with his doctor, dentist, and banker, with his former boss's counterpart at OutListen, a representative from the Chamber of Commerce, and someone in the governor's office. He explained, in so many words, that he was contemplating putting together an advisory board for GQF and that while he had no financings planned for at least the next year, he also wanted to meet people who would be qualified (accredited) potential investors when he ultimately sought OPM. He asked them for advice with respect to organizations that he should join. He told them he was particularly interested in organizations that had mentoring programs or business roundtables in which he could participate. He specifically asked about the organizations to which they belonged—since he figured those organizations were likely to have qualified potential investors in their membership. He asked for suggestions on potential members of an advisory board.

JT's attorney recommended, and was able to get JT a place in, a local-government-sponsored organization for business development, an organization created by local government as part of an initiative to bring business into the area, in many ways like a Chamber of Commerce. JT began attending CEO roundtable meetings sponsored by that organization. He volunteered to oversee a survey to determine what infrastructure (services, facilities) was needed to support local industry and to make the region attractive to industry. In the course of the survey, he took it upon himself to interview the CEO, CFO, and CIO (chief information officer) of every substantial business in the region. Through those efforts, JT met a number of potential candidates for the GQF advisory board (when he was ready to form it) and qualified potential investors. He also became acquainted with a number of qualified potential investors who were involved with the organization.

As suggested by his attorney, JT religiously followed up each interview with a letter thanking them for meeting with him and their participation in the survey, and inviting them to lunch and/or to visit the GQF facility if their schedule ever permitted. A copy of the letter was duly retained in his files. If ever he contacted them in the future regarding the GQF advisory board or investment, he would be able to specifically reference their earlier dealings.

Also at his attorney's suggestion, JT joined a national organization for entrepreneurs. One of the reasons that JT chose that particular organization was that it did not have a local chapter—and JT volunteered to start one. Under the auspices of chairman of the new local chapter of that organization, JT organized a series of seminars and luncheon or dinner meetings. JT approached a number of individuals and/or businesses to participate in the seminars and/or speak at the meetings, including speakers from various Angel networks, government grant programs, venture capital and venture leasing firms, and financial institutions.

The criteria for JT's choices included, of course, knowledge of topics of interest, speaking ability, and "draw" (ability to attract attendance at the event), but also included the fact that they were potential candidates for the GQF advisory board and/or qualified potential investors, and JT wanted to meet them. For the most part, even if they were unable to participate or attend the events, JT was able to make their acquaintance, if not personally, at least by telephone. Just as he did in connection with the infrastructure survey interviews, JT always (particularly when they did not accept the speaking engagement) followed up with a letter inviting them to lunch and/or to visit the GQF facility if their schedule ever permitted. He kept careful records and copies of all correspondence.

JT understood that rich people are often active in charitable organizations—it's one of the ways they give back to the community. He investigated a number of local charities, looking not only at their charitable activities but at the individuals who were on their board of directors and the way in which they raised funds. Based on his investigations, JT chose, and became active in, one of the local charities. After he had established himself within the organization, he volunteered to assist in its fund-raising efforts and in organizing the charity's annual fund-raising Gala, a relatively high visibility "society" event.

JT also understood that he had to pay his dues: Opportunities had to be worked for. Initially, he was assigned the task of finding items that could be auctioned off at fund-raising events. The next year, he was placed in charge of the auction and worked on arrangements at the hotel where the Gala was held. The year after that, however, he worked on a committee of experienced volunteers, most of whom were wealthy individuals, and accompanied one or more of them to meetings with entities that contributed to the charity in the past and to solicit another donation to the charity. The entities were either wealthy individuals or corporations, in which case they met with the CEO or other highly placed management. The next year, he chaired that committee and made the initial calls to the donors himself. Ultimately, he chaired the annual Gala and helped build his credibility within the "society" of the local community.

JT's charitable activities, and particularly fund-raising for the charity, not only permitted him to do a community service but also opened the door for him to meet and become acquainted with many of the high rollers in town—not only the people from whom he solicited donations but also the other people (many of them wealthy) who were involved with the charity.

Ultimately, after he felt that he had built sufficient credibility to attract the right people, JT put together an advisory board for GQF. He approached specific individuals both with an eye to the expertise and experience that they could bring to the table and also, planning ahead, with regard to their viability as qualified (accredited or sophisticated) potential investors and/or their ability to introduce him to qualified potential investors. From that perspective, individuals who qualified as accredited were preferable. However, even if members of the advisory board did not qualify as accredited based on their education and experience, they would be considered sophisticated investors when provided sufficient information.

JT did not actually expect the vast majority of these individuals to accept the offered seat on the GQF advisory board; he tended to aim high with his requests. (George thought that he was crazy to even ask.) There was, however, a method to his madness. Even when individuals declined a position on the advisory board, JT was able to add them to the list of individuals with whom he had a pre-existing relationship that he would be able to approach when he ultimately decided to seek OPM. And, in a number of cases—for example, the corporate vice president who managed the local division of his former employer, OutListen—they recommended (in some cases offered) a substitute even when they declined a position.

By the time JT finally did seek OPM for GQF, he had established a substantial pre-existing relationship with a long list of high-net-worth individuals—qualified potential investors.

JT did it right. He used association with organizations—in some cases actually creating an organization that custom-fit his needs—to:

- "Legitimatize" cold contacts
- Create name recognition within the industry (and potential investors)
- Identify and meet the people he needed to know
- Create credibility through association
- Ultimately create relationships with the right people

So now you know how to create relationships with potential sources of OPM. In the ideal world, you would create relationships with everyone who has resources that you need. In the real world, you may not have that opportunity. Circumstances may not permit you to take the time to create those relationships. You need to be prepared to go forward, even in their absence.

Now that you know how to identify, and get an audience with, the right people, we will explore in the next two chapters how to convince potential sources of OPM to invest in *your* business.

Chapter 8

The Foundation for Attracting OPM: Anatomy of a Successful Business

The Definition of Success

In order to attract OPM and to minimize the cost of using OPM, you typically need to be able to demonstrate that your business is likely to succeed—and succeed *as defined by the source of OPM*. And success means different things to different sources of OPM. Some sources of OPM have greater expectations for profits than others.

Family and friends may invest in your business simply on the basis of their relationship with you, and without any particular expectations. Other types of investors (venture capitalists or Angels) are looking for certain minimum returns on their investment, often referred to as their "hurdle rate". They will not invest in your business unless you can demonstrate that it will be successful enough to provide at least the hurdle rate of return. In those cases, you will have to demonstrate not only a likelihood of success but that you play in a big-enough game (your market is large enough) to generate the threshold returns on investment.

A traditional lender such as a commercial bank is often satisfied if you can show your ability to repay the loan. A (nonprincipal) co-venturer is likely to be concerned with the viability of your business and its ability to perform its obligations (e.g., ongoing participation, or provide support and improvements), but the profitability of your business is often much less important to them than it is to other sources of OPM.

Some sources of OPM are also less risk-averse than others. For example, institutional lenders are notoriously risk-averse. They will typically not provide funding unless there is a virtual certainty that they will be repaid. (Some people would say that they are not willing to lend you money unless you can show them that you don't really need it.) On the other hand, other sources of OPM are willing to assume some risk (some more than others), as long as the potential return on their investment warrants taking the risk.

In any case, the more risk that a source of OPM perceives, the higher the return on investment that the source will demand before it will make the investment. Of course, you are sometimes able to limit the risk to the source of OPM by using a joint venture or licensing structure.

There are entities that will invest in businesses that cannot show a likelihood of success. The question there, however, is whether you would want to have them involved with your business. That type of investor typically has an ulterior motive for the investment—for example, to take over or to acquire the assets of your business. You need to be very careful. It is extremely important that your arrangement with that type of investor is understood and very carefully documented.

The Essential Elements for a Successful Business

Whether you are using your own money or OPM, certain elements are necessary in order for a business to be viable. All of the elements are ultimately necessary, although some tend to be more important during different phases of the growth of the business.

In order to attract investors, you typically must be able to demonstrate either that all of these elements are in place or that you have a plan to put them in place. The more difficult it is for you to demonstrate a clear likelihood of success, the more difficult it is to attract investors. And those investors that are willing to participate must accept more risk, and therefore they expect a higher return on their investment.

How Does a Start-up Demonstrate a Likelihood of Success?

How do you demonstrate a likelihood of success when you are just starting up? Occasionally, an idea or a business proposition is so compelling that it creates credibility on its own. This, however, is typically not the case—particularly when the idea or business plan is untested. The potential investors often do not have the background to make an informed judgment. In many, if not most, cases, investors judge likelihood of success based upon (a) history of success (most often the past success of the management team), (b) demonstrably strong intellectual property protection, and/or (c) association with, or the sponsorship or endorsement of, someone who is already credible. We will discuss the issue of credibility at length later in the book.

So what are the elements necessary for a business to succeed?

The essential elements of a successful business are shown graphically in the B-I Triangle introduced in *Rich Dad's Guide to Investing*, by Robert T. Kiyosaki and Sharon L. Lechter (Warner Books, 2000). There are three foundational elements that form a framework for the business: mission, team, and leadership. Within that framework, there are five essential components: cash flow, communications, systems, legal, and product or service.

B-I Triangle

The Framework: Mission, Team, and Leadership

The framework elements, in effect, define the business. The "mission," which is often both business and spiritual in nature, defines the purpose, focus, and direction of the business. This is particularly true in the early stages of a business's development. The mission may not always be easy to see and is sometimes a bit intangible, but those businesses and business-people who are "on a mission" are driven toward making their business a success.

The "team" provides the business with all of the different types of special expertise and skills necessary to operate in today's complex marketplace. The team includes not only the principals and the employees of the business but also the outside advisors (and virtual employees obtained through strategic co-ventures). The necessary expertise includes not only things like legal and accounting expertise but also the skills necessary for day-to-day operations and management, such as (depending upon the nature of the business) sourcing, manufacturing, order taking, fulfillment, human resources, marketing, customer service, and warehousing.

The "leadership" provides vision and decisiveness. It keeps the business focused on, and moving in the direction of, the corporate mission.

The Elements: Product, Cash Flow, Communications, Systems, and Legal

As noted, all of the elements are ultimately necessary for a successful business, although some tend to be more important during different phases of the growth of the business, and some elements can sometimes be supplied through OPR—by strategic relationships (e.g., licensing or joint venture arrangements) with other business entities.

PRODUCT OR SERVICE

The business must, of course, provide some type of product or service. The product or service should be consistent with the business mission. In fact, it is commonplace for the mission to be based upon the product or service; many times someone will have an idea for a product or service and then build a business around that idea. In any event, however, merely having a product or service is typically not enough for success; the product or service must be supported by a foundation formed by the other components of the B-I Triangle.

CASH FLOW

The cash flow component of a business provides the base of the foundation upon which the business is built. "Cash flow," as we use the term in this book, includes not only income generated by the business but also the money available to the business both on the company's books (financial capital) and through immediate credit (credit lines). The critical component, however, is the term "flow." Timing of when cash comes in and when it is needed to go back out can determine the success or failure of a business. The business must have sufficient cash/capital to permit it to meet operating expenses and to execute its business plan. Preferably, it will also be able to take advantage of opportunities as they arise. Cash flow management is a large part of this element. All of the orders for product in the world will do a business no good if it cannot purchase/procure the materials needed to produce the product. Of course, this is one of the classic situations where a business can use Other People's Money.

COMMUNICATIONS

The communications component of a business, as we use it in this book, represents the interfaces and interaction between the leadership and the team and between the business and the outside world—things like reputation and goodwill (internally within the business as well as with customers, investors, employees, and suppliers), public relations, marketing, and sales. The best product in the world is essentially worthless in the marketplace if no one knows about it or if your reputation for service is so bad that potential customers are reluctant to do business with you.

Trademarks Communicate

The reputation and goodwill of the business are connected to its products by its trademarks and to its services by its service marks. Trademarks "brand" goods/products, identifying the source of the goods/products. Service marks are in essence the same thing when applied to services instead of goods/products. In this book, we use the term "trademark" to cover both trademarks and service marks. Using your trademarks in connection with your products tells your customers and prospective customers that the product in fact comes from you.

SYSTEMS

The systems component of a business represents the underlying processes that define the way the business functions, the way it does business. Systems—defined processes or standard procedures—are the mechanisms for leveraging the expertise of one or more individuals to (for implementation by) a larger and/or less skilled/less expensive group while still ensuring quality control. Typical business systems/procedures involve such areas as customer service, order taking, order processing, delivery and fulfillment, sourcing, manufacturing, assembly and inventory control, quality control, billing and accounts receivable, accounts payable, human resources, marketing, product development and record keeping, interfacing with advisors (such as attorneys and accountants), marketing, and facilities.

LEGAL

The legal component typically involves, among other things, choosing and forming the appropriate form of business entity and observing the legal formalities associated with the particular form chosen; ensuring owner-ship of, and exclusive rights to, intellectual property assets and protecting those rights; and negotiating and documenting agreements defining the relationship between the participants in the business and between the business and other entities.

If a building does not have a good foundation, it is likely to collapse. In direct analogy, if a business lacks a good legal foundation, it is at risk. And just as in the case of a building, the foundation needs to be laid first; it is very difficult to come back after the fact to put in the foundation.

Consider how painful it would be to find out the hard way that the fail-ure to observe legal formalities made your personal assets available to cred-itors of the business, or that you were paying half again as much tax as you would otherwise have paid if you had chosen a different business entity. How would you like to try to explain to your investors that your competi-tors were legitimately able to copy the things that gave the business a com-petitive advantage because you had inadvertently failed to establish or maintain rights to valuable intellectual property? The best product or ser-vice in the world provides no competitive advantage if your competitors can simply copy it.

Competitive Advantage and Barriers to Competition

To be successful, a business must also have some form of advantage over its competitors. To stay successful, the business must be able to sustain that competitive advantage. You can find a competitive advantage in any one or more of the components of the business, and it can derive from other factors as well. Let's touch on some of the sources of competitive advantage.

LOCATION

A location that makes the business more convenient or less expensive for con-sumers can be a source of competitive advantage. For example, if you are the only hardware store within a ten-mile radius, that tends to give you an advan-tage over more remotely located competitors—at least with respect to those consumers in that ten-mile radius. However, this type of advantage is difficult to sustain—it will evaporate as soon as another hardware store moves into your area. Of course, with foresight, you can use the period during which you have a "captive audience" to develop a good reputation and long-lasting goodwill with the customer base that will give you an advantage when the competitors begin to invade your territory.

The advantage of physical location is also being eroded by "e-commerce." With the possible exception of shipping expenses and sales taxes, the location of an enterprise tends to be transparent to Internet shoppers.

PRODUCT OR SERVICE

Having a product or service with a feature that is (or that is perceived by consumers to be) unique, or better than that provided by the competition, is clearly a source of competitive advantage. The same is true with respect to a product or service that is particularly distinctive or that includes a particularly distinctive feature—for example, one that brings the product or the business to the minds of potential customers before they think of the competition, or one that is, in effect, a status sym-

> For further discussion on how to protect your intellectual property rights, read my book *Protecting Your #1 Asset: Creating Fortunes from Your Ideas* (Warner Books, 2001), one of the Rich Dad's Advisors series books.

bol. Of course, unless the appropriate legal foundation is laid to protect intellectual property rights, competitors will be able to legitimately appropriate/copy the feature, and the competitive advantage will be lost.

SYSTEMS

Business systems and procedures that are more efficient or effective than those of the competition, or are distinctive in the minds of potential customers (e.g., by creating recognition and/or goodwill), can likewise give a competitive advantage. For example, consider the advantage that could be gained from the following business systems: a fulfillment system that unerringly puts goods into a consumer's hands within twenty-four hours of an order, when the best your competitors can do is three days; or a manufacturing and/or quality control process that decreases rejects and/or returns to a fraction of those of the competition; or a scripted procedure for greeting and helping customers that makes the customers feel like "family."

Here again, unless the appropriate legal foundation is laid to protect intellectual property rights in the business systems, competitors will be able to legitimately appropriate/copy them, and the competitive advantage will be lost.

COMMUNICATIONS

A good reputation and goodwill in the marketplace acquired through communications (e.g., marketing) and interaction with customers can provide a huge competitive advantage. Customers can be attracted to the business because of the business's reputation or their past history with the business. They know that they can expect a certain consistent level of quality (they know that the product or service is good) and/or fair treatment from the business. Customers can also be attracted because there is something distinctive about the business or its products or services that brings it to the consumer's mind before they think of the competition. All else being equal, a consumer will go to the establishment that comes first to mind. In some cases, the reputation and goodwill established by a business are so strong that the business's product or service becomes a status symbol.

CASH FLOW/CAPITAL REQUIREMENTS

One of the competitive advantages that market giants enjoy over their smaller competitors is a cash flow that permits them to move more quickly to capitalize on opportunities, develop products, and/or develop and execute marketing strategies. (The advantage of moving quickly, however, is sometimes at least partially dissipated by bureaucracy in some of the big boys.)

Certain types of businesses involve the use of specific equipment or facilities. Conventional wisdom is that if they are sufficiently expensive or otherwise difficult to obtain, the necessity of acquiring them can present a barrier to the entry of new competitors into the marketplace. In other words, the more expensive it is to enter your marketplace, the fewer people will do so. If you already have the equipment or facilities, that gives you a modicum of competitive advantage. In many cases, however, when the only obstacle to your competitors obtaining the equipment or facilities is its expense, your competitive advantage from already having that equipment tends to be fleeting. For example, a television broadcast station requires, among other things (including government licenses and permits, as we will discuss), expensive television cameras and transmission equipment. Acquisition of the equipment is necessary before someone can enter into that field. Conventional wisdom says that the cost of that equipment will dissuade potential entrants into the field.

The fact is, however, that the cost of necessary equipment provides no competitive advantage against anyone else who also has that equipment, such as already established competitors. Further, if a potential entrant has credibility, such as someone who had a television station in another location or had run a television station for someone else (perhaps you) and the market was big enough and/or he could demonstrate a competitive advantage over you, he would in all likelihood be able to acquire the necessary equipment using Other People's Money. In addition, the "barrier to entry" tends to evaporate when technological advances make the equipment less expensive or make used but still good equipment readily available. The mere expense of entry rarely provides a sustainable barrier to competition.

LEADERSHIP, TEAM, AND MISSION

Leadership and/or team (and to some extent mission) that give the business credibility, make it distinctive, or add to its reputation in the marketplace can provide a competitive advantage. Consider, for example, a celebrity performer starting a nightclub or a well-known chef starting a restaurant. More often, a management team and outside advisors, by virtue of reputation and experience, give the business credibility within the investment community, as opposed to the marketplace. This, of course, gives the company an advantage when competing for investment capital and a cash flow advantage in the marketplace to move quickly to exploit opportunities as they arise. In fact, as we will discuss, the business leadership and management may be the determinative factor for a prospective investor.

To a lesser extent, the same considerations apply to a company's mission. For example, a company's mission can enhance its goodwill. All else being equal, the public would rather do business with a company with a mission that they perceive as helping people and making the world a better place than with a company whose mission is perceived as merely to make money or as being otherwise self-centered.

LEGAL

A business can also gain a competitive advantage through, for example, exclusive or otherwise advantageous agreements with vendors, or sources of materials, distribution outlets and/or resellers, or sponsorships with celebrities. Consider the advantage the business would have over its competitors if it locked up the rights to a material necessary to provide a particularly desirable feature of its product or service, or if it entered into an agreement under which the largest distribution channel around would carry only the business's products and not its competitors'. Unfortunately, contracts tend to be of relatively limited term. At the end of the contract term, it must be renewed/renegotiated, or the competitive advantage is lost. Of course, goodwill created during the term of the agreement may be helpful in obtaining a renewal and, in any event, may be a continued source of competitive advantage in the marketplace.

Competitive Advantage through Legal Position

Imagine that you own a fast food restaurant and find an obscure article from the 1930s that reports that cooking food in triple-distilled psyllium seed extract instead of conventional cooking oils not only prevents fats in the food from being assimilated when the food is eaten but converts any bad cholesterol that would result from eating the food into good cholesterol. You test it out and determine not only that all of the claims in the article are correct but that the food cooked in the extract tastes fantastic. You then determine that there is only one company, Psyl-Co, that can produce the extract at a reasonable cost, and you enter into a contract giving you the exclusive rights to Psyl-Co's entire output of extract. When your new line of great-tasting, inexpensive, nonfattening, anticholesterol foods is introduced, it is an immediate success.

Your competitors, of course, will seek to emulate what you are doing. Imagine their chagrin when they find out that your contract with Psyl-Co ties up the only cost-effective source of the extract. The contract gives you a major competitive advantage, at least for its duration, or until your competitors are able to find another source for the extract.

But what happens when the term of the contract is up and must be renegotiated? You may lose your competitive advantage at that point: The price of the extract could go up, or you could lose the contract to a competitor. This is especially true if Psyl-Co knows that your competitors are anxious to obtain a source of the extract. Of course, with a little bit of planning and good "communications," you can take steps to reduce that risk. You may be able to establish such a good relationship and goodwill with Psyl-Co that you would have a leg up in a competition for a new contract. You may also be able to take advantage of your period of exclusivity to establish such a reputation and goodwill in the marketplace that even with loss of a price advantage for the extract, your competition will face an uphill battle.

Let's now change the scenario a bit. Assume that the article described using psyllium seed extract as a laxative for horses and that *you* discovered the benefits of cooking in psyllium seed extract (as opposed to someone else's discovery that you read about, as in the original scenario). Assume further that you obtained patent protection of your discovery. If the patent was properly and thoughtfully drafted, you would clearly have a sustainable barrier against competition. This patent protection can be *in addition to* tying up the source of psyllium seed extract with contracts and consciously building distinctive trademarks reflecting goodwill and consumer recognition. It also puts you in a much better position when the contracts must be renegotiated.

Sustaining Competitive Advantage

Establishing a competitive advantage is only half of the battle. You must be able to sustain the competitive advantage, or the results of your efforts will be short-lived. Typically, when competitors, particularly the market giants, find themselves losing ground in the marketplace because you have an advantage, they study the situation, "adapt," and, to the extent possible, "adopt." ("Adopt" is a polite way of saying "copy" or "appropriate.")

Most sustainable competitive advantages result from having a legally protectable, exclusive right to intellectual property, the intangible asset resulting from ideas, creativity, innovation, know-how, and relationships. Intellectual property is typically your number one asset. You need to be able to identify intellectual property assets and know how to protect them. Better yet, you should consciously look for opportunities to build intellectual property assets in your business. To do this, a proper legal foundation must be laid. This means developing a strategy and planning ahead. It is all too easy to inadvertently lose the rights to what would otherwise be very valuable intellectual property. For example, prematurely disclosing a product or

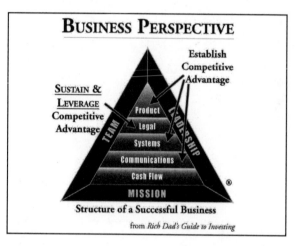

offering it for sale can preclude patent protection. To learn about protecting intellectual property, and the pitfalls for the unwary, you should read my book *Protecting Your #1 Asset: Creating Fortunes from Your Ideas* (Warner Books, 2001), one of the Rich Dad's Advisors series books.

Armed with an understanding of the foundational building blocks of a successful business, we are now ready to start preparing for the quest for OPM.

Chapter 9

Preparing to Embark on the Quest for OPM

At this point, you have decided that you are seriously interested in raising Other People's Money. Perhaps you have a business already, which you wish to expand, or have an idea that you are ready to pursue, and you have also decided that your personal financial resources are not adequate to accomplish these objectives. For whatever reason, you decide to pursue the more conventional approaches to OPM—you want to raise money. So, what now?

As we noted earlier, there is homework that you need to do. A proper foundation is necessary to attract OPM. And more, you have to be able to communicate the fact that you have that foundation—and that you have all the ingredients necessary for success—to the source of OPM.

So how do you prepare for an effective, successful "capital formation" experience? In a nutshell, you need to anticipate the type of information that a potential source of OPM will request, and have that information at your fingertips, in a form that is "friendly" to the potential OPM source.

In the hypothetical presented in Chapter 3, Ivan and Manny went to Angelo, Manny's employer, with a prototype and demonstrated that the appliance worked, but they provided no information with respect to the marketplace. In that case, Ivan and Manny were lucky—presumably because of the pre-existing relationship between Manny and Angelo. Typically, sophisticated sources of OPM demand much more information and that it be presented in a concise, user-friendly manner.

As you might expect, the type and extent of the preparation that is necessary, both the information necessary and the way that it should be presented, will vary considerably depending on how much capital you wish to raise, the nature of your business venture and how complicated it is, and which OPM sources you expect to approach. Let's take a simple example. Assume that you have the opportunity to purchase a duplex rental property across the street from your home. You have a number of choices as to amount, nature, and source of OPM. For the purposes of this example, assume that you believe that the purchase price of the property is much less than its value and that the appropriate approach is to obtain $30,000 OPM in the form of a loan (as opposed to "sale" of an equity interest in the property). Let's also assume that you have two ready sources of OPM: your well-to-do brother-in-law and your local banker. What do you need to do to lay the foundation for obtaining the OPM?

Going to your brother-in-law to raise $30,000 for the purchase of the duplex across the street requires somewhat less formal preparation than going to the bank for the loan. Your brother-in-law will likely be satisfied by:

- Looking at the property with you
- Reviewing the comparable properties pulled off the multiple listing service by your Realtor
- Reviewing some cash rental income and expense numbers that you jot down together
- Knowing that you have already obtained a five-year rental agreement with the local Methodist church to use both apartments as housing for their mission families

With a "deal" as simple as purchasing a relatively small property, the bank's due diligence would be somewhat, but not immensely, more intense than your brother-in-law's. The bank will require a formal appraisal (typically, they will pick the appraiser) and your personal financials and tax returns. Depending upon your financial situation, the ratio of loan amount to the appraised value of the property and/or the nature of the loan (i.e., is your personal liability involved, or is it "nonrecourse" to you and the bank has only a security interest in the property?), you might have to "sell the merits of the deal" to the bank. The bank might ask for the rental history and rent roll of the property, although this request is more common for properties with more units than a duplex. Consider how effective it would be to have all the information that the bank is likely to request neatly assembled and prepackaged for presentation to the bank.

The more complicated the business being financed, the more difference you are likely to see in the information required by different sources of OPM. Let's take a little more complex example. Assume that you are seeking capital to develop the family farm into lots for building single-family houses. In this case, the loan officer at the bank will have a much greater appetite for information, not only about the land parcels making up your family farm but also about many of the following items:

- Appraised value of the land after rezoning and subdividing the land into lots
- Pro forma financial model that shows cost of land preparation, horizontal improvements, sale of lots over what period of time, etc.
- Your own qualifications for successfully managing this project
- Sales plan and marketing costs for selling the lots
- Local market data on lot absorption (how fast lots sell in your community)
- Competitive information about other similar developments in the community
- Legal, planning, and accounting advisors and their costs
- Contractors and architects who are being hired for this project and their experience
- Your financial statement so the loan officer can evaluate the strength of your personal guarantee

So we cannot specify exactly what level of preparation will be necessary for the particular source of OPM that you approach, but we will go through all of the factors that you should think about, prepare, and use in your quest for OPM.

Who Are You and What Do You Bring to This Party?

For the purposes of our discussion, we assume that you are the leader of the quest for OPM. You may not actually be the president of your company, and there may be other key people involved (and we will get to your team in a minute), but all sources of OPM are going to look to you and/or your team as the most important ingredient in their decision to invest—*entrust*—you and the team with their money! It is no secret in the venture capital business, and survey after survey backs up this conclusion: *Investors invest in management!*

You can have the greatest technology in the world or the best restaurant site in the town, but if your management team cannot execute the business plan, or if they alienate the customers or cannot hire and manage good people, then the business will fail and investors lose their money. So put on your best face and get ready to sell yourself and your team—the other key person or persons who will be there every day making things happen.

There are a number of good reasons why investors tend to base their decision to invest on management teams. There are many imponderables about any emerging business. Sometimes a great business idea simply cannot succeed on its own strength alone. The idea may be too revolutionary or otherwise lack sufficient credibility. Sometimes conditions in an industry or market change significantly and quickly. Good management teams are flexible. They can spot the issues and changes and are skilled and objective enough to be able to adjust and grow as business conditions require.

Know When to Hold, Know When to Fold

One of the reasons that investors look at management as a major factor in the investment decision is that investors can rely on good management to protect their investment—in both good times and bad. That means that good management will know when to cut the investors' losses. One specific example of this comes to mind.

A start-up company was in the process of developing a software product. It was still in the development stage and had no source of income. The company brought in a high-powered CEO to help attract OPM. This particular fellow had an impressive track record of building successful companies. In large part because of the CEO's participation, a group of investors bought equity in the company to fund the development of the product. Within a few months, however, the CEO had analyzed the company and realized that there was no way that the investors' expectations could be met. He determined that the market for the product was nowhere as large as everyone had thought and that it could not support sufficient sales to provide the investors' hurdle rate. He realized that failure (from the perspective of the investors) was inevitable and that by continuing development efforts, the company would simply burn up money. Rather than let that happen, the CEO presented the situation to the company board of directors and proposed that they shut the company down.

The company's assets, including its intellectual property, were sold, and the corporation dissolved. In this way, the investors were able to recoup the bulk of their investment. The investors suffered losses, but they knew that they could rely on the CEO's judgment and would not hesitate an instant to invest in any company that he ran in the future.

Investors tend to look closely at the experience and track record of the management team. They are primarily interested in experience that is relevant to the specific needs of the company. For example, experience in a Fortune 100 company may not be particularly relevant to running a start-up company. In fact, a common perception is that when someone's experience is entirely from big companies that tend to throw money at a problem, there's a question as to whether that person would be sufficiently flexible to deal with a small company environment where inexpensive alternatives are necessary. Industry-related experience is also important. Experience in the fast food industry may not be particularly germane to a software development company.

However, experience, skill, and pedigree are not the only factors that investors look for in management. They also look for integrity and commitment. They want to see a high level of work ethic. They need to feel comfortable that all of the key players have a high commitment to, and enthusiasm for, the company. (For example, many investors consider it important that members of management have "skin in the game"—i.e., have themselves invested in the company.) They want to know that they can trust you and your team with their money. They want to know that you and your team will be fair in protecting their interests.

Sometimes the company's product or technology is simply too complex for the potential investor to understand, or market projections are simply too speculative. The history of the management team may be the only solid, understandable information that the potential investor can rely on. If the management team has the relevant experience and a successful track record in the relevant industry, it gives the product, technology, and/or projections more credibility; a good management team makes the potential investor more confident that the business is likely to succeed.

Investors are also interested in the "completeness" of the team. Do you have, or is there a plan to place, a strong individual in all of the important positions? Depending upon the nature and stage of development of the business, critical positions can include chief executive officer (CEO), a chief financial officer (CFO), a chief technology officer, a chief information officer (CIO), and a director of sales and marketing.

What is necessary to sell you and your team? A résumé is the key component. It should showcase your experiences in the best light possible, given the responsibility you will have in this business. And the information on the résumés better be true and verifiable—even aside from ethics, you can assume your OPM source will check the facts.

Your financial statement is also important, especially if you are looking for borrowed capital, since you will probably be asked to personally guarantee the repayment of any borrowed monies. Even if the loan will be larger than your net worth, your banker knows that your personal guarantee will assure that you keep your eyes on the shop and your hand out of the till.

So collect and polish the résumés and financial statements of your team, along with an organizational chart understandable in the context of your business.

Investors Look for Business Plans!

A business plan is the investor's window into the opportunity. No investor can evaluate an investment opportunity without a clear statement of what the business is, how it will succeed in a competitive world, how it will make money, and most important, how that investor will get his money back with the return on investment that he is expecting. The business plan describes your "idea," the market problem, proposed solution, business and revenue models, marketing strategy, technology, company profile, and competitive landscape as well as financial data for coming years. (It will also tell the investor about the management team.)

A good business plan serves dual purposes. Not only is it a vital tool for attracting OPM, but it is also a tool for business operations. A business needs to carefully think through and plan the organization's mission, goals, objectives, and strategies in order to make sure that the business and all involved are headed in the same predetermined direction. You and your team need to think through and plan how the company will be run for the next three to five years. What are the marketing, operational, and financial strategies of the company? What are your milestones? What resources (physical and human) will you need to implement those strategies? When will you need those resources? The process of preparing a good business plan will force you and your team to systematically address all of those issues.

A Business Plan for Every Occasion

One school of thought contends that the actual operating business plan should be used to attract OPM, whereas a second school of thought believes that custom business plans should be drafted specifically for the purpose of attracting OPM. The use of different separate special-purpose business plans crafted specifically for different types of potential investors is espoused primarily by the "marketing types." That approach has the advantage of presenting the information in a manner targeting the particular investor and eliminating details that might be important to business operations, but not to the investor. Ignoring other considerations, the custom document approach is probably more effective in attracting OPM.

However, the custom document approach tends to scare the devil out of some attorneys, particularly those who try to keep their clients out of litigation, or at least try to put their clients in the best position in the event of litigation. Use of different business plans for different purposes creates a risk that some disgruntled party down the line will contend that the particular version of the business plan that he or she was provided was somehow incomplete or misleading when compared to the other versions. It can be uncomfortable to be put in the position of having to justify the differences in the business plan provided to investors from the business plan actually used by the business. Perhaps you can get away with using different business plans for business and investor disclosure purposes, but, at a minimum, you have to be very, very careful.

The more conservative approach is to use the same business plan for both operations and seeking OPM. The trick is to prepare a business plan that covers all bases. The executive summary is then sometimes customized for particular investors. Of course, care must be taken even with customized summaries.

To be effective as a tool for attracting OPM, the business plan should tell the investor what's in it for him or her. Investors will tend to focus on those aspects of the business plan most relevant to meeting *their* goals. That means different things for different investors. For example, a bank will probably focus on the business's cash flow during the term of the loan. The bank wants to be sure that you will be capable of making the debt service payments, paying back the funds, and paying the interest rate. Equity investors, on the other hand, will typically focus on those aspects of the business plan relating to the growth of the company. They want to be sure that their equity interest in the business will appreciate in value enough to provide them with a minimum hurdle rate of return.

The business plan should tell a succinct but persuasive story showing not only where your business is going and why and how you and your team will succeed in getting there but how and when the investor will receive an expected level of return on the investment and how and when the investor will be able to "exit" (extract the investment from the venture). You want to convince the investors that your team has all the skills and expertise needed not only to actively manage the company but also to seize opportunities and solve any problems that arise. You want to convince the investors that you have a viable plan to bring your product or service to market, that you have, or will have, the right type of resources, and that all of the component materials and other resources that you will need will be available.

Investors want to know that the business actually has a carefully thought-out plan for growth. The sophisticated equity investor is typically interested in the answers to at least the following questions: What is the size, nature, and level of sophistication of the market? Will it understand the need, and be willing to pay for, the product and/or service? What is the competitive position of the business? What competitive advantage does the business have, and how will it sustain that competitive advantage? How complete is the management team? What is their experience and history: with start-ups and IPOs, in the specific relevant industry, and with building teams? What is their commitment to the company? What is the relationship of the company with, and what is the position of, the inventor/founder? What are the capital needs of the company over time? Are there product price or cost margin issues? Are there collateral assets available for securitization? Is there demonstrable cash flow? When will there be return on investment (ROI) and how much? While you may not want to answer all of these questions directly when preparing a business plan, they should definitely be kept in mind.

There are numerous sources, in libraries and on the Internet, to assist you in preparing your business plan. There are numerous books, teaching tools, computer programs, and seminars on the subject. (For example, a number of sample business plans are available at www.bplans.com.) There are also consultants whom you can hire to assist you in preparing the business plan. Most of the larger accounting firms have "emerging business practice groups" that can help you prepare your business plan. Many are willing to initially discount their fees for the sake of creating a long-term relationship. Needless to say, the business plan is very important, so if you have not done a business plan before, try to find a friend or advisor to help you through the process.

There are many ways to prepare business plans, and they vary by business type, by investor or capital source, and by size of the venture. They can be ten pages or fifty pages, but shorter is better as long as they are complete and credible, given the complexity of the business and the financial plan.

BASIC ELEMENTS OF A BUSINESS PLAN

It is beyond the scope of this discussion to show you how to prepare a business plan. However, the business plan should be logical, absolutely accurate, and professional in tone. In general, the basic elements of a business plan are:

- Summary: for quick understanding of the business *opportunity*—and to generate enough interest to continue reading
- Description/history of the business or the investment opportunity, including the "story" that lays out the need/desirability of the product or service
- Products or services: the nature of the product, potential applications of the product, how it fills an unmet need in the marketplace, the "unique sales proposition," the stage of development of the product—in terms of milestones already met and milestones to be met
- Intellectual property protection and bases for sustaining competitive advantage
- Operations: facilities, equipment, availability of personnel and materials
- Strategic partnerships and/or other important contractual relationships
- Market information: industry and market segments to be targeted, size of the market, growth rates, profiles of potential customers, government regulations, future trends

- Marketing information: how the market will be developed and penetrated, pricing, distribution channels, promotion
- Competitor information: who they are, relative strengths and weaknesses, product comparison
- Résumés of management team, including advisory board and in some instances legal and accounting advisors
- Existing/proposed capital structure: how the ownership is currently shared or proposed to be shared among owners and contributors
- Financial plans, projections, statement of cash flows: history (if any), revenue models, and three to five years of estimated financial performance
- Amount of capital required
- Proposed uses for this capital
- Exit strategy: how and when the investors will get a return on investment and how and when they can get their money back

Some of these key elements are treated in more detail below, but the most critical elements to any investor are:

- Management team
- Financial plan
- Unique selling proposition and sustainable barriers to competition

So spend most of your effort on assuring the best possible showing on these elements.

GENERAL RULES FOR PREPARING A BUSINESS PLAN
There are a few general rules that you should follow with respect to preparing a business plan:

- Do not state that you are selling stock or what price you might think is appropriate for a share of stock or for a percentage of the business opportunity. There are two primary reasons for this rule. First and foremost, you need to avoid discussions about stock or direct investment solicitation to be sure that you comply with the state and federal securities laws that apply to all investor conversations. When you are raising money for a business from passive investors, you are typically considered to be "selling securities." As we've already noted, and as a general proposition, unless you have registered with the SEC or qualify for certain exemptions, you are not allowed to make "general solicitations" to potential investors, and the materials that you provide them must comply with specific requirements as to content and form. It is easy to inadvertently violate these laws. You definitely do not want that to happen. This issue will be treated in more detail later.

It is also typically best not to prejudge the potential investor's view of the value of your business. In other words, do not include your own estimate of the value of the business now or at the exit stage. All you accomplish is to place an upper bracket on negotiations for valuation. Investors will draw their own conclusions about value and even about how the equity or debt should be structured. And if you are unrealistic about your expectations, they may just say "no thanks" even if they like you and the business, because they think your valuation views are too far apart. (One indirect and more helpful way to treat the valuation issue is to include comparable data on the valuation of other similar businesses.) It is typically best to start with just telling your story—selling you, your team, and the opportunity. After that, discussions about valuation become much easier and more comfortable for both sides.

• Be accurate. Do not make statements or draw conclusions unless you can provide specific details in support. Accuracy is very important, and facts relied upon must be carefully verified. As will be discussed, a sophisticated investor will test all of your facts and conclusions during a due diligence investigation before making any investment. It takes only one mistake or overstatement to absolutely destroy credibility. Be concise in your language and qualify or explain statements in order to maintain credibility.

• Use independent third-party data whenever possible. Information (facts, charts, study results, data, and the like) from credible third parties substantiating your important positions goes a long way to bolster credibility. Include references or citations to your sources. Important but longer documents (market or competitive studies, copies of patents, etc.) can be added as appendices.

• Make sure the business plan is well written and error-free. Edit and proof the plan carefully. Go through it with a fine-tooth comb. Incorrect grammar and typographical errors will reflect poorly on you. They are at best a distraction and may give the impression that you are either ignorant or careless. While it is not necessary to spend a lot of money dressing up the final plan in special bindings or color paper, it is important to make sure it is professional in appearance and presentation, well written and clear, and without errors.

Investors Look for a Financial Plan!

A financial plan tells a potential investor where the business has been and where it is going. If you have an existing business, you should already have a financial history of that business (monthly financial statements, tax returns, etc.). And your plans for the future must also be reduced to financial data, which is the best possible summary of the business activity, results, and capital return. If you do not have a financial background, you should consider seeing your accountant or another advisor for help in this area. Finance information is the language of the banking and investment community, and it must be prepared and explained with care. And consider including an experienced financial advisor on your team, for the extra value and confidence this will bring to your OPM source.

Assuming there is an existing business, your financial plan should include:

- Profit and loss (P/L) statement for two to three (maybe up to five) fiscal years of history, broken down by month for the last twelve to eighteen months (enabling your OPM sources to easily understand trends)
- Balance sheets for each year and month of the P/L
- Cash flow summary statements for each year and month of the P/L

Every business's financial plan, existing or not, must also have three to five years of pro forma financial statements (operating statement or profit and loss, balance sheet, and cash flow) for the future, along with detailed assumptions, so an investor can understand how these estimated or pro forma statements were derived.

This requirement is often a difficult one for first-time entrepreneurs.

How can anyone predict how many widgets we will sell in the third quarter of this year, much less three or four years from now? How many employees will we have selling in the plumbing department in year two? Your reaction is very understandable, because this is a difficult task. But it is necessary, so you will need to work at it, probably with an experienced advisor who has done it before. And not every CPA or public accountant can do this work either. They are far more comfortable dealing with "what happened" than with "what will happen." Try to find an in-house controller or CFO from the industry or market segment your business is in, so you are assured of some special knowledge about your business. These inside accounting people are used to preparing pro forma financial plans to support their own internal planning and budgeting requirements.

With financial projections, reasonableness and credibility are paramount. You are far better off underpromising and overdelivering than the other way around. Generally, all the projection must do to satisfy the investors is show them that they are likely to exceed their hurdle rate. You do not want to project unrealistic growth. Unrealistic projections are a recipe for disaster. Either the potential investor will recognize them as unrealistic and you will lose credibility, or he or she will believe them and go into the venture with expectations that you will not be able to meet. Avoid "hockey stick" projections, where the business starts out growing at a modest rate, then suddenly begins growing exponentially. Again, unrealistic projections are counterproductive. Exaggerated numbers in projections do not accomplish anything other than to damage your credibility.

How to Prepare a Financial Projection

My youngest brother, Bobby (Robert B. Lechter), is a CPA practicing in a Maryland suburb of Washington, D.C. (his Web site is www.rbl-cpa.com). When I was working on this section of the book, it occurred to me that he did a lot of financial projection work. I sent him an e-mail to get his thoughts on financial projections. His response follows.

From: Robert B. Lechter (info@rbl-cpa.com)
To: Michael A. Lechter (mal@MLechter.com)

Mike —

You asked for any words of wisdom that I might have for someone preparing a financial projection for a business plan. Here they are:

Preparing a bombproof financial projection is vital to raising capital. I am going to illustrate a partial financial projection for a medium-sized privately owned restaurant. I chose this industry because most of the basic concepts are universal to all financial projections and . . . because everyone needs to eat.

A financial projection is a prospective financial statement that presents, to the best of the responsible party's knowledge and belief, an entity's anticipated financial position, results of operations, and cash flows, given one or more hypothetical assumptions. Accordingly, a financial projection consists of three essential elements:

- The summary of significant assumptions
- The summary of significant accounting policies
- Prospective financial statements, which reflect the stated assumptions, prepared in accordance with the accounting policies that are to be adopted.

Summary of Significant Assumptions

The summary of assumptions is probably the most critical element of your projection. This is where "sophisticated investors" (or their financial advisors) will turn to first, when presented with a solicitation memorandum. This is where they determine whether or not the accompanying prospective financial statements (and your credibility) hold water. The general rule for the summary of assumptions is "No bull!"

Assumptions are based on *key factors*, not just subjective ballpark estimates. Although the use of estimates is allowed in all financial statement preparation, even audited financial statements, those estimates must be based on competent evidence or methods generally accepted by the industry. Many of the required key factors for your assumptions are developed in the initial business planning stage. For example, two mandatory key factors for a restaurant profit and loss projection are the estimated number of seats in your restaurant and the estimated average number of times each seat will "turn"—that is, how many times a seat will be used for a completed "ticket" during the respective mealtime of a day. At lunch, the average number of turns will usually be less than the dinner estimate. On some days, lunch turns (or bar tabs) may be higher than on other days. Additionally, the estimated average sale per seat for a lunch ticket and a dinner ticket (don't forget the bar tab) must be established. All of this is required before operating revenues can be reasonably projected. And all of this must be documented in the summary of significant assumptions. Other sources of information for key factors and your assumptions can be found in industry statistics reports available from local and national trade associations, the Internet, knowledge gained by personal experience within the industry, and talking with prospective vendors and other restaurant owners in the area.

(Here you can elaborate on what information you can get from the various sources mentioned above. For example, industry statistics can provide "percentage-of-revenue" information for food and beverage cost, certain operating expenses, etc. The Internet can provide manager salary information, etc.)

Notice that I use the word "estimate" for everything. That's important because your projection must disclose to the user that the prospective financial statements result from applying estimated amounts to your hypothetical assumptions and that actual results will vary from the projected amounts, that some differences may be significant, and that some results may not be achieved at all. From here on, I'm leaving "estimated" out.

Summary of Significant Accounting Policies

The summary of significant accounting policies is very similar to the required disclosures that accompany historical financial statements. They are quite specific in presentation and content. The disclosures will inform the user of the type of entity form that will be used and the method of accounting that will be used (cash or accrual). Significant related parties are identified. A disclosure is required regarding the use of estimates in prospective financial statements. Descriptions of the type of property and equipment owned and the respective depreciation methods are required disclosures. Also included will be disclosures regarding capital lease and operating lease obligations, prospective credit arrangements, long-term-debt terms, equity capitalization, employee contracts, and any other significant areas requiring disclosure in order for the projections to be meaningful and complete. This is also where the user will find a disclosure of the federal income tax implications to the entity and the individual investor.

Prospective Financial Statements

Prospective financial statements are classified as either *financial forecasts* or *financial projections*. We are dealing with a financial projection because it is based on one or more hypothetical assumptions. The complete set of statements includes the following:

- Statement of financial position (balance sheet)
- Statement of operations (profit and loss statement)
- Statement of cash flows (statement of sources and uses of cash)

However, pursuant to the *Minimum Presentation Guidelines* for prospective financial statements, issued by the American Institute of Certified Public Accountants (AICPA), the balance sheet and statement of cash flows may be omitted. Minimum presentation statements may be limited to the following items:

- A description of what the responsible party intends the prospective financial statements to present, a statement that the assumptions are based on the responsible party's judgment at the time the prospective information was prepared, and a caveat that the prospective results may not be achieved
- Summary of significant assumptions
- Summary of significant accounting policies
- Sales or gross revenue
- Gross profit or cost of sales
- Unusual or infrequently occurring items
- Provision for income taxes (if applicable to the entity)
- Discontinued operations or extraordinary items
- Income from continuing operations
- Net income
- Basic and diluted earnings per share (optional for non–publicly owned corporations)
- Material changes in financial position

Here are some basic rules to which you should adhere when preparing financial projections:

- Prospective financial statements should take the form of basic financial statements (recommended by the AICPA).
- Follow your assumptions to the letter. If your projected financial results look strange, they probably are. So be flexible and challenge your assumptions ferociously. Change them if necessary. And be prepared to defend them!
- If you elect to omit the statement of cash flows, at a minimum you should present a statement that identifies the source and amount of cash raised for the venture and what it will be used for.
- Any amounts that can be cross-referenced must tie in to their related statements. For example, until the entity is generating positive "cash from operations," there should be a corresponding figure ap-

pearing on the statement of sources and uses of cash, labeled "Cash required to fund continuing operations." This amount should equal the total negative cash deficit accumulated up to the first period that results in positive cash from operations.

- Operating revenues should be separated into major categories so that you can develop and utilize different assumptions more clearly and to your advantage.

- Have a cost of sales category to match each respective operating revenue category.

- Group other operating expenses as either variable (those that fluctuate with sales volume) or nonvariable (those that are fixed regardless of sales volume) whenever possible. (There is a good explanation for this strategy, and it should be elaborated on.)

- Properly distinguish between capitalized start-up expenditures, which are accounted for as intangible assets and amortized over sixty months, and current operating expenses. This improves the bottom line of your profit and loss projection. (You need to discuss what expenditures qualify for this treatment and the timing test for when to begin amortization. For tax purposes, to ensure that the amortization is tax deductible, a proper election must be filed with the initial tax return for the entity.)

- Classify purchases of tangible property that will provide benefits for future years as depreciable assets rather than current operating expenses. (More explanation needed here on what qualifies as a capital asset, depreciation strategies, etc.)

- Separate significant expenses into more specific categories. For example, manager and owner salaries should be listed separately rather than grouped with other employees' wages.

- Obtain actual quotes from anticipated vendors whenever possible. (insurance, equipment maintenance agreements, etc.).

- List items such as initial marketing programs and onetime consulting fees separately.

- If the projection is for more than one year, and a provision for income taxes is applicable to the entity type, don't forget to include the impact of any initial-year net operating loss carryovers.
- Some components of the financial projection, like payroll tax expense, are easily determined after the more difficult task of estimating salaries and wages. Here you simply apply statutory tax rates to the payroll figures to project the expense. Remember to consider the various cutoff thresholds where certain taxes stop.
- Show estimated depreciation and amortization expenses after net cash generated or used by operations.
- If book accounting and tax accounting methods are different, be sure to disclose this in the summary of significant accounting policies and, if material, consider illustrating the effects in a note to the prospective financial statements.
- Don't window-dress your projection by overstating revenues or understating expenses. Don't taint your key factors or assumptions because of subjective feelings or personal sentiments. This will be seen through immediately by a sharp investor or financial advisor.
- Eighty percent of all new businesses fail within the first five years of existence. Have foresight of prospective problems and risks that are inherent in owning a business. In the summary of significant accounting policies, briefly describe these risks and your plans for coping with cash flow deficiencies, seasonal declines, new and existing competition, loss of a major vendor or customer, etc. (This should be elaborated on in greater detail in your "concepts statement.")

These financial plans must be supported by separate statements of assumptions that will help an investor or banker understand how this future financial plan was developed. These assumptions may take up a page or two in the financial plan but are key to a proper understanding of the plans and will significantly improve the investor's understanding and comfort with the financial plan.

How do you include the financial plan in the business plan? The most common approach is to include a section in the business plan that shows—in summary form—the historical and pro forma statements for the business for two to five years of history (if any) and three to five years of future performance, all by fiscal year. A general explanation of assumptions can be included with this summary. The detailed financial statements and assumptions can be included as an appendix to the business plan for more detailed review, assuming your investor candidate is interested enough to devote the additional effort.

Third-Party Studies and Data

If you were an investor, what kind of information would be most credible to you? If a business owner comes to you for capital and makes certain statements about his or her market or about competitive pricing, you are sure to be skeptical or, at least, "from Missouri." So when you are preparing for your discussions with capital sources, make sure you collect all of the third-party studies and information that you can. For example, what is the size of your market? Having a market study that details all such information can be just the factor that provides the right amount of credibility to your plan.

Make sure that you make proper citations to your sources and preferably keep copies of those sources. You cannot imagine how much time can be wasted searching for the source of data if it is not properly "footnoted" or trying to find a copy of a survey or article. Do not rely on simply noting the URL of the Web site where you found a copy—the content of Web sites changes regularly.

In our earlier example concerning two very different real estate ventures, having objective data about the value of that duplex or proposed subdivision will dramatically improve your chances for success with your OPM source.

Investors Look for Co-venturer Commitments or Prospects!

Earlier we described the potential value of having strategic co-venturers contributing to your business asset base or, conversely, reducing the capital requirements you have in the early years. These co-venturers allow you to rely on OPT and/or OPR (Other People's Time and/or Resources) in advancing the objectives of your business. To the extent you can, make sure that these co-venture relationships are reduced to writing or contracts that you can share with your OPM sources.

For example, if you are going to be able to share facility space and some of the direct labor for manufacturing your product, having that commitment in a contract will be very important. Otherwise, your OPM sources will have to go out and verify the reliability of that relationship, or they may discount its value significantly, since they cannot verify it.

Your advisors are to some extent co-venturers as well. So if you have a statutory and/or advisory board, how are you compensating these contributors? Do they really understand what you expect of them? This is often a tricky issue, since you may not wish to pay them in cash, if cash is dear to you in this early stage, and paying them in-kind or in equity may be problematic as well. For example, your CPA or lawyer may not be able to accept an ownership interest. But your investor source will be much more willing to believe in the contributions expected from your advisors if there are written agreements in place. (And these do not have to be complicated legal agreements when a simple letter may confirm their willingness to contribute and how they expect to be compensated, now or later.)

Investors Invest in Intellectual Property and Sustainable Competitive Advantage!

A business rarely succeeds unless it establishes—and sustains—some form of competitive advantage. This means that the ability to establish sustainable competitive advantages is often a critical factor in the investment decision and should figure prominently in your business plan.

More often than not, a competitive advantage involves some form of intellectual property (IP), the intangible asset that results from ideas, creativity, innovation, and relationships: information and data, special expertise and know-how, designs, inventions, works of authorship (such as marketing literature and manuals), the layout of semiconductor integrated circuits, and/or trademarks, trade dress, reputation, and goodwill. There is no question that your business has many forms of intellectual property assets. For example, your knowledge of the business, customers, suppliers, and market—your know-how and expertise—is an intellectual property asset of your business. Certain IP assets are so significant to your business that it is necessary to specifically address those assets in your business plan. Your business plan should make it clear that you indeed have rights to the asset and that you have taken the appropriate steps to protect your rights.

The exclusive right to use IP is established through patents, trademarks, trade secrets (protected by confidentiality provisions in agreements), copyrights, and mask work registrations. The business plan should describe any of those that you have obtained and the status of your efforts to obtain them.

The business plan should also make clear that you in fact own the rights to developments. For example, if you and your team have developed a software product, it is important that the proper agreements are in place to assure that you or your business is the owner of that asset. Your lawyer can assist you in making sure that paper trail is adequate. You may have engaged a third party (independent contractor) to help with development or licensed some technology from a third party to include in your product or service. The assignment and license agreements would be an important piece of information for your investor sources. It may not be necessary to include it in the appendix of your business plan, but describing it and its value is important. You can also expect your investor to review that document and maybe even speak with your contractor or licensor as part of due diligence, a subject we will address below.

Any third-party evaluation of your IP is also important. Showing an investor documentation of the success of the IP in another business (not competitive to your product or service) will be helpful to understanding its value to you. If you are paying royalties or are paid royalties on that IP, an industry survey (if you can find one) that illustrates the common royalty scheme would also be helpful.

Investors Look for a Marketing Plan!

A key ingredient of any successful business plan is an effective presentation of how that business will attract and retain customers for its products or services. Paying customers are the lifeblood of any business (although some investors, to their ultimate regret, lost sight of this during the dot-com craze of the 1990s). This explanation should deal with all characteristics of the sales and marketing plans necessary in the post-investment period to meet the revenue and margin projections in your financial plan. And, of course, the plan must be achievable under whatever spending expectations you show in your expenses in the business for each year. Although the marketing approaches used in businesses differ too much for this book to specifically treat all of them, normally included in such a presentation would be the following:

Identity. What will be the identity of the business and its product and service? What image do you want your customers and suppliers to associate with your business? If you have lots of competitors, how will anyone remember you and distinguish you from the other guys? Are you cheaper, better, easier to find and deal with? Do you already have a Web site and brochure or data sheet examples? Will your business's location and signage generate most of your business from traffic passing by, and what will make them stop? A great identity plan is a good first step in establishing credibility with capital sources. If they buy your act, then they may believe your customers will buy your product.

Promotional plans. Promotional plans are sometimes called "marketing communications plans," consisting of advertising, Web presence and Web marketing, e-mail or fax solicitations, and similar forms of keeping your business name and product in front of customers. Where and how will this occur, and how much does it cost? Can you attend trade shows in Las Vegas every year and get all the customers you need? Will your new copy/mail center franchise find enough customers using your local mailbox or newspaper stuffing service? Do not forget that all these plans that involve spending money have to be consistent with expense projections in your financial plan.

Sales process and personnel. Now, here is where the rubber really meets the road. Almost every business has some person or process that generates leads (names, addresses, etc., of potential customers or maybe just anonymous "eyeballs," as the Internet world calls them) and another person or process that solicits and accepts an order from those prospects. If you are one of the lucky ones that rely entirely on location and visibility to attract walk-in/drive-in traffic, then your product or service and your in-store personnel will be the glue that completes the customer transaction. Otherwise, you will need a credible explanation of how you find and close prospects, that your cost of that process is consistent and competitive for your industry, and that you know how to manage it effectively to maintain the profits on the product or service that you are projecting.

Customer service. Once you have a customer, how do you assure that the sales experience is a satisfying one for that customer, so that he or she will return and that positive referrals to other prospects are likely? While this subject is often not treated in business plans, a source of OPM will be impressed if you do include your own personal philosophy of how to assure satisfied and happy and returning customers.

Again, it is important to stress that this explanation of marketing and sales will be a key measurement tool for the capital source. And someone on your team must have experience in the market or industry you have chosen, or at least in an industry similar enough for the experience to be useful. For example, if you and your partner are opening a new catering service aimed at supplying corporate social and meeting functions, your experience in the wholesale food distribution business may seem very appropriate. And it may convince an investor that you will know how to buy your foodstuffs from the right suppliers at the right price, but one of you should also have experience selling some product or service to corporations, since they are a unique customer set with their own ways of procuring and paying for services.

Investors Look for Viable Exit Strategies!

To deal effectively with this part of your business plan, you must really put yourself into the shoes of your potential capital source. If a future "liquidity" event when the potential investor will recover the full loan or investment, along with the interest rate or expected return on investment (ROI), is not readily apparent, the potential investor will quickly lose interest in your opportunity. Don't resist it, because unless you understand and address your investor's perspective on return of capital and return on investment, you cannot be successful. Remember, one of the first rules of persuasion is to tell him what's in it for him.

Sources of OPM are going to vary wildly in their expectations for capital return, interest or ROI, and the timing for both. In all cases, we refer to the investor's exit strategy as the manner—how and when—the investor receives his capital returned along with his ROI (although in some instances, there may be "payouts," often in the form of dividends, to the investor prior to the extraction of the original investment from the venture). The exit strategy may involve actual extraction of the original investment, or a "liquidity event," where your investor remains a holder of an ownership interest but in a stock form that allows for sale, or liquidity, at a time of the investor's choosing.

The most common form of liquidity, but more rare than you might expect, is that your business will become a publicly held company (giving your investors shares that are publicly traded) or that your business is acquired by another public company, by an exchange of shares, so that you and your investors then own shares in that acquiring public company, allowing you and your investors to sell at any time. (There are usually additional restrictions in both of these liquidity events, but that is a subject for another time.) The purchase of your business—for cash as opposed to an exchange of stock—is a classic exit mechanism.

Let's consider the differing expectations of certain categories of investors regarding exit or liquidity events.

Lenders. Your source for debt capital will have very specific expectations about their required return on capital loaned to your business as well as their usual security interest in assets and, typically, your personal guarantee. As discussed earlier, debt does have a lower long-term cost usually, but your risks may be higher. Lenders expect to be paid back, with interest, on the schedule negotiated and contracted as part of your financing transaction. There is usually very little flexibility in these situations, so your business and financial plans must contain sufficient predictability that you are comfortable that you can meet these commitments. If not, and your business goes into default with that lender, you will have to immediately repay all the debt and interest, which may have serious consequences for the business and you personally.

Equity investors. Sources of capital who agree to invest in your business as equity or stock investors are usually longer-term investors willing to accept more risk (no committed exit timing, no specific ROI, etc.) in exchange for a higher expected ROI. This is not the case for all kinds of equity investors, as we discussed earlier. But for purposes of this discussion, let's deal specifically with the pure equity investor, one whose terms for investment are very close to yours as an owner. They are typically willing to accept an equity investment without that clear date for exit or liquidity. This does not mean, however, that they do not have specific expectations in those regards.

It is absolutely crucial that you clearly understand their expected rates of return and the time period in which they expect to have their capital returned, or at least converted to a more liquid form of capital. As we will discuss in more detail, these patient capital sources may be individual investors or professional investment groups or firms, and so their expectations may be very different. When discussing your opportunity with these equity investors, make sure you understand very specifically the timing of their exit expectation and the ROI they desire. And your business plan must demonstrate that your objectives in owning and financing the development and maturation of your business are compatible with their liquidity expectations.

Due Diligence Preparation

We have mentioned several times that capital sources will be very interested in verifying everything they can about your business opportunity. The banker has an obligation to his management and shareholders and a legal obligation to the depositors to protect his loan, so he will want to know as much as possible about the opportunity. The equity investors, who may have more risk, may actually do more verification than your banker. As I'll discuss shortly, I was regularly hired by sophisticated investors to review the intellectual property position of businesses that they were considering for potential investments.

The due diligence process, in effect, eliminates the reasons not to invest. There are typically a number of facets to investor due diligence. The investigation usually includes business factors such as background checks on the management and key personnel (no criminal issues, bankruptcies, or bad reputations, verification of résumés); analysis of the business model and systems; analysis of the marketplace to verify the data provided in the business plan; and analysis of the general financial issues related to the business (e.g., sales figures, expenses, tax returns, accrued debts). The investigation also typically covers various legal issues such as whether the company has been properly formed and all legal formalities (e.g., annual meetings, corporate minutes) have been observed; the intellectual property position of the company; whether there has been compliance with all applicable laws (e.g., employee benefit plans, any necessary government licenses); whether there is any threatened or pending litigation; and the status of any legal contractual agreements (with employees, labor unions, customers or suppliers, licensors or licensees, landlords, and the like).

Intellectual Property and Legal Foundation from the Investor's Perspective

Over the years, sources of OPM—venture capitalists and the occasional Angel—have regularly engaged me to help evaluate businesses as potential investments. Why hire a patent attorney to help evaluate a potential investment? I'll tell you: because intellectual property is such an essential component of a successful venture.

Most sources of OPM require assurances that investment in a business is economically justified. This typically involves a review of not only a number of business, marketing, and financial factors but also issues relating to the legal foundation and competitive position of the business. That is where the patent attorney comes into the picture. Simply put, unless a company has both a proper legal foundation and a favorable competitive position, it is not an attractive investment.

Many questions regarding intellectual property and competitive position are asked during due diligence prior to investment. Does the business clearly own all critical technology and intellectual property? Does it have the right to use any third-party technology and/or intellectual property that it uses? Have the necessary steps been taken to identify, establish, and protect potential intellectual property assets? Are necessary agreements in place with (a) the inventor/founder of the business, (b) third-party developers and consultants, and (c) employees and principals? Have appropriate nondisclosure agreements been used? Are all important business relationships the subject of a written agreement? Assuming that written agreements are in place, are the terms of the agreements adequate? What is the nature and market power of competitors? Are there barriers that would prevent the company from entering into the marketplace, such as yet-to-be-obtained government licenses or approvals, or applicable third-party patents? Beyond that, as previously mentioned, a business rarely succeeds unless it establishes—and sustains—some form of competitive advantage. This means that the ability to establish sustainable competitive advantages is often a critical factor in the investment decision.

The exclusive right to use intellectual property is established through patents, trademarks, trade secrets (protected by confidentiality provisions in agreements), copyrights, and mask work registrations. Sophisticated investors look for a strategic plan with respect to intellectual property that includes establishing branding and obtaining the proper scope of patent protection.

Patents can represent one of the strongest barriers to competition, and the existence of, or the ability to obtain, patents is often pivotal to the investment decision. However, from the perspective of a sophisticated investor, the mere fact of having patents is typically not in itself enough. To be effective, the patents should be part of an overall business strategy, have claims of appropriate scope, and be competently prepared.

Trade secrets can provide a barrier to competition, but they tend to be vulnerable. To the extent that information can be ascertained from publicly available materials, the information is not a trade secret. Beyond that, trade secrets are only as good as the confidentiality provisions in agreements signed by the entities that access them.

Trademarks and the goodwill that they represent can also present a significant competitive advantage. However, some trademarks are more protectable than others (the less the trademark describes the nature or characteristics of the product, the more protectable it is). Moreover, certain countries require that trademarks be registered in that country in order to be protected.

Unless the necessary steps are taken to establish and protect intellectual property rights, the competitive advantage will not be sustained over time—the competition will be able to legitimately appropriate the intellectual property. Having the largest viable market, best management team, and the most marketable revolutionary product means little if whatever it is that gives the business its advantage in the marketplace isn't actually owned by the business or can simply be taken away by competitors as soon as the business begins to achieve success.

For more detail, see my book *Protecting Your #1 Asset: Creating Fortunes from Your Ideas* (Warner Books, 2001), one of the books in the Rich Dad's Advisors series.

You need to be particularly forthcoming with the potential investor during the due diligence process. Confidentiality agreements should be in place by this time. Open communication with the investor will tend to build rapport and confidence in you and your team. On the other hand, if the investor feels like he or she is being stonewalled, that you are trying to hide something, you are unlikely to get funded. If there are negative facts, you want to specifically call those facts to the potential investor's attention. In that way, there are no surprises, and you can avoid the appearance that you are trying to hide something and control the "spin."

You want the due diligence process to go smoothly and to make the process as easy as possible for the potential investor. Due diligence should be a tool for showing the potential investor how organized and forthright you are. The process should demonstrate your ability and willingness to communicate, your integrity, and your level of enthusiasm. So as you are preparing your business plan, try to anticipate all the things that might be important to this due diligence process, which typically occurs after there are serious discussions and preliminary agreement on the terms of a possible loan or investment. The simplest way to do this is to accumulate all of these items in a set of files or file drawers as you are preparing and going through your capital formation process. Catalog the files and create an index as you go. Then you will be ready for the due diligence activity when your capital source begins asking the questions.

What sort of things should go into your due diligence collection? What would you want to see if you were considering investing in a business? The answer is everything that is important to the health of the business and the business operations or that otherwise verifies or provides support for statements in your business plan.

If you are raising money for an existing business, the collection may become a sizable group of papers, including such minutiae as your organizational documents (e.g., articles of incorporation, bylaws, shareholders' agreements); corporate minute books from the first date of incorporation; copies of all important agreements; company and personal tax returns; personnel records on all management and key employees; payroll records; sales tax returns; patent, trademark, and copyright documents and related agreements and papers; documents relating to your business systems (and particularly management information systems); billing records for critical customers; bank statements for one or two years; data collected on the market and on competitors. For a new business, of course, there will be much less volume, but the process is no less important. Here is where your trove of third-party information will go a long way to building credibility for your business plan conclusions.

Tools to Sell Your Opportunity to the Investor

Now we are ready to begin approaching capital sources. We have already spoken about the importance of doing your homework and being prepared. What tools can you utilize to make the process more effective? Here are some suggestions to consider.

Elevator speech. When you first begin approaching capital sources, especially equity investors, you may have only a few minutes (by phone or by e-mail, even) to make a good impression and gain a willingness by a potential investor to "invest" his or her time in hearing more about you and your opportunity. Therefore, you must develop and practice (on friends, advisors, and other well-wishers) your quick summation of your plan and opportunity—hence the elevator speech, an effective three-minute pitch giving the essence of the opportunity and why it will be successful. Again, you may be saying to yourself, this can't be done! Well, it has to be done. You may not get that thirty-to-forty-five-minute presentation opportunity unless you can get interest established in the first introduction. So develop, refine, and practice it on your spouse or friends until they immediately "get it" and that blank look is replaced by a smile and the slight nod of understanding.

Web site and effective online presence. Unless you are a very local business with a very narrow customer audience, a good Web site and effective online presence can be a persuasive introduction to your business, especially if the Web is a good way for you to communicate with customers and interact with your suppliers. E-mailing an investor with your canned electronic elevator speech and an attached executive summary (which follows) may be good enough to get your investor prospect to review your Web site and understand a lot

Caution—Securities Law Alert

You have to be careful about whom you approach about investing in your company. The typical scenario where you are raising money for a business from passive investors involves securities as far as the law is concerned. Remember, as a general proposition, unless you have registered with the SEC or qualify for certain exemptions, you are not allowed to make "general solicitations" for investments. In other words, no cold calls or broadcast e-mails. You are limited to people with whom you already have some form of relationship. We will discuss this more later.

about your opportunity. Especially for a new business, a great Web site can give a real impression of solidity and permanence to enhance your credibility.

Executive summary. This is your "fishing document," a two-to-three-page summary of your business plan that can (subject to the applicable securities law) be sent by e-mail or fax, or act as an introduction to your business plan and be the first selling tool with real information about your opportunity. The executive summary should be a concise and clear overview of what your company is all about and what's in it for the investor. It will contain the crucial information about the opportunity, its assets and competitive positions, and its team of contributors, along with a summary of financial performance. You "throw" this summary into the hands of your capital sources with the intent that it intrigues them sufficiently to get them to commit to spend additional time getting to know you and your opportunity. It is the primary way to open a substantive discussion with a capital source. But unless the executive summary catches the investor's attention, things very often go no further.

Business plan and financials. This item has been covered previously and will be used with your capital source after he or she has agreed to consider your opportunity. Professional appearance, completeness, and accuracy are key.

Electronic slide show presentation. Microsoft Office, WordPerfect Office, or some similar office suite is no doubt part of your computer skill-sets. If you are approaching equity investors, it is very likely that you will need to develop an electronic presentation that will be used in meetings or phone conferences with them. Not only does it allow you to conduct a concise and organized presentation of information to these prospects, but it gives them a chance to see you and your team in action together. If you have not prepared many of these presentations, get some help from your advisors and practice it like you did your elevator speech. If you do get the chance to present your opportunity in a personal or phone meeting with your investor prospect and/or his partners, this is your key selling opportunity. This is what every businessperson seeking OPM is hoping for. And you need to be well prepared to take advantage of it. As often as not, you won't get a second chance.

Product demonstrations. If your business is based on products or services that can be demonstrated for a capital source, this is an opportunity that should be taken advantage of. And if it's a new product, it better work—the first time and every time.

Offering Memorandum

In a later chapter, we will discuss the effect of state and federal securities laws and regulations on your capital formation process. But at this point, note that any solicitation of capital investment, whether a loan from your brother-in-law or the sale of equity to a venture capital firm, is subject to laws and regulations governing such transactions. If you are soliciting capital from individuals, even professional investors, you may need to prepare an offering memorandum, or prospectus. This document is an extended version of a business plan, with lots of other informational and presentational requirements. And there may be requirements to register with government agencies as well. So an experienced securities lawyer is an essential requirement for this part of the capital formation preparation.

Securities Law and Investors: Charles's Sister-in-Law Hypothetical

Let's look at a hypothetical example that addresses the issue of the documentation that the securities law requires and some of the special issues involved when the investor is a close friend or relative.

"Hey, Mike, I need your advice," Charles announced as he walked over to me. "I'm in one of those damned-if-you-do and damned-if-you-don't situations."

"How so?" I responded.

"You know my new product—the one that your guys just filed a patent application on for me? Well, we just finished the field test, and the performance was ten times better than we expected. We want to manufacture this one in-house, so now I've got to go out and raise the funds to set up production."

"So what's the problem?" I asked.

"The problem is that my sister-in-law wants to invest in the business. If I let her in and things don't go the way we expect them to, I'll never hear the end of it. For that matter, even if things *do* go the way we expect them to, I'd probably still never hear the end of it. I've never seen her satisfied with anything. I mean, I've seen that woman complain that her ice cream was too cold.

"On the other hand, if things do go the way we expect them to and I don't let her have a piece of it, I'll never hear the end of it. Damned if I do, damned if I don't."

We laughed at his joke for a moment. Then Charles continued in a more serious tone.

"The real thing is that if things don't work out, she really can't afford the loss. I'd have a real problem with that."

Charles's description of his sister-in-law may have been half in jest, but there really were a number of serious issues with letting his sister-in-law invest. Some investors—particularly less sophisticated investors and investors who are stretched financially by the investment—are simply too "high-maintenance." They require constant reassurance and hand-holding to the extent that it can get in the way of running the business. I'd met Charles's sister-in-law—she lived here in town—and my guess was that she fit in that category.

A second issue was even more serious. There is a significant emotional burden when you have an investor, particularly a friend or family member, who cannot afford to lose his or her investment. You have to be able to live with yourself (and your family) if things don't work out the way you expect—because sometimes they don't. Are you prepared to guarantee their investment? Are you prepared to live with the consequences if you don't?

A third issue related to the securities law. It actually provided Charles a way out.

"Problem solved," I said. "Blame it on the attorney. Tell her that your attorney told you that you can't let her invest."

He grinned and motioned impatiently with his hand for me to go on.

I continued, "The securities law makes a distinction between investors based on net worth and income. There are accredited investors and nonaccredited investors. Accredited investors are basically institutional investors or individuals that meet certain net worth and income requirements. I don't think sister-in-law qualifies as accredited."

"That's right! I'd forgotten about that," Charles said. He dropped the pitch of his voice, the way that Bill Cosby did in some of his old routines. "The law says you have to keep all the good deals for the 'rich folks'! Only rich folks are allowed to invest in the fast-track pre-IPO—"

"Nope. Not so," I interrupted. I wasn't sure how serious Charles was, but the conversation had taken a weird turn. "At least that's not its intent. The se-curities law is designed to protect widows and orphans from big bad busi-nessmen like you." That certainly got Charles's attention. He looked at me with a quizzical expression. I continued, "The law is not intended to prevent people from investing. It's intended to protect them—to make sure that they are given enough information to make an intelligent decision when they are considering an investment. So the law tells you what information you have to give to investors and the way you have to give it to them—that's the offering memorandum. I'm sure Chris or Greg at Squire, Sanders has talked to you about an offering memorandum at some point." Chris and Greg are Charles's corporate and securities attorneys. Charles shrugged.

The law also requires you to meet very stringent requirements—in some cases limits on the amount of money that you are raising and on the number of nonaccredited investors you can have—or makes you go through a regis-tration process with the Securities and Exchange Commission, but I wasn't going to get into that with Charles at this point.

I got back on my soapbox. "Anyway, it's not that the law is trying to give accredited investors—rich folks as you call them—an advantage. Quite the contrary: It assumes that the rich folks *don't* need to be protected. So an ac-credited investor is not necessarily entitled to as much information as the av-erage Joe. You are not required to give an accredited investor an offering memorandum that meets the specs set out in the law like you are for non-accredited investors. The law doesn't tell you what information you have to give to accredited investors—as long as it's not misleading.

"The thing is, though, you want to make sure that you give all investors the same information," I said. "Otherwise, you run the risk that one of the in-vestors who didn't get the full package will complain that the information you gave them was incomplete—and therefore misleading—and drag you into court. So, as a practical matter, if you have any nonaccredited investors, you end up providing a formal offering memorandum to everybody.

"Anyway, from a business perspective, it's just a whole lot easier—and safer—to raise money strictly from accredited investors if you can."

What I didn't say was that while the rules were intended to protect (since it is so much easier and less risky to deal with only accredited investors), the practical effect of the rules is to prevent nonaccredited investors from participating in many fast-track deals. Letting them participate is just too much trouble and risk for many businesses seeking investors if they have accredited investors as alternatives.

"In this case, you won't have any trouble raising the money that you need through the local Angel network—all accredited investors."

Charles nodded. He knew that as long as he did his homework, with his contacts and track record, raising the money from accredited investors would not be an issue.

"In any event," I concluded, "you have a legitimate excuse for not letting your sister-in-law invest, if that's what you want."

Chapter 10

Friends and Family— Your Personal Network of Potential Investors

In our daily exposure to print and electronic media, we are bombarded with information about the economy and what is causing it to ebb and flow through its business cycles. Those of us who are practicing entrepreneurs or are preparing to become entrepreneurs no doubt follow this information flow more than others.

A lot of this information routinely deals with the popular finance topics: the stock market, the venture capital industry, and, to a lesser extent, the banking industry (and its famous regulator, the Fed). From this media attention, you would assume that these three industry segments are the principal sources for the capital that drives business formation and growth.

But there are two other very important sources of OPM, which are not as widely publicized but which are the most commonly used sources of start-up capital available (other than an entrepreneur's own capital). And you would probably not have read this far if you had the personal resources to finance your investment (or have the resources but, for whatever reason, prefer not to use them).

Can you guess what the two primary sources of OPM are? (The title of this chapter gives a pretty good hint as to one of them.) The two primary sources of OPM are your friends and family and the Angel investors who are present in every community. Together with an entrepreneur's own capital and resources, these two OPM and OPR sources are by far the main source for start-up capital and expansion capital for local or small businesses. So tapping into one or both of these sources, either at the same time or at different times in the evolution of the business, is usually a standard step in financing the start-up and growth of a business. And don't forget that both of these categories of sources may yield both financial capital (OPM) and in-kind resources (OPR).

Let's deal first with the friends and family sources and leave Angels for the following chapter.

Threshold Issue: Your Personal Responsibility

Before ever deciding to approach your personal network of friends and relatives, you must deal with one very important issue. Asking close personal relations for money carries emotional commitments that go well beyond mere "business." Acquaintances—people on the fringe of your circle of friends—will typically decide whether or not to invest in your business based on the merits of the investment opportunity. However, your close personal friends and relatives are likely to make their investment decision more because of their relationship with you than because of the merits. They may also feel some sort of social or moral obligation to assist you—invest *in you*—even if the investment is risky and whether or not they can actually afford the risk. On the flip side of that coin, you may feel some pressure to let them "take advantage of the opportunity," even if they are not qualified investors. (Remember Charles's sister-in-law from the hypothetical in the preceding chapter?) In any event, if they agree to invest money in your business, they will tend to look directly to you to make sure that the business performs and for the return of their capital. This responsibility may not be a legal liability, depending on how their investment is structured, but it may be a much stronger responsibility in their (and your) mind.

Remember, we are talking about the people who are involved in your life. If they invest in your business, you still want to be able to go on with your life and relationships come what may. How will your life be affected if they invest in your business and things go bad? When friends or relatives invest in your business, it's all too easy for the problems of the business to affect your relationships and for problems in your relationships to affect the business. Just think of the horror inherent in these statements: "My 'partner' is my *ex*-brother-in-law" or "My *ex's* father is my biggest investor" or "My biggest investor *used to be* my best friend." So before you go forward with this source of OPM, look yourself in the mirror and ask yourself these questions:

- If I ask these folks for money, will I be able to continue to see them every day or every week or every month or every family holiday and comfortably deal with the pressure of their expectations and reliance on me?
- How will the act of asking these folks for money affect our relationship?
- Will they feel unduly pressured?
- Will I be able to handle it if they say no?
- Can they really afford to make the investment?
- Am I prepared to guarantee their investment—or to live with the consequences if I don't?
- If they were not friends or family, would I ask them to invest?
- Can I really afford to give them the special attention that they will need?

We cannot stress the importance of this issue enough. Of course, you will (and should) feel responsible for all of the investors in your business, and you better be ready to accept it in those other cases as well. But asking close personal relations for money carries emotional commitments that go well beyond the mere business nature of the relationship that you as entrepreneur will have with your other investors. And that relationship can be significantly stressed as long as you are using their money.

Look at this issue from another perspective. If you are asking your brother-in-law for a loan of $30,000 so that you can purchase that duplex we discussed in Chapter 9, you can probably assume that he is well equipped, in terms of both knowledge and experience, to assess the risks of that loan and to request from you the legal protection to assure that he gets his money back if the investment is not successful. But when you collect $30,000 or $50,000 from each of several relatives to assist you in buying a franchise for insurance restoration services, and you have never been in that business before, and you know that they know even less about it than you, the ethical issues become more challenging. It becomes far more difficult for them to assess the risk that you may not be successful or to measure how long their money may be tied up in this business and other important issues. So they are significantly handicapped in assessing the risk that they will lose all their capital or that it will be unavailable to them for a long period of time.

The relationship may be more complicated and with ramifications other than the personal relationships. Let's say your spouse has been employed in the same construction firm for many years. You convince several of the partners in that company to invest in your opportunity, and things do not go well. You are forced to obtain capital from another investor, and all of you are now substantially "diluted" (reduced in percentage ownership) from that first investment. You can be sure that if your relations with those investors become strained because of the devaluation of their capital interests, it can have a similarly stressful impact on your spouse's employment prospects.

But at this point, let's assume you do believe that you can comfortably ask Aunt Bessie to invest her retirement money in your opportunity and still go to her house for Thanksgiving dinner each year and enjoy it. What tools and ideas can we offer to try to reduce the ambiguities and complications of these personal relationships so that everyone is as comfortable and protected from misunderstanding (or even more important, conflict) as possible?

As we mentioned before (and we want you to keep this thought in the top of your mind throughout the planning for your own capital formation experience), *all solicitations for capital, whether loans or equity,* are subject to regulation by the federal securities laws and the securities law of each of the states. In a later chapter, we will try to give you a good lay understanding of this regulatory framework (but not enough to make you feel like you do not need good legal counsel to guide you). But for purposes of this discussion, we can benefit from several principles that underlie the securities regulations.

The basic principles behind securities regulations are to assure that (a) investor prospects know enough to make an informed decision to accept the risk of investment and (b) these investors have adequate financial strength to afford the loss of their investment.

So how do we use these principles to avoid problems in your investor discussions with friends and family? Like your brother-in-law and the duplex opportunity, your investor prospects should have the knowledge and experience to evaluate the risks of the business opportunity in which they will participate as well as to understand the flexibility and protection of the form of investment you are offering. If you are buying an insurance restoration franchise, but you have little knowledge of the business now, and hope to learn enough at their training program, then this opportunity is highly risky for you and your investors. And an understanding of that risk is one of the key pieces of information your investor prospects need.

Of course, if you are borrowing money from your uncle who spent years working as an insurance adjuster and owned a home remodeling business on the side, then he may know more about it than you do and can really be helpful not only as an investor but as an adviser. In this case, your OPM source has enough personal knowledge and experience to evaluate the opportunity. But in other cases, you may have a significant obligation to educate to assure a knowledgeable investor.

In some cases, the amount of money also becomes very important, when compared to the net worth and income of your investors. Asking your dentist to invest $25,000 in your new business opportunity may seem like a good idea. We all believe that our dentists make a very good living, right? But if his net worth is only $45,000 and he is about to begin sending his three teenagers to college, then he may not be an appropriate candidate to tie up his capital in an investment that is not accessible for some long period of time. So when considering which friends and family should be good candidates for OPM, you should determine who has the knowledge and experience to evaluate the real risks of your opportunity and the nature of the investment. And all information necessary to evaluate those risks must be discussed with them, so "overdisclose" to these close personal relations to avoid problems later. And finally, if you do not think they can suffer the loss of that money, or at least go without access to it for a long period of time, they may not be the right OPM source either.

Do It by the Book!

You should not consider investments by friends and family or other so-called amateur sources of OPM to somehow be "different" than if you were dealing with professional investors or the bank. This is a piece of key counsel. Friends and family are *not* a special category as far as the law is concerned. You may believe that your brother-in-law or your aunt Bessie should just hand over the capital you are seeking just because of your relationship. Or that somehow your friends are not being loyal to you if they are reluctant to provide financial backing to your newest opportunity. Or maybe your friends or relatives feel obligated to invest in your business because of their relationship or because they are afraid of being perceived as unloyal. There is a tendency to go forward on an informal basis—to gloss over the details and documentation.

Our view is that when your prospective investors are friends or family, it is just that much more important to be formal from both a sales perspective and a legal perspective. The reasons for this view will become clear as we go on below and in later chapters. In fact, you may find that the personal relationship may actually make this class of OPM *more* difficult to sell an opportunity to! And why is that? Although professional investors may be harder to reach, or even to find in the first place, and your personal credibility has to be built from scratch with them, the investment business is, after all, their main business. And so they are very interested in finding and completing good investments and usually quite efficient about the process once they are sold and ready to go.

But with family and friends, getting them to listen to your pitch is usually pretty easy. Just make an early dentist appointment and take your business plan, or invite your neighbors over for hamburgers and spring it on them casually. But you will find that the personal dynamic may make it much more complicated to have a relaxed and effective conversation about the opportunity that you are offering. For example, your colleague at the office who is always flush with money, driving a new car every two years and taking long vacations to Europe, may become quite uncomfortable in a conversation about investment, because he may hate to admit that he just cannot afford it. Or due to the personal relationships, your aunt cannot find a nice way to say, "I wouldn't invest money in one of your crazy ideas if I won the lottery!" So getting to your sources' real feelings about their financial strength and their impressions of you and the opportunity may be difficult.

But the great thing about friends and family is that many times they will be happy to see you and talk about the opportunity, and they may be extremely supportive of your entrepreneurial drive and may even have the cash liquidity to participate. And even if they don't, they may be able and quite happy to introduce you to other people with the liquidity and experience to invest with you. That good referral from a friend may be all the additional assistance you need to get access to good, local sources of OPM. And each time you present your opportunity to a prospective investor, your ability to effectively communicate your vision will improve.

To return to our point, do not treat your personal network much differently than you would a banker or professional investor. Show them the courtesy of approaching them with a formal process. Maybe this process will be slightly different than with your banker or other sources, and it should take into account your personal relationship, but it should be as careful and thorough as you can make it. This is a very serious step and one with great consequences for your personal relationship, so treat it with the care it deserves.

For example, your personal relationship may change the way you decide to have a meeting with your retired contractor uncle, but you should not ambush him in the wrong setting or put him in a position where he does not have the opportunity to waive you off from such a discussion. Our recommended approach is to tell your prospect that you are in the midst of a new business planning exercise and that you would like to have his comments on it. Ask him if he would schedule a time to meet with you and see if he would like to see some materials in advance to review. In this fashion, you give your prospect some indication of your specific objective and you can then gracefully allow the conversation to lead to your decision to look for OPM and give him the chance to offer to help or run for cover. You will have to carefully consider the various factors present in every close relationship to assure you have approached this prospect properly, so customize your formal sales process for each candidate.

Things to think about in preparing for this interesting but challenging OPM source:

- Review your formal investor sales process and modify your approach and tone to suit the relationship you have with the person you are approaching.
- Give your prospects clear warning that you are about to impose on your relationship to have them look at your opportunity.
- Continue to follow your formal sales process if you continue to get favorable reactions along the way.
- Make it plain to them that you care about their real feelings and encourage their honest and direct feedback.
- Be very sensitive to nonverbal cues that you may be pushing too fast or too hard and that your prospects just don't want to tell you they are not interested or cannot afford it or cannot understand it, etc.
- As you identify your prospects, tailor your information and your requests for further discussion to their experience and their financial ability to participate.
- Make sure that you *overdisclose* information necessary for them to make an informed decision.
- If you get a favorable conclusion, be sure to follow carefully all legal requirements to protect you and your prospects and to assure that both of you have a full understanding of your "deal."

Identifying Your Personal Network

Now that we have discussed the unusual characteristics of friends and family as a personal network of OPM sources, just how do you find sources of

OPM within that network? Who among your family and friends should you go to for OPM?

Once again, we are in favor of a pretty organized approach.

Family is the easiest. You can quickly list the individuals in your family circle, on both your side and your spouse's side of the family, along with aunts, uncles, and cousins. Then it is preferable to prioritize those individuals by:

- Their experience and maturity. Can they understand your opportunity, and are they experienced and mature enough to make a "business" rather than a family judgment about their participation?
- Their economic health. Have they developed the personal liquid wealth that they can safely consider your investment opportunity?
- Special expertise or contacts. If they have experience relevant to your business, not only can they be of particular help, but they may have a special interest in helping.

Turning from family to friends obviously opens up the universe of prospects significantly. And there are orderly ways to approach this identification process as well. But for each name you identify, be sure you would feel comfortable approaching this person to ask for his money. But even if you are not sure you can call him for this opportunity, put him on the list and decide later. You may become more comfortable discussing this opportunity as you go along, and it may become easier to approach more distant friends and associates.

The easiest way to work up your list is to examine your "network" in ever-expanding circles:

- The current circle of closer friends and business associates of you and your spouse
- Other individuals you know through family members
- Your professional relations (doctors, dentists, lawyers, accountants, car dealers, etc.)
- Your clubs, church, and other social groups

- Former bosses, coworkers, suppliers, partners, etc.
- Your college and graduate school friends

Once again, prioritize the list in favor of the closest friends who are financially strong enough and have the business experience appropriate for your opportunity. They should be your best prospects.

And do not forget about the potential "noncash" investor. In an earlier chapter, we discussed the valuable potential contributions of noncash or in-kind investment that can be a very important way to leverage your opportunity or other strategic collaborations or combinations with other companies. So when you are going through your personal network, be alert to other potential contributions from these sources, either as team members, advisors, or in-kind investment that can be just as valuable as their cash.

Whom Do I Approach?

At this point, you must choose whom to approach, how to approach them, and how to properly educate them about the opportunity and its suitability for them. Here is where your personal responsibility intersects with your objective of raising capital. You must base that initial decision of whom to approach on your personal decision that you will be comfortable with the responsibility of having that friend or family member as an investor.

The matter of approach and the style of education and selling will depend on your assessment of the relationship. Based on assessment, you must determine how best to accomplish your conflicting objectives of "overdisclosure" and whether they can afford the investment versus closing the deal.

Be Prepared for Rejection and Don't Take It Personally

The list of family and friends now assembled may be from twenty-five to fifty people or even several hundred. Do you really need that many? We cannot predict how many prospects you need, but you can assume that only a very small percentage of these personal network prospects are going to even be interested in listening to your pitch. And many who will agree to listen do so only so they do not have to tell you they are not interested. Others will listen just to be supportive. But listening is not the same as investing. So prepare for these conversations very well. Your elevator speech should be crisp, and you should be ready with more information if they even show a glimmer of interest. But also prepare for rejection, because most of these prospects are not going to be investors.

You should also be prepared for a certain amount of "fickleness" on the part of this group of capital sources. When you deal with professional investors, they are usually much more businesslike in their decision making and follow-through. They are probably harder to reach and harder to sell, but when they make a decision and a commitment, they generally follow through in a predictable way. Your personal network, most of whom we must place in the amateur investor category, will be much more unpredictable in their decision making, the depth of their commitment, and their own processes for completing the investment.

So be prepared for some ebb and flow in the ranks of your participating friends and family. You may have done a great job of selling and really believe that Uncle Jack is going to write that check, but do not be surprised when he sheepishly tells you he has changed his mind, or that your aunt said, "No way!" Many of them will suddenly find their personal situation to be changed, so they cannot participate, or their accountant said they had to pay more taxes, or some similar excuse. Do not take it personally. It may have nothing to do with you or your opportunity. And it is better for you. Anyone who is not happy to participate and take the risks and rewards of that participation will be a difficult and unhappy investor in the long run.

One other point. Many amateur investors will have their own advisors who have great influence over their financial decisions. That person may be their accountant, their stockbroker, their banker, or their lawyer, or maybe just a more experienced business associate. So they may send you to this third party, and you may get to go through your whole pitch again for that advisor.

While referring you to their advisor may look like a "buying signal," evidencing their strong interest, your work is just beginning. Few of these out-side advisors are going to be very comfortable giving their client or friend sup-port or encouragement for making a private venture investment. They will no doubt know that many such investments are not successful, and they do not want to accept responsibility for recommending participation in a venture they cannot effectively evaluate, at least not without a lot of work. Now, if they are being paid to do this evaluation by your prospect, then you may get a bet-ter and fairer hearing. So give it your best shot and hope for the best. But this is not likely to be a helpful alternative for you.

Learn from the Experience

The process of selling, gaining commitment, and then collecting money within your personal network will be a great training ground for you and a real test of your emotional quotient. Even if you believe that your personal network will not have adequate capital to cover your requirements, these sources will be a great place to practice your pitch and get very important in-formation about how other people look at your opportunity.

Learning to listen to their questions, preparing great responses, and reading their reactions will be very helpful if and when you go on to talk with Angel investors or professional investors outside of your circle of friends and family. And pay particular attention to their nonverbal com-ments as well. Their body language and their visible comfort level in deal-ing with you on this subject of money and your opportunity are very important. You can save both you and your prospect a lot of time and dis-comfort if you quickly pick up any signals that you are wasting your time and theirs, or that they are happy you have this new project and love spending time with you, but they are not interested and are just too nice to say so.

Who Is an "Eligible Investor" — Family, Friends, and the Securities Law

We have already discussed in some detail your responsibility for culling your personal network of those prospects who are not appropriate for this investment. Let's review some of those conclusions and add another important one. Your personal investor prospects should be screened by the following criteria:

- Are they people whom you wish to involve in your business?
- Are you willing to accept the risk that the problems of the business will affect your relationship with these people or that problems in your relationship will affect the business?
- Do they have the business and financial knowledge and experience to properly evaluate the risks and rewards of their investment in your opportunity?
- Do they have adequate liquid capital so they can invest and still not damage their current living standard if the money is either lost completely or is not available to them or their family for a long period?
- Are you prepared to guarantee their investment—or to live with the consequences if you don't?

And then the final screening must take into account the securities regulatory framework. When you are raising money for your business from "passive"

> *The securities laws do not contain any exceptions or "safe harbors" for blood or family relations. You are not relieved from complying with the securities law just because your source of OPM is a friend or relative.*

investors (investors not significantly involved in the management of the business), the law is likely to view it as selling securities. We will get to the issue of whether or not your fund-raising efforts come under the securities law later. For now, however, it's a pretty good assumption that they do.

Unless the investment that you are offering qualifies for very specific exemptions, you are required to register the transaction with the SEC and/or an analogous state agency. Since you are raising money from friends and family, I think that we can safely assume that at this point you have not yet gone through the expensive and time-consuming process of an initial public offering—registering with the SEC. We will touch on what is involved in "going public" and the pros and cons in a later chapter. Depending upon their circumstances, participation of your friends or relatives may prevent you from qualifying for certain exemptions from the registration requirements or require you to meet specific requirements with respect to the information disclosed to your investors and the form in which it is disclosed.

In order to qualify for an exemption from the registration requirement, you must meet certain criteria. One of those criteria is that all investors, whether friends, family, or otherwise, must be "qualified." Sometimes the potential investor must have a certain net worth and/or income level (remember the issue with Charles's sister-in-law in the preceding chapter), have a certain level of experience and expertise, or reside in a specific state. Most of the time the investor also has to be someone with whom you have an existing relationship. (You can't reach the investor through general solicitation or advertising.) However, since we are talking about friends and family, I think we are safe on at least that front.

The requirements for being a qualified investor depend on the particular exemption that you are relying on. For example, as we've noted before, the securities law draws distinctions between investors based on net worth and income and on their level of sophistication, knowledge, and experience. We touched on this, among other places, in connection with Charles and his sister-in-law. Do you remember the difference between accredited investors and nonaccredited investors? Accredited investors are basically institutional investors or individuals that meet certain net worth and income requirements (e.g., a millionaire or having an annual income in excess of $200,000). To qualify under certain exemptions, all of your investors must be accredited. Other exemptions have limits on the number of nonaccredited investors that you can have. Still others require any nonaccredited investor to be "sophisticated" (have sufficient business and industry know-how to understand the issues). In addition, unless an investor is accredited, you have to observe some very strict requirements with respect to the information that you provide to the investor and the form in which you provide it. In fact, if any of your investors are not accredited, as a practical matter you will have to comply with the "disclosure" requirements with respect to all of your investors. We will get into the exemptions and specific requirements to qualify for them in a later chapter.

The Care and Feeding of the Amateur Investor

When you have commercial bankers and/or professional investors providing capital to your business, you will receive a pretty clear set of requirements for reporting to and participation by that capital source. Your banker will require regular financial statements (which may have to be audited annually by a CPA firm approved by them), weekly or monthly borrowing base certificates, audits of inventory and receivables or other security and annual renewals. Not only will the usual venture capital deal include that same kind of financial reporting and monitoring, but you may get one or two new members of your board of directors, certain new decision-making processes, and even recommendations for new members of your management team.

If you are fortunate enough to find adequate equity capital from amateur investors, you should be well prepared to set an expectation with those investors about their participation in the business. They may not think about it at the time of making the investment, but you should have already decided what kind of information you are going to provide and what kind of participation, if any, they can expect in the business on a day-to-day basis. If these commitments are designed and articulated at the time of investment, your future relationship with these investors will be smoother.

At a minimum, you should provide annual financial statements to shareholders, although there may be other legal requirements in your state, so check with your lawyer. It is also prudent to have meetings with shareholders more often than the one annual meeting required by your state law (in the case of corporations) or the shareholder meeting periodically required by the need to have shareholder approval of certain decisions. It is always better to keep shareholders informed about the business in a regular way, rather than to surprise them with shareholder meeting requests and important decisions in a rush, without proper time to prepare them. If this kind of corporate governance is new to you, your lawyer may be able to make some good suggestions about how to manage an investor family and minimize conflict and other difficulties. Having a board member or two with significant experience in this regard can be very helpful as well.

Other forms of business organizations, such as limited liability companies and partnerships, may have different requirements. But the objectives are the same. It is important to keep "stakeholders" informed about the business so they can participate in their required decision-making roles with good and timely information. Surprises, unless they are good ones, are to be avoided. It is not unusual for businesses to send out monthly or quarterly financial statements and provide periodic written reports of important business activity.

Amateur investors may make little or no demands on you for information or participation. But they may also be just the opposite. They may feel like an "owner" and may feel entitled to any information they wish and to participate in many more decisions than you would like them to. They may also want to visit or even hang around and get involved. This can be good or bad depending on the business and the investor. Do not be surprised to get a phone call asking to borrow the company truck for the weekend to move a relative to a new house. Or even worse, they may want to get "free stuff," or heavily discounted products and services. For this reason, setting expectations early about information, updates, decision making, and participation can go a long way to preventing problems in the later relationship.

Proper Documentation Can Save Heartache

After all of our discussion so far, this topic should already be implicitly clear. There may be a temptation to be informal or even to completely dispense with contract and other legal formalities when dealing with friends and family. Do not give in to that temptation, even if it seems overly stiff or formal at the time.

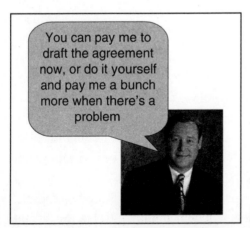

Your uncle may have loaned you $1,000 for that car in high school, and you both were happy with a handshake deal. But when he gives you $50,000 as a shareholder in your new dry-cleaning business, go through the formal steps of legal documentation as if he were a professional investor.

Many people dislike—make that *despise*—paperwork. And

they tend to like the involvement of attorneys even less. Paperwork and attorney involvement are often inconvenient and expensive. However, they can not only keep you out of lawsuits but preserve your relationships.

Formal documentation can prevent misunderstandings in the future. If an investment is not properly documented—if there is no comprehensive written agreement and no formal offering memorandum—it is very easy for legitimate misunderstandings to occur. Over and above that, it is an unfortunate fact of life that memories tend to become clouded or, worse yet, selective—because, inevitably, some people tend to remember (only!) what they want to remember.

It is extremely important that everyone agree on the nature of an investment—for example, whether it is a loan or an equity participation. Who determines when the money comes out of the business? When money comes out of the business, who gets paid first? Are there guaranteed returns?

All too often, particularly when friends or family are involved, formalities are ignored. This is when the misunderstandings tend to arise. For example, let's assume that you tell your rich brother-in-law Bill that you need $100,000 to get your product to market, and he writes you a check. Is it a loan or a purchase of equity—an ownership interest—in the business?

A misunderstanding is all too possible. Brother-in-law Bill may well think that he's making you a loan when you think he is buying equity, or vice versa. In that case, your brother-in-law expects to be paid back even if things don't work out so well for your business. You, on the other hand, think that your brother-in-law, as an equity participant, is assuming the risk of failure, and you do not contemplate having to pay him back if things go bad.

Even if there is no question that the money was a loan, in the absence of a clearly written agreement, there is still all too much room for misunderstanding. What is the term of the loan? What is the repayment plan? Bill may think that you will pay him back in monthly installments, whereas you don't plan to pay him back until it is convenient. Is the loan interest-bearing, and if so, what is the interest rate?

Conversely, it is also possible that you think that the money is a loan, whereas Bill thinks that he is buying an interest (to his mind, 50 percent) in your business. Imagine your surprise when, down the road, you go to pay your brother-in-law back his $100,000 and he tells you that he expects 50 percent of the value of your wildly successful business. In either case, things will not be very comfortable between you and your brother-in-law at the next family get-together.

Let's take another example. Suppose you have raised that same $100,000 from your brother-in-law Bill as an investment in your dry-cleaning business, and for that sum, you informed him that he was to own 33 percent of the business. If you do not properly document that event at the time it happens, then both sides may have different expectations concerning the 33 percent. But if you actually give him a certificate for 1,000 shares and you issue yourself the other 2,000 shares, then his ownership is clear. Five years later, you may have bought two other dry-cleaning shops and received new investments from new investors, and there may be 6,000 shares in the company. If you had only an oral agreement with Bill for 33 percent, would he think he was entitled to 1,000 shares (one-third of the original company shares) or 2,000 shares (one-third of the company shares five years later)?

What if Bill thinks he is going to receive one-third of the profits every month, or maybe receive a paycheck every week? You, however, intended that Bill should get his one-third later, only when the business is sold. After all, Bill won't be there to fold the laundry or man the counter like you are on those days when you are shorthanded.

So it is important to go through formal documentation of the investment process, even if it does delay events and costs money, because it is the best way to assure that there are no misunderstandings that lead to conflict along the way. We all know that even the best and most expensive lawyers papering every transaction as completely as possible cannot prevent all conflicts, but there is no better way to avoid most misunderstandings in advance, and it provides a helpful tool to resolve conflicts if and when they do happen.

Another very good reason to follow a formal documentation process is that *the law may require you to do so.* This is particularly true in a number of areas, such as setting up and managing limited liability business entities, local, state, and federal tax regulations, and, of course, under the securities regulatory framework. For example, without the proper documentation, you will not have limited liability. You can read more about the requirements for setting up a limited liability entity in *Own Your Own Corporation,* by Garrett Sutton, Esq. (Warner Books, 2001), one of the books in the Rich Dad's Advisors series.

Let's go back to the example of your brother-in-law contributing $100,000. Assume he thinks it is a loan. However, because of lack of documentation, not only is his contribution deemed to be for equity, but there is no limited liability. Assume the business gets sued and he is named as a party. Just imagine the conversation around the table at the next family holiday dinner if he is held responsible for some liability of the business.

In addition, if you don't provide the proper disclosure materials to investors, you may be at risk under the securities law. We will get to the requirements under the securities law later in the book. My best advice on this point is to find an experienced business lawyer to help with the formalities of complying with the securities law.

There are some who say that you should not do business with friends or family. However, to follow that advice would deprive you of perhaps the largest, and certainly the most supportive, source of OPM. The best advice with respect to friends and family is simple: Give care and thought to the special problems that doing business with friends and family presents. And if you do go forward, treat them with all the formality that you would a professional investor.

Chapter 11

Angel Investors— Your Source of Heavenly Capital?

In the preceding chapter, we discussed compiling your list of friends and family who may be potential sources of OPM and OPR. Maybe that list is too short. Or maybe its members are unable or too financially conservative to support your capital requirements. Or they don't want to get involved because they still think of you as a little kid on a tricycle. Or maybe you have already tapped into that source of capital. Or maybe you simply know that you need to access larger amounts of capital than are available from your personal network.

So you know you need a source for larger amounts of capital. But you also may know that your capital requirement is too small for the professional venture capital community, or maybe you know that your opportunity needs some time and more success before you want to tread on the doorsteps of the dreaded "vulture capitalist." What other source of OPM might be appropriate for this in-between stage? If you need capital that exceeds $100,000, yet is less than $1 million, then finding an Angel or two might be just the right strategy.

What are Angel investors and how do you find them? More important, how do you get them to participate in your opportunity? Almost everyone who compiles their list of friends and family finds someone in that group who has some experience investing in new or expanding business opportunities. Perhaps the person has chosen to become a source of capital for several businesses. That experienced investor actually meets the standard of Angel investor.

Angel investors come in all types and guises and have very different expectations about the amounts of money they will invest and the kinds of opportunities that interest them. But their main characteristic is that they inhabit a middle ground between the "amateur" investor that we described in our friends and family discussion and the "professional" investor we will discuss in coming chapters.

Some Background on Angels

The most famous story about Angel investing is the former Intel executive who provided some cash and a personal guarantee of a bank loan to help a famous garage start-up find its footing. That company was Apple Computer. Their story was a galvanizing event that opened one of the most dramatic evolutions in capital formation in the twentieth century. But independent wealthy individuals have been providing risk capital for investment opportunities throughout history, from the money lenders banished from the Temple in biblical stories, to later examples of the Renaissance patrons who furnished funding for the creation of art forms of various kinds. In fact, the term "angel" is said to derive from the OPM sources who provided the funds to sponsor the writing, production, and staging of Broadway and off-Broadway plays and musicals. The term was pure flattery, used during appeals for funding, but the term stuck.

The first venture capital firms were usually made up of Angels who got together and pooled capital as a way to spread their risk and involve other contributors of money, expertise, and work effort and to professionalize the investment process. When pension funds and other institutions, either through regulatory changes or simple strategic choices, began to invest in venture firms, the success of these firms drew greater and greater amounts of capital.

These larger portfolios eventually required these firms to limit their investments to larger and larger investments in a single company. You would not be surprised that it takes as much effort and time for a venture capital firm, with its contractual responsibility to its own investors, to make an investment of $1 million as it does to make an investment of $10 million! So getting the attention of a venture capitalist for your $350,000 investment is exceedingly difficult. This natural evolution in venture capital firms creates special characteristics that we will deal with in more detail in a later chapter. (We will also treat one of the newer forms of venture capital firms, included in the Small Business Investment Companies program (SBIC), that have evolved to service that investment size from $1 million to $5 million.)

Mirroring the growth of the venture capital industry, we have seen several estimates of the growing influence and organization of the Angel community. One estimate puts the approximate amount of capital from individual investors in the range of $50 billion annually, of which $40 billion is thought to come from friends and family and $10 billion from Angels. Another estimate, from the Small Business Administration (SBA), counts about 250,000 Angels, investing about $30 billion annually. The inconsistency in these numbers is not too surprising due to the difficulty of drawing clear lines between the "friends" in the friends and family category and the "Angels" who are repetitive investors and the difficulty of gathering such "private" statistics. Whatever the actual amounts, it is clear that Angels are providing significant share of capital for new businesses that are either in too early a stage or too small for the professional venture capitalist. And we are also seeing a trend toward more organization and professionalization even among Angels, a point we will address a little later.

A study of Angels by MIT's Entrepreneurship Center ("Venture Support Systems Project: Angel Investors," MIT Entrepreneurship Center, February 2000) categorized Angels into four groups:

- Guardian Angels, who are value-added investors, usually with some background in the industry of the companies they take positions in

- Entrepreneur Angels, who have started their own companies and use their earnings to invest in other early-stage companies
- Operational Angels, who bring cash plus substantial operational and financial expertise often earned in their careers in large, professionally managed companies
- Financial Angels, who have money and invest principally for financial return, presumably as an intentional diversification strategy for their own portfolios

You might wonder about the usefulness of these categories to you, since you may be initially indifferent to anything but the "color of their money"! But it is crucial to identify the interests and objectives of these Angel prospects for two reasons: (a) to carefully craft your message to meet their objectives, prejudices, and interests and (b) to understand when and why you are not successful or seem to be not holding their attention. There is no reason to waste time on prospects when there is not a fit between your investment objective and their financial, industry, participatory, or operational objectives or approaches.

Another point to remember: Guardian (value-added) or Operational Angels may be doubly important to your opportunity, since they may bring both OPM and OPR. Consider seeking out attorneys and accountants as potential Guardian and Operational Angels. This is an area in which I have had a great deal of personal experience as an Angel. No matter how hard I try to prevent it, whenever I make a significant investment in an emerging business, I always find myself contributing my time and legal expertise in addition to the cash, spending more time than I had anticipated developing strategy and supervising legal matters for the business. You will find that many good attorneys and accountants are the same way.

Why Would an Angel Consider Investing in Your Business?

Before we go into specifics about accessing Angels as a source of OPM, or even better, OPM and OPR, let's look at early-stage investing from the standpoint of an Angel. Before you go and begin selling your opportunity to an Angel, it would be great if you knew pretty well how he or she was going to be viewing this opportunity.

Your Angel source is usually going to be a high-net-worth individual, who has either inherited his or her net worth or earned it in a successful business of his or her own. They are often making these venture-style investments for one of two reasons: (a) as an intentional diversification of their own investment portfolio, similar to the way a pension fund may put 1 percent or 5 percent of its total portfolio into venture firms for investment in high-risk, high-yield opportunities, or (b) because they love to be involved in young entrepreneurial business opportunities. Or both. Understanding their reasons for investing may provide a real boost to the persuasiveness of your pitch.

An Angel's Perspective of the Deal

You can already see that these investors differ substantially from your typical friends and family investors. Most friends and family investors do not regularly see high-risk investments as opportunity and saw yours only because of your personal relationship. And your friends and family already know you pretty well, so your involvement is a known quantity. (We are intentionally ignoring the fact that some of your family and friends network may also be Angels. Angels may be within your circle of friends by coincidence—*or by design through your networking efforts.*)

Your Angel prospect is a different animal in many ways. Here are the key characteristics of *their* perspective when looking at your opportunity:

- They don't know you. Here we get to the same issue raised earlier in our discussion of preparation for your quest for OPM. The experience and image of you and your team become terribly important, so be ready to sell yourself. And one other consideration: With Angels, it will make a huge difference if you are introduced to them by someone they know and trust who will give you a strong reference. That gives you at least a running start. (Of course, if your networking efforts were already successful in acquainting the Angel with you, you are just that much further ahead of the game.)
- An Angel's dollars are going to be unreachable for some time. Unless you are borrowing money from an Angel, with a set repayment schedule, it is likely that his money will be tied up in your business for quite a while, maybe five to eight years. This is a major commitment for anyone to make

with his personal money. That is half a generation, a time in which his life will change dramatically, and his requirements for money may too.

• Your opportunity is very high-risk. Most entrepreneurs do not really believe that their opportunity is high-risk, and yours may not be. But your Angel prospect is going to believe that it *is* high-risk and will need to have very reliable assurances that you and your team have thoroughly analyzed and understand the risks and are prepared to manage them as close to zero as possible. Again, this issue will depend heavily on your personal credibility.

• ROI must justify the risk and period of investment. If he is putting his investment in your opportunity at high risk and it may take six or seven years for him to receive his return *of* capital and return *on* capital, then that return on capital has to be proportionately high. So your investment package should show a possible return on investment that compensates him for this risk and for the entire period of investment, on a compound interest basis. And that ROI will, of course, be different in different economic times. If he can make 12 percent per annum in a liquid investment, where he can access or borrow against his investment anytime, then your return, with its higher risk and its illiquidity for five to eight years, probably needs to show an exit event that will throw off a return of two or three times that of a more conventional return.

• Can and will they help out? Many Angels are active or retired entrepreneurs or businesspeople. They may have great skills, knowledge, and advice to offer, assuming they have the time and inclination to be involved in some way. This is important data, since they may have great contributions to make, and their involvement may go a long way to satisfying their desire to control risk. If they are involved enough to know what is happening, they can also feel some ability to anticipate and avoid risks that you may not see or appreciate, making them more comfortable in making the investment. The involvement may also be something that they enjoy. So finding a useful participation for them may go a long way toward facilitating their investment.

• How much capital will you need after them? If your business plan shows that the Angel's capital is not the final capital you are going to be raising, then their risk goes up quite a bit. Why is that? The dreaded word is "dilution," which is the same risk you as a shareholder have in raising money in multiple rounds. Your own equity position, and that of each team member and each of the early investors, face potential dilution from later rounds of new investors. If the business does well or is pursuing a licensing and/or joint venture strategy, then that dilution may not be too bad. But the Angel investor knows that a conventional investment round after him will likely be much larger and that it will come from a professional venture investor, and both of those characteristics raise the risk of substantial dilution of his equity stake. So he will be particularly sensitive to the business plan's financial objectives and the likely timing and size of that next round so that he can gauge the risk that the valuation at that later funding stage will justify an investment that enhances his stake or that hammers it.

These items should help you understand your Angel capital sources better and should help you position your sales pitch and your discussions with them more appropriately.

Finding and Selling Your Own Angels

Individual Angel prospects are typically located by personal networking and word of mouth. The best source for these references is your own network, similar to the way you tapped into your friends and family network. Instead of approaching these contacts and asking for their money, you ask them for introductions to people they know who have the inclination and experience to invest in your kind of opportunity.

If your advisory board is already in formation, its members will be a good source. Your lawyer, banker, accountant, and similar professional advisors can also make the right introductions. And remember, a personal reference and introduction is the best way to meet Angel sources.

The Angels in most communities become pretty well known as capital sources. And for that reason, they are regularly being contacted ("besieged" might be a more accurate description) for their capital, so you have to find a way to get through their self-imposed screening mechanisms. They are being sought after not only by other entrepreneurs like you but also by every charity and nonprofit in town. (You will find this to be the case later when we talk about venture capital firms as well.) So if you have not been a salesperson in your career, with good experience in knocking on doors and tastefully evading the secretaries and assistants who guard access to these capital sources, you might want to find some help in that regard.

Your objective is to get a twenty-minute meeting, preferably in the next month or so, and to have a willing listener. The absolute best way to get this first meeting and to have your Angel prospect be ready and willing to meet with you is to have that personal introduction from someone known and trusted by the Angel. You can imagine how helpful it is if your lawyer can call this capital source and say something like this:

"One of my clients has a great business started, and he is in the process of raising money for expansion. I have known him for many years, and he has been successful in everything he has done. I think the business would be interesting for you to look at, and maybe you will wish to participate. Can I have him call you and set up a meeting?"

That kind of introduction is a terrific help in getting someone's time and, more important, his attention. He knows what you want, and he will be listening with interest to see if it is something that can be good for him as well.

Now here we get to the hard part. That twenty-minute meeting is a crucial performance opportunity for you. Your elevator speech and your short introduction to you and your team and your plans will be the thing that makes or breaks your opportunity with this prospect. Of course, this Angel may not want to have anything to do with your chosen industry, or he may not be interested in investing the amount of money you need, but at least you got a good chance to state your case. And if you do a good job, you can then ask him for introductions to other potential investors who might have an interest in your opportunity. But if he is interested, then you can manage the selling process to get him (and his advisors, if he sends you that route) the information and materials they need to make a positive decision.

Now, what do you do when you have a list of potential Angels and no one can make an introduction? If you are able to find out what organizations the Angel is active in, join those organizations. Or become active in an organization that would give you the opportunity to call on the Angel. Or do all of the things that JT did in the example of Chapter 7. And if none of those things are possible or don't result in your meeting the Angel, what then? *Well, before you do anything else, you go to your securities attorney and make sure that a cold contact to the Angel will not disqualify you from an exemption to the registration requirement or otherwise run afoul of the securities law. In many cases, a cold call or unsolicited e-mail to a "stranger" will be a technical violation of the securities law. And if the Angel is located out of state, that may present additional problems.*

Let's assume for the purposes of discussion that you find one of the *rare* instances when a cold contact is cleared under both federal and state securities laws. Then what? This is where your sales experience (or if you can corral a sales expert advisor to help, that is even better) will come into play. Contacting an angel that you do not know except by reference or by reputation is a daunting task. How does one do that to preserve the best opportunity for success?

If you can get an e-mail address, the easiest, most efficient (for both you and your prospect) form of contact is a very carefully worded, but short, e-mail introduction to you and your opportunity and a request for a meeting. This, of course, presumes that your e-mail can make it past the potential investor's anti-spam software. Once again, we see the importance of that elevator speech, the crucible of information that will immediately garner your prospect's interest and prevent immediate depression of the delete button. More information can be included, say, with the Web address of your company Web site and an attachment with your executive summary. These items alone must convey enough information for a motivated prospect to decide if he will schedule a meeting with you and meet you and listen to your pitch.

Then what do you do? The greatest thing that could happen is that sometime in the next week you get a return e-mail saying a meeting is a good idea and giving you some dates. Of course, this almost never happens. In fact, if your e-mails even get read at all, you should be pleasantly surprised.

Remember, these prospects are well-known sources of capital, and they are constantly being recruited for many financial opportunities, both profit and nonprofit. And they are usually quite busy with their own obligations, even if those obligations are to lower their handicap or schedule the next visit to their Montana ranch. Seriously, most of them are also working hard, even if they are retired or semiretired. Most of them did not obtain their wealth by inheritance, and even if they are not working for a living, most of them are hard at work at something they care about.

What will happen is generally nothing. You will have to take another step and follow up on your e-mail. And that generally requires a phone call to the potential investor's house or office, and that is the worst kind of cold call. Here your expert selling advisor may have some good ideas about how to get through to your prospect, navigate successfully whatever screening device or people are placed in the path of well-meaning solicitations, and get the desired hearing opportunity. And that hearing may not be a real meeting, but only a phone meeting. In fact, if you get to talk directly to your potential Angel, he may tell you to give your pitch right then and there on the telephone instead of setting a time for a meeting. So, once again, the importance of your impromptu selling skills and opportunity summary become extremely important.

If you are successful in getting a phone interview, you do not even have your physical appearance to help you out, and you have no way to read your prospect's body language; it is just two voices over a phone. This is the toughest task you will face, since any failure to maintain interest will result in a pretty quick sign-off by your prospect. And again, you likely will not get a second chance.

For your out-of-town prospects, this first meeting is almost always a phone meeting, so honing your phone selling skills is a good thing. As you are putting together your pitch materials, carefully craft several phone selling scripts, to make sure you are well prepared to launch a quick summary of your reasons for calling, whether you get voice mail or happen to accidentally get your prospect to pick up the phone. There are no second chances in any of these meeting events; it is "one strike, you're out!"

If you have not done a lot of cold calling and similar selling activities, you will need to get some good training or assistance. One of the biggest issues will be your own reluctance to be confronted with this single opportunity to sell and the fear of failure or rejection. You may find yourself putting this off any way you can. There is no easy way to prepare for this process, but getting some training and practicing

For more on sales and dealing with rejections, you may want to read *Sales Dogs,* by Blair Singer (Warner Books, 2001), one of the Rich Dad's Advisors series books. You can find other sales training tools through the Sales Dogs Web site, www.salesdogs.com.

on your friends are good ways to prepare. On each day that you plan to do some cold calling, warm up by calling and talking with people you are comfortable with and even make some practice calls with patient friends.

And do not let your imagination make the process worse. For example, if you have sent out ten e-mails or left ten messages, and no one is responding, it is easy to begin to wonder if there is something wrong with your pitch or even with your opportunity. No response is just that and only that. There is no other message you should take from it—no interpretation for you to place on it—except that you got "no response." In fact, since there are hundreds of possible interpretations of "no response," there is no point in trying to pick one. So just keep going, keep trying, until you get some real data to help you understand your prospect's level of interest. But there is a point—when you have left three or four voice mails at an office, or where several e-mails and follow-up e-mails over some weeks have not generated any response, at locations where you know that prospect is working or living or answering other e-mail inquiries—when you have to realize that "no response" means "no interest," and you have to go on to other prospects.

We expect that you will find that most of these prospects are basically nice people, and they may let you down quickly when they talk to you, or they may avoid you so they do not have to say no. And many of them will be so busy and so bombarded by inquiries that they cannot take the time to listen and tell people no in a nice way. So they let silence speak for them.

We do not have the space here to teach cold-selling techniques. Get help if you need it. Do not be bothered by rejection. Continue to fine-tune your materials and presentation skills and keep going. Entrepreneurs are distinguished by their passion for their cause and by their persistence in the face of adversity. If you are bothered by failure or rejection, you are probably in the wrong business, or you should recruit a team member with the experience or grit to do the hard selling necessary to close the capital you need. It is a worthy skill and a useful person to have on the team. Getting your necessary supply of OPM is not the last challenge in making your opportunity into the reality you have visualized. And raising money may happen at a number of stages in your business's evolution.

Can I Find a Group . . . a Cohort . . . a Flock . . . Even a Choir of Angels?

As you read the preceding section about identifying and accessing angels, your first thought was probably, why can't I find them in a group and sell to them all at once? Well, you can. And we can thank the Internet investment boom and the Internet as a communications tool for this enhanced access to Angel investors. The boom 1990s created many more well-heeled entrepreneurs, still young enough and energetic enough to want to participate as active investors in other people's ventures. Many of them realized that banding together to share the work effort and their knowledge and experience might make the investment process work better and accomplish more with less effort. They also realized that they could give consideration to opportunities that may require higher levels of funds if they could pool their funds and share the risk with other Angels. These Angel networks are now an established part of the capital formation opportunity in the country.

The first summit of organized Angel groups occurred in April 2002 at the Massachusetts Institute of Technology, coordinated by the Marion Kauffman Foundation and resulting in a paper called "Business Angel Investing Groups Growing in North America." The paper cited research conducted by Jeffrey Sohl, at the University of New Hampshire's Center for Venture Research, who estimated that there were about 50 formal business Angel groups in 1997 and as many as 170 formal and informal organizations throughout the United States and Canada in 2002. The organizations have many things in common but vary in methods and organization and how their members participate. Key characteristics useful for you to know are:

- Their choice of organization and forms of membership participation are really not too important to you (until you successfully exit from your current venture and wish to join as an Angel, perhaps).
- Their methods of selection and their appetites in terms of industry, type, and size of investment should be researched well before contact.
- Introductions are often critically important in most networks, although many do accept "over the transom" executive summaries which are screened through their Web sites or administrative personnel.

- Some invest as a group, using commingled funds, relying on a single offer to an investment opportunity, while others follow a more informal process where individual Angel members take a lead role for opportunities they like and bring in other members as required.

You can find Angel Web sites easily on the Web and much useful information concerning Angel investing. We discussed this earlier in Chapter 7.

For your opportunity, you must find those networks that are active in your community or in cities near enough to be convenient travelwise. Angels, like many professional venture capital types, prefer to invest near where they live. And this trend toward "neighborhood" investing has accelerated since the post-2001 travel restrictions have increased the time involved in air travel. Try to find networks within two hours of your business if you want to get their attention and involvement. If they are located in your state, it may also make it easier for you to qualify for an exemption from the registration requirement of the federal securities law.

Angel Eccentricities

Whether you are dealing with Angel investors you have located one at a time through your own personal network, or organized Angel groups, you will still be dealing with "amateur" investors who are investing their own time and their own money in listening to your pitch and, assuming you are successful in gaining their trust, in your business. While some of the organized networks have built a formal process and group dynamic that may resemble the professional venture capitalist (VC) firm, the vast majority of them are more loosely organized and will just provide you a more efficient forum to get your group of investors together.

Unlike the professional investor (venture capitalist), investing is not the Angel's "job." It is a VC's daily responsibility to find, evaluate, and decide to invest X dollars. VCs are typically under pressure to find a place to put X dollars in Y number of deals every year in order to make their investors happy. So the VC partner is hungry to find good deals, and when he does, he is happy to get it done and the checks written. This is not the perspective of Angel investors. They are not under the same pressures. So you can expect the process of selling and closing the sale and, more important, collecting the cash from the Angel to be more challenging. He probably has lots of activities to take up his time; *and* it is not his job to invest money in risky ventures; *and* he isn't making this kind of decision every day; *and* he has no partners or investment committee to share the decision-making responsibility (although he may be surrounded by naysayers); *and* he has many, many other, safer places to put that money. So what are the eccentricities you can expect to see?

The most important characteristic of Angel investors, like friends and family, is that they are almost always investing their own money. (Sometimes it may be their children's trust fund or a relative's money, but this is pretty rare. And if you do have that case, then you have additional legal issues to be concerned about.) Even if they love your opportunity and want very much to invest, they still have to get over the hump of having to write that personal check. And this is going to be very, very hard for many of them, and impossible for some of them.

Even though angels may be investing their own money, most of them have a spouse, or perhaps a trustee of their funds, or an advisor, or some other influencing factor that may act as a brake on their enthusiasm for your opportunity, and may even act as a final veto.

Since you are dealing with individuals, you are going to be faced with the myriad of personalities, idiosyncrasies, cultures, biases, and other differences in each of them, so you cannot have a unified approach or strategy. Each will have to be treated differently, will have different experiences and knowledge, and will make their decisions in their own individual and peculiar way. Because many have generally been successful in business and in life, the Angel may have the type of personality that likes to control things a bit or perhaps just likes to have things his or her own way.

The decision to say yes will likely take longer. In all investor situations, the pace will be slower than you, the entrepreneur, would like. But with Angels, you can expect it to be very drawn-out. And even when you get the "yes," do not celebrate yet, since you are only sure of a "yes" when you actually have a check and it is cleared by your bank. And that may not be the end of it even then, since Angels sometimes ask for the money back; "buyer's remorse" is a disease rampant among Angels.

Angels may also take special "care and feeding," an issue we discussed in the case of friends and family. While they are generally experienced enough not to expect "free stuff," they will usually expect lots of information and may be very free with their opinions. And if they perceive any reluctance on your part to listen or to follow their advice, then your relationship may become strained. On the other hand, because it is their money, they will often be very willing to help out when they can, so use their skills and experience if it works for the business. It is important to manage the relationship with each of your Angel investors, on an individual basis, to assure continued good relations and support and to use whatever contribution they can make.

Remember earlier we spoke about the fact that some of these Angel investments may last for five to eight years. This means that you may have to live with these eccentricities for a good long while. Some people searching for OPM will probably approach the Angel concept with the idea in mind that beggars can't be choosy. However, you should make certain that you are at ease with the eccentricities of the Angel before entering into a relatively long-term relationship with him or her. You may indeed want to be "choosy" about the source of your OPM.

While these last few observations may make one pause when considering pursuing Angel prospects, there are some very definite benefits to an Angel round of investment. We have already discussed the significant contributions that some Angels can make to your business, lending their years of experience and often free work effort to help make your business successful. Their contacts with other investors, both Angel and professional, and their contacts with strategic partners and potential board members (both advisory and statutory) can help in many ways to make your business successful.

But the two main reasons why Angel rounds can be very good for your business capital strategy are these: (a) If you are not dealing with a monolithic investor, you are generally in control of the valuation, and (b) for the same reason, you are generally in control of the deal terms, contracts, and similar important characteristics of the transaction. In both cases, the fact that you are dealing with several, or even up to ten to fifteen, individual Angel investors does not mean that any of them have the clout to negotiate valuation or deal structure or to demand board seats. This is the primary benefit of an Angel round, which provides access to a larger amount of capital without the corresponding loss of control of the transaction, which often occurs in deals with a lead venture investor. Not to mention you may get some very valuable volunteer help in running your company and managing its future.

One final point about Angels requires our standard caveat about legal and securities compliance matters. Even though these investors may appear to be experienced investors and wealthy enough to sustain the potential loss of their investment, you must still comply with the requirements of the securities laws and regulations. You will likely control the paperwork, but an offering memorandum is still likely to be required, and full documentation of the transactions will be necessary. You may be in control of that documentation, but it still needs to be done as carefully as you can.

Chapter 12

Venture Capital

There are billions of dollars available to businesses in all stages of development from venture capitalists (VCs). As outlined earlier, venture capitalists are professional investors and may be in the form of venture capital funds, corporate venture investors ("direct investors"), or professional Angels. The fundamental similarity of venture capitalists is that they are in the business of investing in businesses, which means they are generally very involved in the businesses in which they invest. This is in contrast to many investors from the friends and family, regular Angel, or debt investor categories.

Active vs. Passive Investors

As professional investors, venture capitalists are usually very active in the trade or business in which they invest. They typically add value to the business they invest in based on their business expertise and experience in addition to the money they invest. In most cases, they will want to share control of the business as well as share in the success of the business. If you are bringing in a venture capitalist, you must be willing to accede some control in the way you operate your business. Some people are unable to do this. Many entrepreneurs fail to recognize the difference between passive investors and active investors and the impact this difference may have on their business and the everyday operations or management of the business.

What Do Venture Capitalists Look For?

As professional investors, VCs, no matter what form they take, have definitive investment strategies and criteria. The three most critical areas they look for in a potential investment are competitive advantage, exceptional management, and extraordinary growth potential.

COMPETITIVE ADVANTAGE

Like many of the other sources of OPM mentioned in this book, the venture capitalist looks for a company to have a competitive advantage through proprietary products or services. The ownership and existence of patents, trademarks, copyrights, and other rights demonstrate a company's advantage over any existing or potential competitors. They will look at all the factors that we discussed earlier that make your product, service, or business better, unique, or distinctive. They will also want to make sure that the competitive advantage can be sustained over time. They know that the competition will recognize the competitive edge of your business and will adapt and, to the extent possible, adopt.

Over the years, "financiers," typically venture capitalists and the occasional Angel, have regularly engaged me to help evaluate businesses as potential investments. Why hire a patent attorney to help evaluate a potential investment? I'll tell you.

Most venture capitalists (certainly the ones that are successful) require assurances that an investment is economically justified. This typically involves a review of not only a number of business, marketing, and financial factors but also issues relating to the legal foundation and competitive position of the business under consideration. That is where a patent attorney comes into the picture.

Simply put, unless a company has the proper legal foundation to build on, it is not an attractive investment. Has the appropriate type of business entity been formed? Does the business clearly own all critical technology and intellectual property? Does it have the right to use any third-party technology and/or intellectual property that it uses? Are necessary agreements in place between the business entity and (a) the inventor/founder of the business, (b) third-party developers and consultants, and (c) employees and principals? Have appropriate nondisclosure agreements been used? Are all important business relationships the subject of a written agreement? Assuming that written agreements are in place, are the terms of the agreements adequate? Have the necessary steps been taken to identify, establish, and protect potential intellectual property assets? Does the company have potential liabilities (contractual or otherwise) to others? Beyond that, a business rarely succeeds, unless it either outspends the competition (which is not at all attractive to the investor) or establishes—and sustains—some form of competitive advantage or barrier against competition. Having the largest viable market, a crackerjack management team, and a dynamite product or service means little if whatever it is that gives the business its advantage in the marketplace isn't actually owned by the business or can simply be taken away by competitors as soon as the business begins to achieve success.

Accordingly, VCs typically scrutinize the competitive position of a business before investing. They study the nature and market power of competitors. They want assurances that there are no barriers that would prevent the company from entering into the marketplace, such as, for example, yet-to-be-obtained government licenses or approvals or, typically most significant, applicable third-party patents.

On the other hand, the ability to establish sustainable competitive advantages is often a critical factor in making the investment decision. In general, you have a competitive advantage when (a) an aspect of your business is unique, better, or distinctive as compared to competition or (b) you have acquired or achieved a difficult-to-acquire-or-achieve requirement to enter or remain in the marketplace—that is, you have overcome a "barrier to entry"—that is still a "barrier against competition." Competitive advantages can come not only from products or services but also from internal business procedures and systems, or communications and relationships with the external world. Occasionally, a competitive advantage can, at least for a time, come from things like the location of facilities (the facility is more convenient and therefore "better" than the competition); or the requirement that competitors invest in expensive capital equipment or obtain government licenses or approvals already held by the company. More often, a competitive advantage is derived from a strategic exclusivity, typically in the form of contracts or partnering arrangements with key customers, suppliers, distributors, or strategic allies.

Most of the time, however, sustainable competitive advantages involve some form of intellectual property—the intangible asset that results from ideas, creativity, innovation, and relationships. This includes not only invention but also information and data, special expertise and know-how, designs, works of authorship (such as marketing literature and manuals), the layout of semiconductor integrated circuits, and trademarks, trade dress, reputation, and goodwill. Barriers against competition are typically based upon the exclusive right to use intellectual property established through legal protection mechanisms: patents, trademarks, trade secrets, copyrights, and mask work registrations. Of course, unless the necessary steps are taken to establish and protect intellectual property rights, the competitive advantage will not be sustained over time. Unless legal protections are in place, the competition is typically at liberty to legitimately appropriate the intellectual property.

The nature and scope of the company's intellectual property protection is critically assessed. Is there an agreement regime in place to protect trade secrets? Is there a strategic branding plan? Have trademarks been registered in the United States and any other relevant market? Are there procedures in place to identify potential intellectual property assets and to assure timely pursuit of appropriate protection? Have patents been granted or applications for patents timely filed?

The existence of, or the ability to obtain, patents is often a critical factor in making the investment decision. However, merely having patents is typically not in itself determinative to sophisticated and professional investors. They usually need assurances that patents are part of an overall business strategy and are competently prepared. Occasionally, the reputation of the company's patent counsel is enough to give the investors those assurances. However, in the more typical case, the scope and validity of the patents are investigated and analyzed in excruciating detail.

EXCEPTIONAL MANAGEMENT

Exceptional management is another key ingredient important to the VCs. They must be confident in you and your management team's ability to grow your business. The more experience and depth of knowledge you can demonstrate, the easier you will be able to convince the venture capitalist of your opportunity for success. There are times, however, when the VC may recognize an opportunity to "add value" by strengthening your team. The venture capitalist wants to know that your management team is both credible and credentialed. Again, an advisory team with the same qualities will help your cause.

EXTRAORDINARY GROWTH POTENTIAL

The typical VC is not interested in being a big fish in a small pond. Venture capitalists want to invest in companies that possess extraordinary growth potential and are playing in a big game. A typical return on investment strategy is one of five times the original investment within three years, or ten times the original investment within five years.

In what kinds of businesses can the venture capitalist find that kind of return? To interest the venture capitalist, your business must have one or more of the following characteristics:

- A growing industry. Companies in the biotechnology and other technology industries have been popular investment targets based on potential growth. Many venture capitalists were beat up quite badly when the dot-com bubble burst. Nevertheless, VCs still tend to be attracted to cutting-edge technologies. Many VCs only invest in specific industries.
- A growing market. Does your company possess a large market share in your market, or does it possess the opportunity to capture market share? Is the market large enough to support your explosive growth?
- A qualified market. Does your market understand the need for your product or service? Will they pay for your product or service?
- Strong margins. Do your company's operations generate significant operating margins (35 percent or more)? The stronger your margins, the more attractive you become.

- IPO, merger, or acquisition candidate. Is your company positioned to grow quickly enough to successfully complete an initial public offering, to become attractive as a merger or acquisition for a bigger company in your industry?
- Business strategy. Do you have a strong business plan with a defined strategy that conforms with the strategy of the venture capitalists' goals?
- Exit. Understand when considering all of these factors that the venture capitalists' primary goal is to provide a significant return on investment within a specific time period (typically three to five years). The exit strategy may be an IPO, merger, or acquisition, or even a buyback of the venture capitalists' position (based, of course, on the greatly increased value of the business), but there will be an exit strategy defined *before* the investment is made. To most venture capitalists, the exit strategy is an absolute requirement because exit time is payoff time.

To the venture capitalist, the extraordinary growth potential is the reward for taking the extraordinary risk on your new and untested business venture.

How Do You Prepare for a VC?

Venture capitalists are deluged with "investment proposals" all the time. The typical firm may receive a thousand proposals a year and 90 percent of them are rejected quickly because they do not fit the established investment criteria of the firm—or they are not properly prepared or presented. Here are several tips that may help you in selecting venture capitalists and how to get them interested:

- Do your homework. Research the venture firms or funds that invest in companies similar to yours and/or in the same industry as yours. We discussed the wealth of information available on venture capital firms in Chapter 7. For example, you may find this information in *Pratt's Guide to Venture Capital Sources* (Securities Data Publishing), *The Directory of Venture Capital & Private Equity Firms* (Grey House Publishing), and the membership directory for the National Venture Capital Association (NVCA), a U.S. venture capital industry trade association, all available at your library or local bookstore or through numerous Web sites. Ask your accountants and attorneys for recommendations and referrals. Attend meetings within your industry to establish a network of contacts. Many VCs attend these industry association meetings to keep abreast of new developments within the industries in which they invest. If you are a technology start-up, you do not want to spend your time chasing a venture fund that specializes in consumer product retail businesses.

• Prepare your business plan. We discussed business plans in Chapter 9. It is imperative that you clearly define your business, its financial history, and financial projections. Be realistic with your financial projections. You want to satisfy the venture capitalists that you are prepared for the next level of growth and that you have the right management team in place to get there. Write a dynamite one-to-two-page executive summary to catch their interest (remember you are one in a thousand). How do you highlight yourself above the rest?

• Practice your pitch. This is another opportunity to benefit from your family and friends. Practice your presentation on friends and advisors, encourage them to play devil's advocate and question you. Fine-tune your elevator speech. You never know when you'll have an opportunity to pitch your company as an attractive investment. Remember, your only opportunity to make the elevator speech to the venture capitalist at the top of your list may actually be a chance encounter in the elevator. Always be ready for that chance meeting. You should be your own number one salesperson.

• Think BIG. From a VC's perspective, size does matter. VCs want to know that you believe in the growth potential of your company and that your vision and passion are big enough to meet their investment criteria. Remember, venture capital funds typically make investments in the range of $500,000 to $5 million. Don't approach a venture capitalist for a $35,000 investment in your bagel business. On the other hand, if you are planning to sell your "better" bagel all over the world and need $1 million to go forward, the venture capital route may be for you.

• Sell your management team. Emphasize your management team's track record, their prior start-up or IPO experience, competence, credibility, and character. Include their prior industry-specific experience as well as team-building experience.

• Know your investment needs. You must be clear on what your investment needs are. How much money will it take to get you to the next level? We discussed this at some length in Chapter 5.

• Know your equity structure. Be prepared to inform the VCs about the current equity owners and their relative equity positions. Be prepared to discuss the equity you are offering in exchange for the proposed investment.

• Focus on how you will use the money. Center your presentation around what you intend to accomplish with the requested investment and the projected return on investment and planned exit strategy.

• Keep your presentation under an hour. Be respectful of the VC's time and clearly and precisely present your business and the investment opportunity.

Understanding the VC Process

Getting the first meeting with the venture capitalist is a *huge* step in getting him or her interested in your company. You may have been referred by someone respected by the VC, you may have presented a concise executive summary that has piqued the VC's interest, or lady luck is on your side. Doing your homework before that first meeting is extremely important to move the process forward.

As mentioned earlier, the VCs have specific investment strategies and criteria. They also typically follow a specific process or system in selecting potential investments. However, they also want to have a steady flow of new deals coming to their attention. Once you are in that flow, and the VC is interested in further information about your company, the next step is the VC's due diligence.

DUE DILIGENCE

Venture capitalists will carefully review your business plan to assess its accuracy. They will verify the industry information as well as the financials you provided. In addition, they typically do careful background checks and reference checks on you, your management team, and your company. The other major part of the due diligence is, as mentioned above, the review of the legal aspects of the business. This will entail review of the business structure, potential litigation, your intellectual property position, and your contractual obligations. The venture capitalists' goal is to maximize their earnings potential while minimizing their risks. Due diligence gives them some idea of the potential hidden risks to their investment.

INVESTMENT VALUATION

If the due diligence phase is completed successfully, venture capitalists move on to determine how much they are willing to invest and, most important, what their price to you is for the investment. They will evaluate the profit potential of the business and then forecast the future value of the business based on their investment. Then they work backward based on their return on investment criteria to determine how much ownership they must possess to achieve their desired return. They will also typically review other investment deals that are comparable to yours in establishing valuation benchmarks. The valuation process is one of the most critical steps in the venture capital investment cycle. Once a valuation has been established, the VC then attempts to structure the deal.

STRUCTURING THE DEAL

In structuring the deal, the VC wants to maximize his return on investment and minimize his risk while also satisfying the entrepreneur's funding and equity requirements. Further, he will want to do it in a manner or using an equity device that (a) gives him some control over the business so he can protect his investment and (b) works toward a liquidity event (exit) within a predetermined period (typically five to seven years). This may be accomplished by combining several investment vehicles. While a straight equity investment in exchange for a percentage of the voting common stock is the normal structure, it is very common that a deal will include the use of several of the following instruments:

- Common stock—new or existing shares
- Debt—loans that may be secured by company assets
- Convertible debt—loans that may be convertible into common stock or preferred stock

- Preferred stock—which may have a guaranteed return and a preferential standing over common stock
- Options—which may be exercised to generate additional dollars to the company and increase the equity position of the option holder. (One option usually represents 100 shares of stock.)
- Warrants—which may be exercised to generate additional dollars to the company and increase the equity position of the warrant holder. (One warrant usually represents one share of stock.)

In structuring the deal, VCs may use one of these instruments or a combination of them. In addition, they may create "stages of funding" with benchmarks that must be accomplished before each additional round of funding. This is popular with the VCs because it adds another element of control as well as limiting the risk of their investment. But in the end, even after establishing a valuation and a proposed deal, success of the deal depends on the negotiation process between the VC and you. You may have to get creative to devise a deal that makes all parties satisfied with their control and return on investment potential.

MANAGING THE VC RELATIONSHIP

As mentioned in the beginning of this chapter, the role of the venture capitalist as an investor is one of an active investor, not a passive investor. As such, the role of the VC after the deal is done and the investment is made must also be defined and implemented. The VC will give ongoing advice to you as a strategic partner as well as a financial advisor. He generally speaks from experience, and his advice can be invaluable. It can also be extremely intrusive in the management of your company. He will monitor your business activities and raise concerns over any deviations from the approved business strategy and business plan. He will even monitor how much money you draw out of your business for salary or bonuses. But bare in mind that the ultimate goal of the VC is the same as yours: to build a successful business that provides a significant return on investment. The trick is to negotiate beforehand an agreed-upon level of involvement with which both you and the VC are comfortable.

EXIT

Since the VCs' return on investment is typically only realized after the business has grown significantly and an exit strategy is implemented, the exit strategy itself is critical. Whether the exit is through an IPO, a merger, or an acquisition, it must be managed carefully to ensure that the expectations of both the VCs and you as the business founder are realized. The VCs' primary concern is to harvest their investment. They are not particularly concerned with continuing involvement in the business. You, on the other hand, may welcome a liquidity event but may not be ready to literally exit from "your baby." Your concerns and those of the VCs with respect to an exit are not necessarily aligned. That is why it is so critical that the exit strategy be carefully planned and agreed upon from the beginning.

Summary

In review, venture capitalists provide an essential element of OPM and OPR. As an entrepreneur, it is very important to understand both the advantages and the disadvantages of working with venture capitalists.

Advantages

- VCs provide an important source of management experience and counsel.
- VCs bring their network of advisors and business contacts (OPR) in addition to their investment dollars.
- Equity investments by VCs provide funding for your business without the need for interest payments (which would be required for debt funding).
- By having more equity from VCs, you can actually qualify for additional debt financing.
- VC investments generally result in a more structured business environment and create a more disciplined approach during a period of rapid growth.

Disadvantages

- VC investors look for very high rates of return on their investment.
- VC investors require shared ownership of your business and active participation in management.
- Looking for VC money may be expensive related to compliance issues and due diligence, including legal and accounting expenses.

- Ongoing compliance and shared management activities and information reporting can become cumbersome and costly.
- You must be prepared to either give up or share control and profits from your business.

Preparing for and pitching venture capitalists on the attractiveness of investing in your company can be a very rewarding experience. By having to analyze your business operations, financial history and projections, market position and management team strengths and weaknesses, you will learn a great deal about your successes and failures of the past and your opportunities for future success. Good hunting!

Chapter 13

Using OPM for a Fee—Institutional Bank/Lender Financing, Factoring, and Leasing

At some point, you have determined that you do not have money available to build your business or pursue your life's ambition. You believe that you are not the least bit creative, and you cannot figure out how to get Other People's Money. Even after reading every chapter in this book, you still have no idea how or where to sell stock in your company or who would possibly be interested in purchasing it. Your cash flow is stretched to the max, and you get that sinking feeling that your business will not be able to succeed or grow. The solution: You do what just about everyone else has done since the beginning of recorded history. You decide to get a loan. You feel comfortable because you always knew that this is *the* traditional way to fund your business. In fact, borrowing funds is a tradition that goes back at least five thousand years. Even the Old Testament has references to this kind of funding activity, including even a code or rules for forgiving debt.[1] You can't get much more traditional than that.

First understand that borrowing is not the worst thing in the world. If you have read some of the Rich Dad books, you know that not all debt is bad. There is such a thing as "good debt." If a person wants to become rich, he or she has to learn how to harness the power of good debt. Further, if you are a borrower, you are not alone. One estimate is that the U.S. loan origination market is a $1-trillion industry.

This chapter deals mainly with the traditional loan. It does not deal with loans from your brother-in-law or the neighborhood loan shark. However, we will touch on some other mechanisms for getting the use of Other People's Money or Resources in return for payment of a fee.

Is It Really Other People's Money?

One of my friends says that borrowing money is really very similar to using your own money. It is different from when you bring in other principals—in effect selling equity in the company. In that situation, you are literally using Other People's Money. But my friend views a loan as though you are using your own money, because eventually you have to pay it back. From that perspective, when you are using your own money, you could look at it as though you have just decided to be your own equity partner, because you are putting money into the business (at least on a monthly basis when you are paying the lender back) instead of bringing in another equity partner.

However, the classical view (which I happen to share) is that with a loan, the bank or lender is an "investor" or "partner." They just take a different type of consideration for use of their money. Instead of getting a percentage of the business, they get a payment of interest.

But here is why using the banker's money really is Other People's Money. When you borrow from the bank, your business (you hope) will soon start to cash-flow. While this is happening, you are, of course, paying back the loan to the bank. But are they getting any of your profits? The answer is no, of

---

1. Deuteronomy 15:1–11.

course not! Let's say the bank loaned you 80 percent or 90 percent of the value of a piece of property or a piece of equipment. Your equipment is producing the goods that you sell; however, you don't give the bank 80 percent or 90 percent of the profits of those goods, do you? Congratulations, you have just taken in an investor that will not take even 1 percent of the profits. If you borrowed for an appreciating asset such as real estate, you get twice the kudos, because your investor (the bank) is also not splitting the capital gains with you. Further, you have just expanded your purchasing power for the equipment or property, because you put in only a small percentage of the total cost. That is known as "leveraging" with Other People's Money.

The Loan Process

One of the easiest methods to obtain a loan is to pull out your credit card. You are still using Other People's Money. The only difference is that the issuer of the credit card is loaning you the money (and the cost—interest— that you pay). The great news is that the loan will almost always be approved up to your credit limit, and you will not have to fill out any applications or worry about credit scores or whether the banker thinks that either you or your business plan is flaky. But using a credit card is not always the best solution to your business's financing needs. Problems arise. First, your credit card may then be filled to the max, so that when you go to the store, you get embarrassed by that look the clerk gives you as your credit card is declined. A second problem is that even if you don't get "the look," your business still needs $25,000 of start-up capital, and unfortunately, your credit card just happens to have a limit of $10,000. A third problem is that credit card debt is usually extremely expensive.

Once deciding that additional credit card debt is not the best alternative, our hopeful business entrepreneur decides to go with a more traditional approach. This usually entails applying for a loan from a commercial bank.

The businessperson assumes that the best bet is to visit the bank where he already has an established relationship. Perhaps he has money on deposit, a previous loan history, or just a good old-fashioned golf buddy on the loan committee. But some businesses are well known enough and/or good enough to be able to generate interest and a bit of competition from more that one banker. Don't be afraid to go down the block in search of your bank loan. Once it is decided which lender or lenders to approach, the loan application process begins.

Applying for Other People's Money

Of course, the first step is to ask for the loan by filling out the loan application in order to qualify for it. This may be harder work than you think. Why is this hard work? The loan application itself is usually not all that complicated; often it is only one page long. The problem is that for the average business loan applicant, there is a great amount of additional paperwork that the lender will want to see before actually approving the loan. Further, the lender may have a number of other considerations and/or requirements that must be met before they will consider giving you the money. The first of those considerations may be whether or not the loan is secured or unsecured.

Security—Secured vs. Unsecured Loans

For those who have read *Rich Dad's Guide to Becoming Rich without Cutting Up Your Credit Cards,* you know that quite simply put, "Secured debt is debt that has collateral backing it up . . . Unsecured debt is debt without any collateral backing it up."[2] For example, the mortgage on your home is typically secured by the real estate in which you live. The same is true if you were to take out a home equity loan. Your auto is the collateral or security for your auto loan and so on. Because the auto loan money is used to purchase the vehicle, it creates a Purchase Money Security Loan Interest in the collateral—your auto. Not every collateralized loan creates a Purchase Money Security Loan Interest. Other assets could secure a loan as well. Your business assets may secure a loan for business expansion. More specifically, the lender may secure the loan with your inventory, your

---

2. Robert T. Kiyosaki and Sharon L. Lechter, p. 62.

accounts receivable, or maybe other tangible assets such as your office equipment or company's vehicles.

Most banks will with broad strokes list every imaginable business asset as their security for the loan, including those mentioned above, and your cash, notes, paper, and other accounts, stock in your company, business investments and their accompanying dividends and/or profits. Many standard form loan agreements will describe the collateral with phrases such as "general intangibles" and even "all other property not otherwise described [in the loan agreement]." The latter two phrases could cover just about anything, including possibly your intellectual property and goodwill. Some loan agreements go a step further: They explicitly include your intellectual property and goodwill as collateral.

The reality is that few borrowers will qualify for an unsecured loan. Typically, only the bank's very best customers with excellent credit, a great deal of assets, and long-standing (and profitable) relationships will be able to obtain the elusive unsecured loan.

The Personal Guaranty

Another major consideration of the lender for any business loan is whether they will require a personal guaranty. What is a personal guaranty? It is a promise by the one who makes it that they are in effect "guaranteeing" to pay the obligation of the borrower. If the borrower defaults, the personal guarantor will be held responsible for payment of the debt. Despite giving every imaginable business asset (and maybe even your firstborn) as security for a conventional business loan, lenders often still require that the loan be personally guaranteed. The personal guaranty may be requested by the lender for loans to either a third party or your business entity.

If there is a default by the business entity and you signed a personal guaranty, then the lender can (and will) go after you and your personal assets to satisfy the loan. This may put everything you own at risk, including your house, auto, IRA, or even that savings account you have for junior's future tuition needs. Under certain circumstances, some lenders may even require your spouse to sign the personal guaranty, thereby jeopardizing any of the spouse's separate assets.[3] If the collection of the loan really went haywire and there was a judgment against your spouse, the lender could even garnishee (attach or seize a portion of) your spouse's paycheck. If this happens, my personal guaranty to you is that conversations around the dinner table will reach a new low!

Relief from the requirement of signing a personal guaranty is reserved for the better bank customers and situations where the value of the collateral clearly and greatly exceeds the amount of the loan. Those companies with an excellent payment history may have a better chance of avoiding the personal guaranty requirement, depending, of course, on many other factors. Once a lender forgoes the personal guaranty without any negative consequence and has positive experiences with the borrower, they are likely to continue the lending relationship with the borrower on the same basis. The lender, in effect, learns to trust the business entity as a borrower.

The personal guaranty document is usually written in a form that gives the bank extraordinary protection. It is almost always irrevocable until the loan is fully paid off and even covers any new money loaned. Usually, guarantors are also required to waive certain rights such as the right to Notice of Default on the loan by the borrower, or Demand for Repayment. This means that if there is a default on the loan, the lender could come after the guarantor without even bothering to contact the borrower.

Sometimes the terms of the personal guaranty will even require waiver of certain legal rights, such as rights to dispute the validity of the underlying debt, the right to dispute the matter or raise defenses in a court of law, or even the right to have the dispute heard by a jury.

Because the terms are so burdensome and risky, some borrowers may decide not to take out the loan and simply refuse to sign such personal

---

3. This common lender practice may be a violation of the Equal Credit Opportunity Act and Regulation B, 12 CFR, part 202, depending on certain specific circumstances. Community property states, joint ownership of secured property, and/or joint credit applications may lead to exceptions to this rule.

guaranties. Before taking this approach, keep in mind that sometimes even the largest corporations are required to obtain the personal guaranty of their top officers or largest shareholders in order to get the loan. For example, WorldCom made personal guaranties to Bank of America for money the corporation loaned to Bernie Ebbers in order to purchase additional stock. Ebbers in turn made a personal guaranty to WorldCom.

Other Issues in Business Loans—the Loan Covenants

The lender may have some additional requirements for the loan. These are actually additional protections for the lender (as if they did not have enough protection with a personal guaranty and security interest) in the loan documentation, loan agreement, or perhaps even in the promissory note. Conditions in the loan agreement, sometimes referred to as "covenants," may set additional burdens for you, the borrower. One common example is that your business may be required to meet or maintain a ratio of debt to equity that is acceptable to the bank. If you decide to go out and borrow more money, the debt ratio might be affected in such a manner that you may have just violated one of the covenants of your loan.

How does your lender know that your debt to equity ratio has been changed and is no longer acceptable? The answer lies in another common covenant: You may be required to provide accounting documents and tax returns on a regular basis to the lender. The bank as lender may also have a covenant that requires you to maintain all of your operating accounts at their financial institution. With this type of covenant, the bank wins the trifecta: (1) it gets to play with your money, (2) it makes its own money-on-deposit accounts look better to state and federal regulators, and (3) it can easily monitor your financial activity like the Big Brother it really is.

Other common conditions or covenants imposed by a lender are loan processing or documentation fees; variable or escalating interest rates; occasionally, prepayment penalties; current and quick liquidity ratios that indicate the borrower's capacity to raise cash to meet a need or needs; and borrowing base certificates, aging of accounts receivable, and inventory listings, all of which may be required to monitor collateral for a line of credit.

If you think the loan agreement must be a really horrendous proposition, it is heartening to know that every once in a while, a borrower may come across something in the loan agreement that may actually be to the borrower's benefit. For example, if the loan is at favorable interest rates and the bank allows the borrower to make the loan assumable, a subsequent sale of the business could be a bit more appealing.

The Loan Review

Now that the application is in and the agreements have been signed, it is time for the lender to make its decision. As mentioned before, the loan decision will often depend on a previous relationship between the lender and borrower. But even with a healthy previous relationship between the two, the lender ought to still consider the financial health of the applicant with each individual lending request. Regulated banking institutions have a general obligation to monitor the borrower's ability to repay loans in circumstances where it is, for example, extending additional credit. Regulators such as the Federal Deposit Insurance Corporation (FDIC) have the authority to deal with any unsound or unsafe banking practice, including practices in the areas such as loan documentation and credit underwriting.[4] State and/or federal regulators may require the bank to adequately document loans even to the best bank customers.[5]

The lender will look at many different items in order to determine if the borrower is sound. Depending on a number of other factors, such as the aforementioned relationship of the bank and the borrower and the strength of the borrower, these could include financial statements, profit and loss statements, credit reports, and business plans. The lender may have already asked you to provide a small pile of documentation when you applied for the loan. The financial statement, along with other documents, helps the lender

---

4. 12 USC 1831p–1(a)—Standards for Safety and Soundness prescribed pursuant to section 39 of the Federal Deposit Insurance Act. Also see 12 CFR §337.11.
5. See, for example, 12 CFR §345.42 requirement by the Federal Deposit Insurance Act.

Discrimination in Favor of the Good Customer

Can a lender treat their customers with long-term relationships differently? Would this be discrimination against other loan applicants? For example, can the lender forgo requesting all of the documentation that it might request from a new applicant? Unequal treatment of loans is not illegal as long as it is not discriminatory because of a prohibited type of discrimination. The possibility of discrimination is why the FDIC "encourages" fair lending practices, but it does not mandate a specific method of treatment of each loan application. Only these "general" rules against discrimination apply, and as stated in the Equal Opportunity Credit Act, the lender cannot discriminate because of a prohibited practice—that is, it can't discriminate based on race, sex, religion, etc.

In general, lenders try to meet the spirit of the law in the following ways: by advertising products and services in a nondiscriminatory manner; by fully disclosing costs and conditions of credit to the customer and allowing the customer to make an informed decision; and by making credit decisions based on prudent underwriting standards that focus on predicting risk and avoiding bias.

understand your financial health by disclosing your assets and liabilities to them. Income statements, also known as "profit and loss statements" (or commonly referred to by their abbreviation P&Ls), will in general terms be indicative of your income and expenses. When applying for a business loan, the bank will undoubtedly require the income and expense statement of your business, but for the average borrower (and/or personal guarantor), the bank will also require a personal income and expense statement. The personal expense statement will reveal your household expenses. It's not that the lender is nosy. The lender doesn't really care how much you spend on clothing or gasoline each month; they are merely doing a thorough analysis on the borrower's financial strength in order to eliminate surprises that may later lead to a default on the loan.

Lenders might also ask for other specific documentation that may raise their comfort level when deciding whether or not to lend money. For example, don't be surprised if they ask you to produce contracts or invoicing information with your customers, inventory evaluations or appraisals, loan documents with other lenders, or lease agreements with vendors. Despite everything said here, the FDIC has a policy statement that claims to allow for evaluation of loans based on performance as opposed to documentation.[6] Banks, on the whole, being rather conservative institutions, will opt to protect themselves by asking for an excessive amount of documentation.

The lender will also consider other intangibles, such as amount of equity invested by the borrower versus the amount that the borrower is asking for from the lender.

Creditworthiness

At the same time that they are looking at the small mountain of documentation provided, the lender will also want to know if you are indeed creditworthy. They will do this by reviewing the credit history from agencies that track such information. There are two different types of sources used for this purpose. If the lender is reviewing your business's credit standing, they will likely run your business's "D&B." The second credit review may be of your personal credit history.

"D&B" stands for Dun & Bradstreet. The Dun & Bradstreet report is a type of credit report for businesses. However, Dun & Bradstreet offers reports that go well beyond the simple credit rating score. They also offer detailed comprehensive reports on a company's financial standing that claim to be able to "predict future payment habits and financial stability." Of course, there is no crystal ball that can truly predict future payment habits, but D&B does so by looking at industry norms, backgrounds of company owners, and certain business asset ratios, among other factors related to the business.

The personal credit history review begins with the bank obtaining your credit report and "credit score."

---

6. FDIC Statements of Policy, p. 5337, *Current through Report Bulletin* 8 (April 29, 2004).

Who's keeping score? The Fair Isaac Corporation scores borrowers who make loan applications in order to help the lender determine creditworthiness. By reviewing debt/income ratios and past payment history, among other things, Fair Isaac is able to come up with a score that most lenders will use to determine (a) if they will give you a loan and (b) what the terms may be. A higher credit score may help the borrower obtain more favorable terms, such as interest rates typically reserved for their better and most creditworthy customers.

CREDIT BUREAUS

Experts on borrowing will recommend that prior to applying for any major loan, the borrower should check his or her credit report and credit score. The purpose, of course, is to make sure that any incorrect negative information is remedied. Since the process of remedying the report can take a few months, it is best to try to anticipate your borrowing needs prior to applying for the loan.

Under the Fair Credit Reporting Act,[7] a consumer is entitled to have the reporting agency reinvestigate matters that the consumer believes to be inaccurate.[8] If it is determined that the information is either inaccurate or unverifiable, the credit bureau is required to delete the information from the credit report. In fact, even if the reinvestigation does not resolve the dispute, the consumer is entitled to have a brief (up to one hundred words) statement added to his or her credit report which explains the consumer's position on the credit information. The reporting bureau is then required to provide the consumer's statement (or an accurate summary or codification of the statement) to those who make inquiries of the credit report.[9]

There are three major credit reporting agencies, one of which your lender will inevitably go to in order to get your personal credit report. They are Experian, Equifax, and TransUnion. For a small fee, you can obtain your credit report and your Fair Isaac score from each of these three credit bureaus. If you have recently been turned down for credit based

---

7. Fair Credit Reporting Act (FCRA), 15 USC §1681 et seq.
8. 15 USC §1681i.
9. Id., (b) and (c).

upon the report, by law[10] you may be entitled to a free copy of the credit report. To obtain a copy of your credit report, contact the credit reporting bureaus as follows:

Equifax Credit Information Services, Inc.
P.O. Box 740241
Atlanta, GA 30374
(800) 685-1111
www.equifax.com

Experian
475 Anton Blvd.
Costa Mesa, CA 92626
(888) 397-3742
www.experian.com

TransUnion
P.O. Box 2000
Chester, PA 19022
(800) 888-4213
www.transunion.com

The Business Plan

Your business plan is an important document for your lender because it will help the lender understand how you plan to pay back your loan. As we have discussed, the business plan is also useful and necessary for convincing investors to join your enterprise.

There are many sources available on the Internet and in books that can help a business owner prepare a business plan. These resources can help any business plan writer with the particulars of writing a good plan. For example, a number of sample business plans are available at www.bplans.com/

---

10. 15 USC §1681j(b).

samples/sba.cfm. For a more detailed analysis of the business plan, review the material in Chapter 9.

However, in summary, almost all business plans contain certain essentials elements:

- A business plan should give a description of the business and the goods and services you are offering.
- The plan should tell something about who is involved in the business by discussing the experiences and background of the ownership or management of the company.
- It should help the lender understand something about the finances of the company, at a minimum by explaining what you need to borrow and how you plan to invest it in the business.
- It should help the lender understand the marketing strategies for the company and how the company is going to get customers for its goods or services.

The bottom line is that a banker somewhere is going to be making a determination if your product or service is worthwhile. Your business plan should help the lender decide that issue in the affirmative.

SBA Loan Programs

Another factor that may come into play and make the lending decision easier for the lender is whether or not the borrower can get the backing of the Small Business Administration (SBA) through one of the SBA's loan or guaranty programs. Almost every type of "small" business is able to apply for an SBA loan regardless of industry sector. However, a business may not be considered a "small business" depending on the amount of its sales or the number of people in its employ. The SBA sets threshold standards of measurement for determining if you are a small business, and the standards vary from business sector to business sector. A heavy construction business can have much greater sales and still be considered a small business than, say, a dry cleaner. However, sometimes the standards vary even within a business sector. For example, in the personal service sector, a dry cleaner may still qualify as a small business if its sales are $4 million, whereas an industrial launderer could show three times that amount of sales before being disqualified for an SBA loan.

IS IT AN SBA LOAN OR A SBA GUARANTY?

There are two general types of assistance that the SBA can give to borrowers. The SBA can help with "direct" loans and "guarantied" loans.

Direct loans are those made directly by the SBA to the individual or business without involvement of a third party. In recent years, this type of loan is a mere footnote to the SBA programs in that it has been available only for very limited purposes. Conventionally, it is available for emergency matters, such as natural disasters.

That being said, almost all SBA loans are really "guarantied" loans. Despite its name, the guarantied loan does not actually provide money that emanates directly from the SBA. The loan itself is in actuality from a private third party, such as a lending institution or bank. The SBA in a sense gives the party that is really giving the money (the lender) a guaranty that the borrower will pay back the money. This type of loan is much more readily available, and the vast majority of SBA loans are this type. The SBA guaranties about $12.5 billion of loans a year.

Don't assume that just because the SBA will guaranty your loan that the bank will automatically lend you money. The bank will still review your creditworthiness and make an independent decision as to whether it will lend you the money. In fact, in a number of situations, it is the bank's determination, not that of the SBA, that carries the most weight. The advantage to the SBA guaranty, of course, is that the risk is reduced for the bank, and as a result, it may be more likely than not to make the loan.

The guarantied amount depends on the specific SBA program under which the loan is covered. There are many different types of SBA programs, and each program has its own rules, requirements, peculiarities and prerequisites. But under the most typical SBA loan programs (known as Section 7(a) loan programs), the risk to the lender may be reduced by up to 75 percent or 85 percent of the amount loaned. Under some representative SBA loan programs, the SBA guaranties 75 percent of the loan, and the guaranty will cover up to $1.5 million of the loan amount. But under other characteristic loan programs, the SBA can guaranty up to 85 percent of the loan if the amount of the loan is $150,000 or less.[11]

Loans under another SBA loan program may be considered more risky for the bank. For example, if the loan is under the program known as SBA-Express, the maximum amount that the SBA will guaranty is 50 percent of the borrowed funds. The SBAExpress loan currently will allow a loan amount up to $2 million. At the other end of the spectrum, because exporting is viewed as an important business activity by the government, under the Export Working Capital loan program, the SBA currently guaranties up to 90 percent of the loan up to $1.5 million in order to encourage lenders to make loans to exporters.

In recent years, the SBA has made great strides toward making the availability of loan guaranties known within a very short time period. The SBA does that by having programs in place for "preferred" lenders or those who are "certified." In a sense, the lender is prequalified so that if they are "preferred," they can handle all loan activities from approval to closing and beyond ("beyond" as in handling default processes). Under the "preferred" status program, the SBA basically defers to the lender decision. If the lender is "certified," the SBA makes the ultimate decision on loan approval, but the SBA only reviews the lender decision instead of conducting its own independent analysis. As a result, the turnaround time for approval is very fast, with an SBA stated goal of three days' turnaround time. Under both of these programs, the certification process is essentially based upon the SBA's past experience with the lender.

Yet another program is known as the SBA LowDoc program. As its name suggests, little documentation is required for certain loans under the program. This program merely requires a one-page application filled out by the borrower, with the lender filling out the back of the form. Then within thirty-six hours, the SBA will give its answer. The SBAExpress program also has a declared turnaround time of thirty-six hours.

Funds from an SBA loan program are a relatively inexpensive form of money. It is because of certain governmental regulations that this type of

---

11. These loan amounts are typical of the SBA Section 7(a) guaranty loan program.

money may be less expensive to borrow. Under most SBA programs, the interest rates are negotiated between the lender and borrower. But the interest rate may not exceed the guidelines set by the SBA for the particular program. The guidelines are usually indexed to the prime rate. This means that the interest rate on the loan may not exceed a certain set percentage or number of points above the prime rate. For example, currently under Section 7(a) loan programs, the rate may range from two and a quarter (2.25) to four and three-quarter (4.75) points above the prime rate, depending on other variables of the loan arrangement between bank and borrower.[12] The variables are the particular loan program, the length of the loan term, and the loan amount.

As mentioned, loan programs from the SBA are plentiful and have varied purposes. In addition to some of the programs already mentioned, one other example is the CAPLines loan program. This is an umbrella lending program under which the SBA helps small businesses meet their short-term and cyclical working capital needs in a variety of situations where such short-term issues may arise. Businesses that have seasonal fluctuations, short-term spikes in labor needs, or needs for building or construction projects fall under the shelter of this umbrella. The SBA's Defense Economic Transition Assistance program, as its name might suggest, helps businesses in the defense industry transition to civilian commercial products when defense needs diminish. The SBA also has a loan guaranty program for assisting qualified employee stock ownership plans (Qualified Employee Trusts program), for helping small businesses finance pollution control programs, and for helping businesses meet their operating expenses when a key employee is called up to serve in the military (Military Reservist Economic Injury Disaster Loan program).

Many of the different programs have common elements. Adequate security is required under all SBA loan programs, although the SBA will not decline a loan based solely on this deficiency. Further, the SBA will occasionally grant small economic injury recovery or physical disaster loans on an unsecured basis.[13] The SBA will also always want to see the borrower put

---

12. Other programs may have rates between zero and 6.5 points above prime. The latest rates are published quarterly in the Federal Register.
13. Under $10,000 if covered by the Physical Disaster Loan program. For loans over $10,000, the borrower must pledge "available" security.

in a sufficient amount of equity in their business. So that the borrower has a sufficient stake in the business, the debt to equity ratio should not exceed 4:1. The implication of this is that business owners should not expect that all of their start-up capital will come from an SBA loan program. Creditworthiness of the borrower is another common factor of the SBA programs, as is the requirement that the applicant's personal and business resources should not be excessive. If the borrower's resources are otherwise plentiful, they are not eligible for an SBA loan.

The most common element of all SBA programs is that they share the rationale of encouraging lenders to make loans to small businesses by reducing the risk to the lender. As a result, many small businesses that may have had difficulty in obtaining this variety of Other People's Money have been able to successfully grow their enterprises.

Alternative Loans of Sorts (Besides Using Your Credit Card)

At the outset of this chapter, I mentioned that this chapter deals with traditional loans. Keeping my word not to discuss the neighborhood loan shark, there are some other types of "loans" that should be considered. Actually, I'm taking a little bit of license here. These are not loans at all, in the sense that you have to pay back a lender come what may. However, in each case, like a loan, you are given the use of OPM or OPR in consideration of payment of a fee. Let's discuss these very briefly.

FACTORING

Dead Beat Company (DBC) is your business's very best customer. The only problem is that it pays its bills very slowly. A further problem is that your company's landlord will not wait for the rent for three and a half months until DBC cuts that big check it owes you. You decide to call a factoring company. Factoring is a practice whereby you take your business's receivables, essentially your invoices, and sell them to a company, known as a "factoring company," at a discount. The factoring company pays the invoice immediately (less the factor discount) and then *it* collects the money from DBC. The downside is that you did not get quite as much as you had invoiced. But the upside is that you can pay your landlord today because you got the money from the factoring company earlier than you would have gotten it from your customer.

Factoring is a great (albeit sometimes expensive) cash flow management tool for a start-up business. Your personal or business credit rating is not really important to the factoring company. The credit rating of your customer will determine the availability of factoring and the factor rate. In fact, because you had the money to pay your bills on time, your credit rating improves. Further, you can give the factoring company only those invoices you choose, and you don't have to spend time, energy, and goodwill acting like a collection agency with your own customer.

The "discount"—the price you pay—is typically a percentage of the face value of the invoice. The factors establish that percentage as a function of the creditworthiness and payment history of your customers and the payment cycle (length of time it takes the customer to pay after receiving the invoice). The amount typically ranges from 2 percent to 6 percent for each thirty-day period it takes your customer to pay the invoice from the time the factor purchases the invoice.

Here's the way it works. When the factor "purchases" an invoice from you, they will initially pay you the face value of the invoice, less their maximum fee (what you would pay if the customer failed to pay the invoice). If and when your customer ultimately pays the invoice, the factor pays you the difference between the maximum fee and the actual fee based on the timing of the payment (although some factors will hold back a portion—retain reserves—against disputes with your customer).

For example, if you factor an invoice for $1,000, you might get an immediate advance of $700 from the factor. The factor holds back an amount ($300) corresponding to their maximum fee. The factor takes on the initial risk of nonpayment—if your customer doesn't pay the invoice, the factor is out the $700. (That's why creditworthiness of your customer is a consideration. If the factor thinks that there is a significant risk that the invoice won't be paid, they will not purchase the invoice.) If and when your customer ultimately pays, the factor pays you the "hold-back" less the actual fee. Let's assume that your customer pays "net 30" and the factor charges a 3 percent fee for each thirty-day period. In essence, you pay $30 for a thirty-day advance of $700. If your customer paid "net 60," you would pay $60 for a sixty-day advance. While the factor does assume the ultimate risk of nonpayment, the advance is a bit pricey—if you annualize the fee, it's the equivalent of an interest rate of 36 percent per annum.

LEASING

It is easy to understand how leasing your business equipment is much like borrowing from the bank to pay for it. Imagine if you had to pay cash for every piece of equipment that your business needs. Even if you could get a bank loan, you will typically still have to put some money down (maybe 20 percent) to finance the equipment loan. As a type of loan, leasing benefits many businesses by allowing them to obtain the equipment they need without any large out-of-pocket expenditures. Even shipping and sales taxes are often written into the lease. In fact, including installation and maintenance expenses in the lease can preserve even more cash. This allows the business to use its capital for other purposes.

Sometimes there are certain tax benefits that also go along with leasing. In many but not all situations, your lease payments are immediately deductible as a current business expense.[14] Yet another benefit of leasing is that some people use it as a creative way to inject capital into the business. Some will refinance the equipment they already own by selling it to a leasing company and then leasing it back.

FAMILY AND FRIENDS

Sorry for breaking my promise not to discuss borrowing from your brother-in-law, but another good source for borrowing funds is indeed your family and friends. Just remember one thing: If something happens and you cannot repay the loan, your friends will not be friends and your family will now be known as the "estranged family."

---

14. Under some circumstances, leased equipment may be treated for tax purposes as though it were purchased as opposed to an operating expense. In such cases, the cost is depreciated over a certain allowable period of time instead. You may wish to check with your accountant prior to entering into a lease to avoid that result.

Be Creative!

While borrowing is a quite traditional method of obtaining Other People's Money, the sources for borrowing are limited only by your creative thinking. In addition to the methods mentioned above, here are some additional sources for borrowing.

Some businesses will borrow from their customers by requesting up-front payments for goods and services or even "advances" as well as outright loans. Others may borrow from their vendors by asking them to finance purchases or asking for favorable terms that delay payment. Some businesses have even been known to borrow from their employees by asking for actual loans or by requesting deferral of payment of wages and/or benefits or concessions thereto. However, one should use caution not to compel, even implicitly, such concessions, because doing so may violate federal or state laws, such as labor laws or a contract that might include a collective bargaining agreement. Payment for goods or services can sometimes be delayed if obtained from a third party by bartering.

Inventive thinking about sources for Other People's Money can be the start of the success of your business.

Chapter 14

Joint Ventures, Licensing, and Strategic Alliances

For the previous nine chapters or so we have been concentrating on raising money—the conventional approaches to OPM. Now it is time to get back to the use of Other People's Resources (OPR).

In Chapter 4, we looked at alternative approaches to meeting capital needs. Do you recall what they are? Assuming that you are moving forward, your basic choices are to self-fund, raise capital (using conventional direct OPM), or use OPR.

Strategic use of OPR can often be the easiest way to get started and the fastest route for a business to get to the "big time." Your business can acquire virtual resources, virtual employees, virtual manufacturing capacity, virtual distribution channels, and so on. You get the benefit of the resources without having to spend the time, effort, and money to develop them yourself.

OPR—Typically More Available Than Direct OPM

OPR is often available for the average business even when conventional OPM is not. Why? There are a number of reasons:

- There are myriad sources of OPR—many more than sources of cash contributions, particularly when you have exceeded the bank accounts of your friends and family.
- The "investment" criteria applied by sources of OPR are typically much more flexible than those applied by sources of conventional money. You don't have to have the history or assets that are often required in order to qualify for a loan from a financial institution. You generally don't have to contend with inflexible thresholds as to "size" or with "standard" hurdle rates as you might if you were seeking capital from a professional investor or Angel.
- You have much more flexibility with respect to limiting risk to a source of OPR than you do when an investor is contributing money.
- Use of OPR typically does not give rise to issues under the securities law.
- You typically have a much wider range of choices with respect to the type of consideration you give in return for OPR as compared to direct OPM. As mentioned earlier, you are limited only by your imagination and your ability to negotiate.

Anatomy of a Co-venture

Use of OPR typically involves some form of co-venture. The co-venture may be in the form of an informal strategic alliance, a contractual relationship, or a new business entity. The formation of a new business entity can be in the context of starting your business together with other founders, or in the context of a joint venture in which your business is one of the principals.

There are two ways to look at a co-venture. You can look at it from the perspective of the formation of the co-venture as if it were a business entity. When viewed in that way, each co-venturer makes a contribution to the co-venture and receives something (e.g., a percentage of ownership, a share of profits) in return. Alternatively, you can look at it from the perspective of your business "paying" some consideration in return for the OPR.

TYPES OF CONSIDERATION

Money

Sometimes you pay money for the use of OPR! This is the case when you outsource tasks, lease equipment, or pay a royalty to in-license (get the use of) technology. Think about it. It's just like paying money (interest) for the use of OPM when you take a loan. You pay for the immediate use of the resources (just like you pay for the immediate use of loaned money), without having to make the initial cash outlay to acquire or develop the resources.

Equity

There may be times when the price of OPR is equity in a (your) business. In fact, this is a relatively common occurrence in the context of a start-up. Sometimes it's just a matter of perspective. Perhaps you see the opportunity to build a business around an idea—but it's your co-venturer's idea. Your co-venturer contributes intellectual property in return for an ownership interest. Your contribution for your ownership interest could be essentially anything—money, services, or other intellectual property.

Or perhaps you have an existing business, and there's someone with special expertise or know-how that you need, but you cannot afford to pay his or her salary. Or perhaps someone has equipment or other resources that you need. Instead of coming up with the cash, you bring him or her into the business. In other words, you pay for the OPR with equity in your business. Of course, you don't necessarily have to sell ownership interests in your business. Payment in equity is only one of your choices.

In-Kind

Many times your "contribution" to the co-venture—the consideration for your co-venturer's resources—will also be "in-kind." Sometimes you might barter—trade—services for the OPR or the like. However, you are typically able to get the maximum leverage from a co-venture when your contribution is intellectual property. We will return to that in a moment.

When intellectual property is involved, irrespective of the type of co-venture, you will typically see one of two types of agreements. There will be an "assignment" transferring ownership of intellectual property to a new entity or a "license" permitting an entity to use the intellectual property without transferring ownership.

Special Breeds of Co-venture

As mentioned above, a co-venture may be implemented through an informal strategic alliance, a contractual relationship, or a new business entity. I use the term "co-venture" to cover not only actual business entities but also virtual business entities created through contractual relationships or through informal strategic business alliances. Let's look at a few of the different forms of co-venture.

STRATEGIC BUSINESS ALLIANCES

Some people use "strategic alliance" as a generic term to cover any sort of cooperation between businesses. We are using it in a somewhat more limited sense. For our purposes, a strategic business alliance is an informal arrangement where the co-venturers consult with each other to ensure that certain business activities of each benefits the other. There may or may not be a written agreement. There may or may not be other relationships (e.g. vendor to customer) between the participants.

For the most part, strategic business alliances involve consultation regarding the direction of research/improvements to products, training, referrals, and promotion of products. In relatively rare instances, you might share expertise or intellectual property with another company to help it develop or improve a product or service that would help sell or otherwise make a market for your products or services. For example:

- You are the manufacturer of a product. You might have an informal understanding with your retailer that if you consult with him with respect to product improvements, the retailer will promote your product.
- Or you are an air conditioner manufacturer. You might provide free training to HVAC company personnel with the informal understanding that the HVAC company will recommend your products.

- Or you are a dry cleaner. You and the tailor down the street might have an informal understanding that you will refer anyone who asks about alterations to the tailor and he will refer anyone who asks about dry cleaning to you.
- Or you are a beverage producer. You and a concert promoter might consult with each other with respect to cooperative promotional activities.
- Or you are a manufacturer of aircraft parts. You might cooperate with a manufacturer of other parts in a bid for a government contract.

Get the picture? In each case, you get the benefit of the efforts of, or additional credibility from, your co-venturer.

OUTSOURCING

Outsourcing is defined as "purchasing a functional service from another business." In recent times, outsourcing has taken on a native connotation. Some people think of outsourcing as moving jobs out of the local economy to take advantage of cost savings in some less expensive foreign region. That, however, is far from the whole story. You can outsource to the guy just down the street.

Outsourcing is a tool to get the immediate use of resources, such as the expertise and facilities, without having to make the initial cash outlay to acquire or develop the resources. Sometimes you can achieve a cost savings by outsourcing. That really is not our focus here. There are many times when you might want to outsource, even though you pay a premium for the services. You are paying for immediate access to the resources. As mentioned above, the premium that you pay is directly analogous to the interest that you pay for the immediate use of loaned money.

When might you want to outsource a task? The obvious answer is when you, for whatever reason, cannot, or prefer not to, go to the time and expense to develop the capability to perform the task in-house. Sometimes the volume or frequency of occurrence of the task simply doesn't warrant the expense. Or a task might require expertise or equipment that you do not have, and you would prefer not to have to raise the money to acquire it. So instead of "buying it," you "rent it." Or a strategic alliance with a particularly strong player may give you credibility.

LICENSING AND IP-BASED JOINT VENTURES—THE ULTIMATE USE OF OPR

Perspectives on Licensing

Licensing is a tool used to leverage intellectual property (IP) assets. When you "outlicense" one of your IP assets, you, the "licensor," enter into a license agreement with the "licensee." Under the agreement, you grant the licensee certain rights with respect to the IP in return for some agreed-upon consideration. For example, the licensee may be permitted to use the intellectual property in return for payment of royalties.

You can view outlicensing as a way of generating income by "renting out" one of your assets (which just happens to be intellectual property). In fact, you can often obtain huge returns on investment—the ratio of licensing income to the cost of developing the IP can sometimes be essentially infinite. We will come back to that in a moment.

However, there is another perspective from which to view licensing. You can view a license as a mechanism to get the benefit of your licensee's manufacturing and distribution facilities and sales and marketing efforts without having to spend the time and money to develop them on your own. It is the ultimate use of OPR. Your product can be manufactured and distributed entirely through OPR—your licensee's.

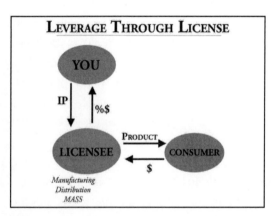

Obviously, the licensee also gains something from the relationship. From the licensee's perspective, they are also using OPM or OPR—yours. They did not have to go to the effort or expense of developing (assuming that they could) the intellectual property that you are licensing to them. They are presumably generating income using your intellectual property and keeping a significant portion of the income.

You typically receive only a portion of the income generated by the licensee's efforts. However, that income may be a huge multiple of your investment in developing the IP. Or the license may permit distribution into a geographical region or channel trade that you would otherwise not be able to reach, and the licensing income is essentially found money. Or if the licensee's resources are much larger or more efficient than those that you could devote to manufacture and/or sales, a small percentage of a large number is often considerably more than 100 percent of a small number. And, depending upon the circumstances, you can sometimes use the licensee's resources and efforts to increase the value of your business far beyond the royalty income generated. We will revisit an example of how that is done in a moment.

> **REASONS TO LICENSE**
>
> - Royalty Income
>
> - Additional source for product may increase market acceptance
>   - Concern about availability
>
> - Particular licensee may give product credibility or create market for other products
>
> - Not economical or impractical to manufacture - but is part of one of your products, or is neccessary to fill out your product line
>
> - Local licensee may create a market in remote geographical area

Franchises

Are you wondering if the use of OPR and licensing is really all that common? Is it a real-world practice or just an academic concept found only within the confines of the pages of a book? The answer to that question is right before your eyes as you drive down the street past a McDonald's, Holiday Inn, Century 21 real estate office, or NAPA auto parts store. These businesses represent one of the most pervasive uses of OPM and OPR in modern culture—the franchise. Franchising is one of the more popular and successful methods to jump-start a business.

A franchise, as that term is used today, is simply a species of license. A "franchisor" grants one or more (typically many) "franchisees" a license to essentially replicate the franchisor's successful business. The license (franchise agreement) provides the franchisee with what is essentially a

turnkey business—typically including all or most of the essential elements of a successful business (the B-I Triangle) that we discussed in Chapter 8.

In general, the franchisor has built a successful business. And has been able to identify and "bottle" the reason why the business was successful! In other words, the franchisor has identified and established exclusive rights to the intellectual property assets that give the business a competitive advantage—that make it a success. This intellectual property can pertain to any (or all) of the elements of the B-I Triangle. It typically includes trademarks and know-how, and sometimes patents and copyrights. The know-how (and patents) often relate to business systems, communications, legal foundation, and product or service that define the successful business. Many successful franchises are built around a great system or method for running the business—for example, a system for quickly serving hamburgers and shakes.

IP—the Foundation for the Franchise

When I lecture about turning ideas into assets (as I often have occasion to do, either as part of the course that I teach at Arizona State University or at seminars), I typically ask the audience to analyze their business with respect to competitive advantage.

A prospective franchisor must do precisely that. What gives the franchisor's business a competitive advantage? What aspects of the business make it unique or distinctive or better than the competition?

Every successful business has such characteristics. There are a multitude of features that may make the business unique, distinctive, or better. Just a few examples of those features are the fact that the business is more efficient, more customer-friendly, has better quality control, looks distinctive, has better business processes, or perhaps it simply has a better product. These, of course, can be valuable business assets. And, quite often, these are the characteristics that make a business a prime candidate for franchising.

Of course, unless the franchisor has established some form of exclusive rights to the things that create a competitive advantage, anyone can copy them, and there is nothing to license. The franchisor must take foundation steps to protect the ideas and assets that will be licensed to the franchisee.

My book *Protecting Your #1 Asset: Creating Fortunes from Your Ideas* (Warner Books, 2001), one of the books in the Rich Dad's Advisors series, provides a detailed survey of the processes involved in protecting those ideas. Another resource that may be helpful is the Intellectual Property Tools Kit available at my Web site www.mlechter.com.

Rather than self-finance or raise capital through conventional means to expand (although many franchises ultimately go public), the franchisor opts to expand their business using OPR. The franchisor uses other people's (the franchisee's) money, resources, and efforts to expand the franchised business (and, in particular, the goodwill associated with the business). The franchisor and franchisee enter into a franchise agreement. In that relationship, the franchisor licenses the franchisee to use the intellectual property to build a business that is modeled on the successful characteristics of the franchise. Of course, quality control provisions are included in the agreement to ensure the integrity of the franchise. The net result is that while the franchisee owns the business, as far as the consuming public is concerned, the franchisee is the alter ego of the franchisor. (This is the primary thrust of a trademark license.)

In exchange for granting the right to use the intellectual property, the franchisor receives fees and royalties from the franchisee. And the efforts of the franchisee help to build the goodwill of the franchisor, increasing the value of the franchise business.

The franchisee, on the other hand, gets the benefit of Other People's Resources—know-how, business systems, and trademarks—without having to expend the time, money, and resources to develop them. The franchisee often also receives the benefit of training, the economies of scale associated with a large business, and cooperative advertising. From the perspective of exploiting Other People's Money or Resources, both franchisor and franchisee can be winners.

In general, license agreements and franchises would be considered securities only if they came within the definition of an "investment contract." Since under normal circumstances the efforts of the licensee and franchisee play a significant part in the expectation of profits, the licenses/franchises are not securities under federal law. However, they may well come within the definition of "securities" applied in various states. In any event, franchises are heavily regulated by both the federal government (through the Federal Trade Commission) and the states, and typically require a form of registration similar to that required with respect to securities.

If you are interested in learning more about franchise, and franchising, you may want to visit my web site www.mlechter.com, as well as the Rich Dad organization web site www.richdad.com for further details.

IP-Based Joint Venture

An IP-based joint venture is very similar to a licensing arrangement. In fact, a license to use intellectual property is typically a cornerstone of the joint venture.

There are many definitions floating around for the term "joint venture." One broad definition is "business undertaking by two or more persons engaged in a single defined project."[15] A particularly succinct definition is provided under the European Union competition rules, where joint ventures are defined as "undertakings which are jointly controlled by two or more other undertakings." (The first time I read that definition I misread the term

---

15. *Black's Law Dictionary,* 7th ed. (1999), 843.

"undertaking" as "undertaker." Actually, an "undertaking" is defined as "any entity engaged in an economic activity.")

I think a better definition of a joint venture is "an association of two or more co-venturers, who each contribute resources toward, and jointly control, a specific business undertaking (business activities)."

A joint venture may take many forms. It may involve formation of a separate legal entity or contractually defined cooperative activities (forming a virtual business entity). In any event, a joint venture agreement would define your rights and obligations and those of your co-venturer. In general, your contribution to the joint venture would be a license to use the intellectual property. Your co-venturer would, in effect, contribute the production and/or distribution resources.

New Legal Entity or Virtual Entity?

Under what circumstances would you typically see a new legal entity created, rather than a virtual business entity? One situation is when both parties contribute intellectual property. Another is when the co-venturers plan to work together to make improvements in technology or on further research and development. In many cases, the new entity would own the resulting improvements and new technology.

There are also instances when you might want to bring on an additional equity investor into a particular facet, but only that one facet, of your business. Do you remember the example we gave in Chapter 4, where you were in the office supply business but came up with an idea for a new way to do business that was applicable to a number of different fields, including the automobile industry? An acquaintance, Otto, with expertise in the automobile industry wants to participate as a co-venturer. You, however, do not want to dilute your ownership interest with respect to the fields of use outside of the auto industry. So you create a completely new and separate entity (e.g., a subsidiary), license the new entity to use the technology in the automotive industry, and sell an equity interest in the new entity to Otto.

There are other similar circumstances that come up from time to time. For example, some countries require a certain percentage of any company doing business in that country to be locally owned. A joint venture with a local co-venturer is one way to meet the "local ownership" requirement.

Joint ventures are also sometimes used when the licensor of particularly sensitive technology wants an added measure of control over the security measures taken to protect confidential information. This approach is commonly used when trade secrets are licensed into a region with "underdeveloped" intellectual property laws.

If a new entity is created, both you and your co-venturer enter into agreements with the new entity. The new entity would be your licensee. There may or may not be royalty payments, depending upon the agreement. You might also enter into an agreement with the new entity to perform further research and development. Your co-venturer would likewise enter into agreements with the new entity to provide the production and/or distribution resources and whatever other contributions are contemplated. Your co-venturer might or might not be paid for those resources, again depending upon their agreement with you. Both you and your co-venturer would take equity positions in the venture according to the relative value of your contributions (taking into account any payments made by the new entity for your contributions).

Alternatively, if no new legal entity is formed (i.e., the business entity is virtual), you would enter into a license agreement with your co-venturer. You would typically take an active role in making business (and technical) decisions relating to the manufacture and sale of the product. Typically, you and your co-venturer would be reimbursed for certain specific expenses, and the two of you would then share the net receipts from the sale of the products. This type of arrangement is often employed when one of the intellectual property assets involved is a trademark. Why do you think that is? We will revisit an example in a moment.

Joint Venture or License?

Why are we referring to this arrangement as a "joint venture," as opposed to a "licensing agreement"? The answer relates to the extent to which you are involved in the "business." While there is no "bright line" between IP-based contractual joint ventures and license agreements, the licensor in a joint venture tends to take a more active role in business, and in a straight license agreement, a more passive role. Frankly, whether a particular arrangement is characterized as a joint venture or a license agreement is strictly academic. The only thing that really counts is the terms of the agreement.

Licensing IP vs. Competitive Advantage

Can you license others to use your intellectual property without giving up a competitive advantage? Yes, you can—as long as you either pick the right intellectual property asset or limit the scope of the license.

You can license someone else to use IP and still retain your competitive advantage if the IP relates to a product or service that has another basis for a competitive advantage (e.g., you have two patents covering a product, but grant a license under only one). The same is true for IP that is not being used in your core business. For example, assume that you are extremely successful in the fast food industry. During the course of business, you discover that if you

YOU LIMIT THE LICENSE AS TO:

- Territory
- Technical Field
- Certain products or lines
- Marketing channel
- Time

mix vinegar and a couple of different chemicals, you get the ultimate disinfectant cleaner. Unless you were differentiating yourself from competition based on the cleanliness of your facilities, you certainly would not hurt your fast food business by licensing someone else to manufacture and sell the cleaning product.

You can also license someone else to use core intellectual property without losing your competitive advantage. You do that by limiting the scope of the license with respect to one or more of technical fields of use, products or product lines, marketing channels, and time.

As a practical matter, you do not lose any competitive advantage if you grant a license that limits the use of the intellectual property to technical fields or distribution channels that are outside of your core business or to geographical areas outside of your present marketing area. This is particularly true if the term of the license agreement is correlated with your plans for expansion.

For example, let's assume that you are located in Florida. You presently sell your product strictly through retail channels in the local Florida markets, and you project that it will be at least five years before you're able to expand to the West Coast. What do you lose if you grant a license to someone giving them the right to manufacture and sell your product, but only in California and only for the next five years?

Or assume that you determine that the people who purchase products in response to infomercials are an entirely different group of people from those who purchase your products through retail channels. Assuming that you are not planning to do your own infomercial, what do you lose if you grant someone else the right to sell your products, but only through the distribution medium of infomercials?

Or assume that you develop video games. You come across a programming technique that lets you generate what is perceived by viewers as a 3-D display on a regular monitor. As it happens, that 3-D display is helpful when viewing spreadsheets. Do you think that granting a license to use the technology, but only in spreadsheets, would adversely affect your video game sales?

PREREQUISITE—PROTECTED IP

In each case, we assume that you have taken steps to protect your intellectual property rights in the products. If you did not, the value of your contribution to the co-venturer would be in question. A co-venturer is not willing to ascribe a high value to IP that can be copied as soon as a product embodying it hits the market. You are unlikely to find a licensee willing to pay a significant royalty to use something that they would be able to copy for free.

For more on how to protect those intellectual property rights, read my book *Protecting Your #1 Asset: Creating Fortunes from Your Ideas* (Warner Books, 2001), one of the books in the Rich Dad's Advisors series.

Ivan, Manny, and Angelo Revisited

In Chapter 3, we considered the story of Ivan, Manny, and Angelo, a hypothetical illustrating how you can build a business using, in main part, non-monetary contributions to the business by the principals, and the equivalent from others—Other People's Resources (OPR).

Do you remember the story? Let's go back and analyze the transactions with respect to the use of OPR.

HOW DID IVAN USE OPR TO START HIS BUSINESS?

How good is your memory? Ivan had an idea for a kitchen appliance product that removed grease, fat, and such from food. He didn't have the expertise to make prototype, so he used OPR by enlisting his friend Manny. Manny was a former mechanic and appliance repairman who had the skills to make prototype. In return for making the prototype, Ivan gave Manny a 5 percent ownership interest in the "business."

If we view the transaction from the perspective of an existing business on Ivan's part, the consideration for the OPR (Manny's expertise and services) was a 5 percent equity interest. (Another way of looking at the transaction is that Ivan and Manny created an informal partnership, where Ivan contributed intellectual property—the idea—for a 95 percent interest, and Manny contributed his expertise and services for a 5 percent interest.)

HOW DID IVAN AND MANNY USE OPM AND OPR TO CREATE IMA, LLC?

If you will recall, Ivan and Manny took the prototype to Manny's employer, Angelo. Angelo assumed the role of an Angel investor. He contributed seed funds to lay the legal foundation for the business, and, more important, he contributed his business expertise. A limited liability business entity (IMA, LLC) was formed (owned 66 percent by Ivan, 30 percent by Angelo, and 4 percent by Manny), and patent and trademark applications filed. Viewed from the perspective of Ivan and Manny's "partnership," the consideration for OPM (the seed funds) and OPR (Angelo's expertise and services) was a 30 percent equity interest. Their plan was to license one of the "big boys" to manufacture and distribute the appliance.

WHAT HAPPENED WHEN IMA FIRST TRIED TO LICENSE THE TECHNOLOGY?

If you will recall, in their initial attempts to license the technology, IMA was not able to negotiate satisfactory terms. They learned one of the basic lessons of licensing: You have to be able to sell your licensee on the merits of your position. And that can sometimes be difficult when you are trying to license technology that has not been tested in the marketplace.

In addition to the basic economic issues and the issue of sustainability of competitive advantage (i.e., protection of intellectual property), a potential licensee will look at a number of factors. Those factors include the amount of effort (expense) that will be required in order for the licensee to bring a product to market, and marketplace projections.

You, the licensor, will have your set of projections. The prospective licensee will have their own, typically much more conservative (at least for the purposes of negotiation) projections. Why should they accept your projections over theirs? That brings us to the issue of credibility.

In general, an invention must be developed to a certain threshold level in order to be licensable on "satisfactory" terms. That threshold level tends to vary from industry to industry. It also varies as a function of your expectations and credibility. If your invention is untested in the marketplace, you may have to temper your expectations in accordance with reality.

How do you achieve credibility? Occasionally, an idea or technology is so compelling that it is credible per se. This, however, is typically not the case—particularly when the idea or technology is untested. In most cases, credibility can be acquired by marketplace success or other empirical data. Failing that, you can sometimes achieve credibility by virtue of your own reputation (past successful products), by virtue of publicity, or by virtue of an association with, or sponsorship or endorsement by, someone who already has credibility in the industry or can otherwise open doors.

The threshold issue is getting an audience with the right individuals in the industry. Beyond that, the less work required of the licensee to bring a product to market, the more hard data you have in support of your market projections and the more demonstrably strong your intellectual property protection, the better deal you will be able to strike.

HOW DID IMA DEAL WITH ITS INITIAL LACK OF CREDIBILITY?

When faced with the initial rejection, IMA set about to build credibility. It used OPR and OPM to bring the product to market and prove market acceptance.

- The product was produced using OPR and OPM. Manufacturing was outsourced to a job shop. While extremely expensive, the job shop provided production flexibility and extended payment terms that facilitated IMA's cash flow management.
- A Web site was designed, managed, and hosted for a percentage of the sales through the Web site (up to a predetermined cap).
- Direct sales through the Web site and to "strategic" customers (fast food franchisors) were augmented by third-party sales on a straight commission basis.

It took a year or so, but IMA established credibility by virtue of market-place success. The profit margin was nowhere near what it should be—the costs of manufacture and distribution were much higher than would normally be the case. However, the sales proved that the appliance was viable in the marketplace. And if manufacturing and distribution costs were brought down to the norm, the business would be quite profitable.

HOW DID IMA USE A STRATEGIC ALLIANCE TO BUILD ITS BRAND?

As you will recall, IMA did not stop with achieving credibility. It entered into a strategic alliance with a fast food franchisor, Flavorful Fligles (FF). In return for favorable pricing, FF, among other things, provided IMA with research to support advertising and featured the IMA Not Greasy trademark in its promotional materials and advertisements. The additional exposure, paid for by IMA's co-venturer, increased the value of IMA's trademark. The IMA Not Greasy brand was promoted though its co-venturers'—FF's—resources.

HOW DID IMA USE A JOINT VENTURE TO LEVERAGE ITS IP?

IMA went on to further leverage its intellectual property through a joint venture. As you may recall, IMA's initial success was in the commercial market. IMA entered into a profit-sharing agreement with HugeCo, one of the biggest of the big boys, to enter the consumer market. The joint venture was structured not only to generate significant income from a new market for IMA but also to further build the value of IMA's business.

In essence, IMA contributed a license to use intellectual property (patents, know-how, and trademarks) to the venture. HugeCo was responsible for manufacturing and distributing the product. Certain costs (which were agreed upon beforehand) were reimbursed from the gross receipts (to IMA or HugeCo as appropriate), and what was left (the profits) were split between IMA and HugeCo. HugeCo's manufacturing and distribution costs (reimbursed out of gross receipts) represented a huge cost savings, and HugeCo's marketing and distribution capability represented a huge increase in volume of sale. IMA made a bundle.

HOW DID THE JOINT VENTURE INCREASE THE VALUE OF IMA'S BUSINESS?

The income stream from HugeCo's sales was only part of the value IMA derived from the joint venture. The agreement was structured so HugeCo's activities helped IMA continue to grow its business.

Sales of the products by HugeCo would continue to build recognition of the IMA Not Greasy trademark. Under the agreement, HugeCo was not only permitted but *required* to use the IMA Not Greasy trademark prominently on all of the appliances, on all packaging and promotional materials, and in all advertising. Certain marketing activities and levels of advertising were also required. In that way, HugeCo's activities would make IMA's trademark even more well known and more valuable.

Sales in the consumer market by HugeCo did not detract from IMA's sales to commercial customers. In fact, the additional promotion of the IMA Not Greasy trademark actually bolstered the sales.

HOW DID IMA KEEP HUGECO FROM JUST "TAKING OVER"?

The agreement with HugeCo kept HugeCo from taking over by limiting the scope of the license to the company, giving IMA a right to participate in management of the business, and building in accountability.

Limited Scope License

The intellectual property license was limited to certain products—the original IMA Not Greasy appliance and "such other products as the parties may agree upon in the future." That permitted IMA to develop other products and sell them under the IMA Not Greasy trademark, taking full advantage—leveraging—of the consumer recognition (and goodwill) of the trademark.

In many instances, but not necessarily all, it would make sense to bring the new products under the agreement (to take advantage of HugeCo's resources). HugeCo might not want to take on that particular product for some reason. However, when it made that decision, it had to keep in mind that IMA had the option to pursue it on its own. In those cases where HugeCo's resources were somehow not applicable to the product (the particular product was directed to a different market or required different manufacturing techniques), IMA was free to go forward on its own or with another co-venturer.

Participation in Management

IMA also retained a say in the management of the venture. IMA not only had veto rights with respect to the products of the venture but also retained design control (although with consultation from HugeCo) and had approval rights with respect to all advertising and packaging and certain management decisions. Specific quality control standards had to be met (quality control is required in a trademark license).

Accountability

Accountability was built into the agreement through complete and precise drafting and a relatively short term, in combination with the leveraging of IMA's business. The agreement very specifically spelled out HugeCo's obligations. Everything that IMA thought was important was included in the agreement explicitly and in detail. The agreement was also for a relatively short term (five years). If HugeCo did not live up to IMA's expectations, the agreement would not be renewed. (That, of course, was a two-edged sword: IMA also had to live up to HugeCo's expectations—or HugeCo might not renew.)

Because HugeCo's activities under the agreement were leveraged to help IMA continue to grow its business during the term of the agreement, if the agreement was terminated for some reason, IMA would not be behind the eight ball. IMA would not have to start all over again and rebuild its market position. That put IMA into a position of parity with HugeCo when the time came to extend or renegotiate.

IMA was well ahead of the game by going forward using OPR from HugeCo. The risk of big-boy HugeCo simply swallowing up or riding roughshod over little-guy IMA was minimized.

As you can see, co-venturing—and licensing in particular—is an extremely powerful tool.

Chapter 15

Grants

In the dictionary, the verb "grant" is defined as "to accord as a favor, prerogative, or privilege," to "bestow upon a person" or "give by possession or entitlement." In plain English, a "grant" is essentially a gift. In this book, we use the term to refer to a type of Other People's Money—where an outside entity provides funds for a specific purpose without an expectation of repayment—in other words, makes a gift to your business. The only real expectation of the entity providing funds is that the recipient will follow certain rules or conditions laid out in the grant process.

A grant—gift—of money sounds like a wonderful arrangement. Having someone give you money certainly sounds better than selling a portion of your business or going into debt. It even sounds better than a joint venture. You receive Other People's Money, at little cost to you, and typically, you will never have to pay it back. The primary issue with "grant money" (other than qualifying for the grant in the first place) is making sure that you can live with the strings that are attached to the money—there are usually restrictions on the purposes for which the money can be used, and sometimes restrictions on the way that you grow or run your business if you accept the grant money. However, if the rules and restrictions that go along with taking the grant money are consistent with your purpose in goals, a grant can indeed be a wonderful arrangement.

Types of Grants

There are many different types of grants available. Most grants, however, emanate from two very broad groups. For the most part, they come from either governmental bodies or private entities. (We also found occasional references in the literature to grants coming from a genie in a bottle, typically in multiples of three. We have, however, not been able to find any material on currently available sources of those grants. If we happen to find any such material, it could be the subject of a future book entitled *Other Apparitions' Money*.) The governmental bodies from which grant money is available include a wide variety of federal and state agencies. Private entities providing the money for a grant are typically a wealthy family, organization, or corporation that has established a foundation for the purpose of giving away money. Certain types of businesses, such as organizations that are engaged in research related to the cure of particular diseases or in providing services to the needy, are also able to attract charitable donations—gifts from organizations and individuals. We will not, however, cover the subject of charitable donations in this book.

Why do governments and foundations give away money? With respect to private (nongovernmental) sources of grant money, altruism plays a significant part. Many private sources of grant money are "cause"-oriented. They support a "cause" and are willing to put their money where their mouth is. For some private sources, the sole reason for existence is to provide financing for "worthy endeavors"—activities that would further those sources' specific cause. What types of causes do the private sources direct grant money to? The causes are across-the-board. Some organizations will give grants in order to cure a particular disease or malady, help the needy, or solve some social issue (e.g., promote education of children or financial literacy) or address an environmental issue (e.g., save the whales). We will provide some examples of these types of grants below.

There is another motive for many of these private donors: tax incentives. Tremendous tax savings can sometimes be realized by giving away money—at least by giving money to organizations that qualify as "charitable" under the tax law. These organizations are sometimes popularly called "501(c)(3) corporations." They derive their name from the section number of the tax code that allows for charitable organizations. Donations by an entity that does not qualify as a charitable organization to other entities that likewise do not qualify as charitable organizations are not typically deductible. In other words, you could not simply give money to your son's for-profit business and deduct the gift from your taxes. However, one of the bases for qualifying as a 501(c)(3) corporation is to provide grants. A charitable organization can provide grants to for-profit entities provided that the funds will remain dedicated to the purposes of the giver and that the nonqualified recipient will use them for those purposes. Likewise, money can be given to individuals provided that case histories regarding the recipients are kept, showing name, address, purpose of award, manner of selection, and relationship (if any) to the donor.[16]

Accordingly, to get money to for-profit entities and take advantage of the tax benefits, some entities set up charitable foundations to provide the grants.[17] The entity makes tax-deductible donations to the charitable organization, which uses the money as the source for grants. However, there are restrictions on "self-dealing" between private foundations and their substantial contributors. The donor or the donor's family, employees, or business managers may not control the charitable organization directly or indirectly.[18] Manipulating the foundation or its board of directors could jeopardize the tax status of the foundation. This is also true of those who, for some other reason, are in a position to exercise "substantial influence" over the affairs of the applicable tax-exempt organization. Violations of these provisions give rise to taxes and penalties against the private foundation and, in some cases, its managers, its substantial contributors, and certain related persons. As a result, the donor should not exercise control over designating grant recipients.

---

16. Revenue Ruling 56-304, C.B. 1956-2, p. 306.
17. Another type of foundation that gives grants is a "publicly supported" type under IRC 509(a)(1).
18. §4941 of the IRC and IRC 509(a)3(C).

Government Grants

Governmental bodies, obviously, are not particularly concerned with receiving tax benefits. So why do they give grants? Just like tax deductions and loopholes, the government gives grants to address public policy considerations—they want to encourage and provide an incentive for certain types of activities. Public policy purposes could be anything that current policy makers in the legislative or executive branches believe will help society. Activities that the government wants to encourage, not unlike private foundations, run the gamut from research on particular technologies thought to affect national defense, to medical research, to economic research or environmental issues, to activities that might help to expand the economy.

Perhaps your industry is adversely affected by imports. If so, there may be a governmental grant available to you courtesy of policy makers through the U.S. Department of Commerce. The free money may give your industry trade association a competitive edge when trying to sell its product in a market dominated by foreign goods. Maybe you are in an industry that government policy makers believe needs to get off the ground. If so, you might want to apply for free money to get your helicopter parts company airborne. Perhaps there is a gap in the way the free market economy is providing goods and services, such as a lack of medical services in Alaska or an inner city. A government grant may cure such a deficiency by providing an incentive—free money—to boost the availability of medical services in those areas.

The examples cited in this chapter are not just theoretical. For example, there really is a grant program for helicopter parts from the Department of Defense. An additional real example: A Chicago-area food flavoring company used a Trade Adjustment Assistance Program grant from the Department of Commerce to finance software and hire a chemist who developed new flavors so they could compete with much larger international counterparts.[19] The grant gave the company the boost it needed for job and revenue growth. But it doesn't take a flavoring company to recognize what a "sweet" deal a grant can be.

---

19. *Crain*'s Chicago business article "Help for Companies Facing Foreign Rivals," by H. Lee Murphy, October 26, 1998.

From the United States government alone, there are numerous grants available from a variety of other departments and agencies. They include the Departments of Justice, Agriculture, Housing and Urban Development, Interior, Labor, State, Treasury, Veterans Affairs, Transportation, Energy, Health and Human Services, Education, and Homeland Security as well as agencies such as the National Endowment for the Arts, National Foundation on the Arts and the Humanities, National Science Foundation, Small Business Administration, and Environmental Protection Agency and agencies dealing with development in the Appalachians as well as mediation and conciliation issues.

Many of these departments and agencies are well-known household names. But did you ever hear of an agency known as the U.S. Institute of Peace? Well, if you are a nonprofit organization interested in "international peace and conflict resolution," there is money available for your organization. The aforementioned National Foundation on the Arts and the Humanities would like to give you $400,000 to $800,000 to help you along with production of your television documentary program or historical dramatization. Just make sure that your television program addresses "significant figures, events, or developments in the humanities."

Not every grant is quite so esoteric. Governmental grants come in all shapes and sizes. Grant programs are known by so many acronyms that even the most entrenched bureaucrat would get queasy trying to remember them all. As stated above, the government issues grants for such purposes as to cure disease, help the needy, or solve social or environmental issues. "Project grants" from the government are available for everything from minority business development to homeownership opportunity (Self-Help Homeownership Opportunity Program) to grant programs for rhinoceros conservation projects. The following are just a small sample of available government grant programs in several interesting areas.

Business

Earlier, in Chapter 13, we discussed many of the loan programs available from the Small Business Administration (SBA). However, the SBA also gives away money in the form of grants. Generally, the SBA does not provide grant money for start-up of businesses, but it does provide grant money to run women's business centers that provide free training and other assistance to women who want to start businesses. For example, one recent program known in short as the Women's Business Center (Grant) Program had the announced purpose "to add to the business community more well-trained women entrepreneurs."

For businesses that are not looking for start-up money, the SBA has a number of grant programs. One particular grant program available through the SBA, although it is administered by the National Institutes of Health, is designed to aid in the creation of technological innovation. The Small Business Innovation Research (SBIR) program is a program for small business concerns to engage in research and development "that has the potential for commercialization." A companion program, also for the purposes of stimulating innovation, is the Small Business Technology Transfer (STTR) program. This grant program is designed to facilitate "cooperative" research and development between small business concerns and research institutions. In other words, grants under STTR can go to a small business concern or a research institution.

Under these programs, grant money is available both for preliminary steps, such as feasibility studies (as much as $100,000), and for the actual research and development stages. The latter stages can qualify your small business for as much as $750,000 under SBIR and $500,000 under STTR. To date, more than $12 billion has been awarded under the SBIR program to small businesses.

As you might expect, the Department of Commerce also has many grant programs designed for the benefit of businesses. You do not have to be a nonprofit organization in order to benefit. One example is a grant designed "for small and medium-sized businesses that are new-to-market exporters or first-time exporters looking to establish long-term relationships with potential customers, distributors, or partners." The government's money is available to expand relationships with overseas partners through (excuse me for using yet another acronym) the SABIT program (Special American Business Internship Training). At the time of publication of this book, the department or its Economic Development Administration agency had other economic development grant programs available that support public works projects, international trade, minority businesses, technology, and telecommunications services.

REAL ESTATE AND HOUSING

In the real estate and housing area, the Federal Housing Authority is more frequently the source of loans and loan guarantees. However, this agency has grant programs as well. Recently, the Senate passed the American Dream Down Payment Act authorizing $200 million in grant assistance per year to low-income, first-time home buyers. The Department of Housing and Urban Development, popularly known as HUD, has the above-referenced Self-Help Homeownership Opportunity Program, which provides grant money to low-income families that are willing to invest sweat equity in their homes.

EDUCATION

Grant programs from the U.S. Department of Education cover a wide variety of subjects. There are grants to help students of all age groups (kindergarten through postgraduate), teachers, school systems, and communities. Some grants are aimed at specific groups, such as low-income or minority students—for example, American Indian students. But even small businesses can receive a grant from this department. If you qualify as a small business concern, funds for research and development projects related to "important educational or assistive technology, science, or engineering" questions may entitle your business to a governmental grant.

There are also grants available to pay for college education. For those who like to use Other People's Money, the education grant is better than any student loan available because, like all grants, it does not have to be paid back. The popular program the federal Pell Grant does not have to be re-paid; nor does a Federal Supplemental Educational Opportunity Grant—one for undergraduates with exceptional financial needs.

The U.S. Department of Education even has a grant program that is evocative of the Rich Dad philosophy. As our loyal Rich Dad readers know, the goal of the Rich Dad organization is to elevate the financial literacy of children as well as adults. In fact, the Rich Dad organization has a foundation to teach the difference between earned, passive, and portfolio income and also educate individuals to convert earned income into passive and portfolio income. The Department of Education has a grant program that is similarly designed to support financial literacy among all students in kindergarten through high school. The Excellence in Economic Education Program grant is awarded to a national nonprofit educational organization "whose primary mission is to improve the quality of student understanding of personal finance and economics." A $1.5-million grant was recently awarded. The objective is not only to increase the knowledge of economics among students and teachers but also to encourage the "best practices and exemplary programs that foster economic literacy." Is someone in the Department of Education a Rich Dad aficionado?

SCIENCE, MEDICINE, AND TECHNICAL

Except for an exceptional few doctors who went into politics, our government's legislators and bureaucrats may not ever actually cure a disease. However, with a number of grant programs, the federal government funds research for HIV-AIDS, Parkinson's disease, and Alzheimer's as well as cancer, leukemia, and arthritis. Individuals can also directly benefit from grants that provide assistance with payment, such as for Vietnam veterans who have children with spina bifida or for their pharmaceuticals, as well as substance abuse.

Congress established the National Science Foundation in 1950 in order "to promote the progress of science; to advance the national health, prosperity, and welfare; to secure the national defense; and for other purposes." As with most agencies, numerous grants are given by the NSF. Some may not sound as though they would have much application to our daily lives, but they exist. Case in point: One particular division has an "award" for research on "Spatial Scaling with an Unusual Food Web Structure: The Case of Azteca Ants in the Coffee Agroecosystem." Let's skip the details on this one in the event that you are sipping your morning brew while reading this book.

TARGETED GROUPS

Sometimes grant money is available from the government for those who fall into specific groups or classifications. If you are one of the following, you might be able to get a grant from the government for any number of reasons: veterans, minority groups, first-time home buyers, artists, musicians, nurses, teachers, researchers, the disabled, farmers, and low-income families. Do you have a proven track record in developing cooperatives? If so, the Department of Agriculture has a grant for you. Are you a historian looking to reach regional or national audiences with an exhibition or symposium? Then you will want to review the grants available from an independent grant-making agency of the United States government known as the National Endowment for the Humanities.

At different times, the Minority Business Development Agency of the Department of Commerce has had a number of grant programs for individuals and institutions for the purpose of encouraging minority business development. One program provided one-on-one counseling and technical assistance for individuals and for-profit firms. The targeted minority groups include African American, Native American, Aleut, Asian Indian, Asian Pacific American, Eskimo, Spanish-speaking Americans, Puerto Rican, and Hasidic Jewish Americans. (Less orthodox Jews do not appear to be eligible under this program.) Another program has the stated use of "developing access to capital, market, and other opportunities on behalf of minority business."

The foregoing gives just a few examples of the types of government grant programs available at the time of the publication of this book. If you are unable to find a program that is suitable for your purposes or business, keep in mind that the U.S. government is constantly announcing new grant programs on a regular basis.

Surprisingly, even the Internal Revenue Service has a grant program. It is actually geared more toward agencies that provide assistance and information to low-income taxpayers than to individuals and/or businesses. But there is a certain irony in the fact that the IRS gives as well as receives.

A word about other governmental grants: Government grant programs are not just limited to those from Uncle Sam. Numerous states, counties, and municipalities also have grant programs. Like the federal government, state and local governments give grants for a wide variety of causes. Oftentimes, these programs embrace many of the same areas that their national counterparts cover. The vast majority of states, for example, have grant programs to aid and assist women and/or minority business owners. Most states also have programs that help economic or job growth in their locality. For example, the Wisconsin Department of Development has an economic development program that gives (also loans) money to business projects based on their potential contribution to job creation or retention in the state of Wisconsin. In

Colorado, the Sales Office of Business Development similarly gives grants to businesses that create or retain jobs for low- or moderate-income persons. Illinois gives research and investment grants for new technology and innovation. Similar programs are everywhere, and your business may be the direct beneficiary of the money that these states are giving away.

A state or the federal government may grant money to a local municipality, which then in turn may grant or loan a portion directly to a business or individual.

The lesson: When searching for grants, don't forget that even among the various levels of government, there are many places to search for Other People's Money.

Grants from Nonpublic Institutions

It is estimated, rightly or wrongly, that more than $32 billion in governmental grant money is available each year. It is uncertain how much free money is given away by private institutions on an annual basis, because it would be a massive undertaking to come up with a survey of those foundations or to inspect all of their returns. However, various news sources have estimated the number to be anywhere from $25 billion to more than $100 billion per year. When you are talking about figures like that, the actual total doesn't really matter. What matters is that there is an awful lot of Other People's Money out there for your use.

The list of private foundations that have grants available for a variety of causes could fill a small telephone book. Clorox, Ford, and Verizon Wireless certainly don't have much in common in regard to the types of products they sell, but like so many of the largest corporations in America, they have established foundations for charitable purposes.

Philanthropic organizations come in all sizes. Funds are available not only from the largest and most famous foundations but also from foundations that act locally that are not household names all over the country. In addition to the Mellon and Ford foundations of the world, there are less well known examples such as the Mosette Levin Trust—a foundation that helps in the medical and health care area.

Grants from private foundations often cover many of the same matters as those covered by governmental bodies. A short list of the scope of those matters follows.

Health and medical. The Mosette Levin Trust gives grants to individuals for cancer treatment. If the individual is under the age of sixteen, this trust will also give a grant toward aiding with childhood illnesses.

Education. Private foundations, of course, give education scholarships. These are a type of grant similar to the ones from the Department of Education. The only real difference is that foundations, corporations, and other organizations are giving them out. The Woodrow Wilson National Fellowship Foundation (roots from Carnegie-Mellon) is one organization that has a number of programs for scholars.

Social issues. Many foundations address social causes. The Infinity foundation gives grants for charitable, holistic healing, scientific, religious, or educational purposes, including grants designed to promote human rights and democratic freedoms in Tibet, as well as grants to fight AIDS and breast cancer.

Targeted grants. Ford Motor Company has a grant program for those who need adaptive driving aids installed on their vehicles. Of course, not surprisingly, one of the requirements of the program is that the vehicle be a Ford or Lincoln-Mercury.

When trying to think of potential private sources for grants, sometimes it is necessary to think of the nonobvious sources. Even the local Masonic Lodge and American Legion Post may give grants for the needy or those seeking an educational scholarship.

Information Sources

The above are just a few examples of the multitude of private and government grant programs. How much information can you use about grants? The answer is limited only by how much time you have to review it. The fact is that there is so much information that a list of all the sources available could easily be the size of this book.

In the past, it was more difficult to find information about grants. It may have involved writing letters to different organizations or foundations, checking bulletin boards at the local college or university or a government office, or obtaining government publications. With the growth of the World Wide Web, these sources have become increasingly easy to uncover. Ink stains from newsprint from government brochures are a thing of the past! Even the professional grant writer—a person who accesses grants for a living (and takes a percentage of the grant money)—may soon go the way of the vinyl record.

If you are looking for U.S. government grants, probably the single best free source listing the widest variety of governmental grants (and loans) is the Catalog of Federal Domestic Assistance from the General Services Administration. It is a database of all available federal programs. It covers grants to all types of groups, businesses, and individuals. While the catalog covers many grants available for nonprofit organizations, you don't have to have an aversion to profit to find some free money. The government's money is easily available for those who are profit-based through numerous programs on the catalog. This laundry list of grant programs is updated biweekly. Better yet, you can access it on the Web at www.cfda.gov/default.htm or http://12.46.245.173/cfda/cfda.html. You can also access grant information from most of the agencies or departments mentioned in this chapter on their Web sites.

Process

So you are finally convinced to go out and get Other People's Money through a grant process. The next step is simply to contact the agency or private foundation that administers the grant program in which you are interested. There the application process begins. It starts with reading all of the requirements of the grant and then writing the grant application.

The grant information will usually describe the "Application and Award Process." The process of obtaining a grant varies as greatly as the types of grants available. Some are simple to understand, and others have more complex technical requirements.

The application should, of course, meet the requirements of the grant program and criteria specified. When you are dealing with the government, understanding the program may require reading through the material more than once. Sometimes a long vague statement of purpose or a criteria statement is the norm. Using our helicopter parts example, one criterion of this program reads that the program is designed to show "potential effectiveness of partnership in further development and application of technology for the national technology and industrial base." Only Uncle Sam could come up with such a phrase!

The grant you are applying for may also have certain eligibility requirements. For example, if you are a milk producer seeking a grant under a certain income-loss program, you may have to show that you "produced milk" and "commercially marketed" it. In the helicopter parts example, the requirement is that you have to show a "significant" amount of research and development in the field. Defining "significant" may make the eligibility requirement a bit vague to some. But often eligibility requirements are quite unambiguous. Using one of our previous private foundation examples, in order to benefit from a grant from the Mosette Levin Trust, one would have to be a resident of La Porte County, Indiana.

Likewise, there may be certain use or restrictions of use relative to the funds granted. There may be complex restrictions as to how these funds are used, or there may be no restrictions at all. One marine fisheries initiative allows for usage of funds in North Carolina among other states, but if your business plans to use the funds across the state line in neighboring Virginia, don't bother to apply.

The process may also lay out certain technical requirements of the grant process. Continuing with our helicopter example, this particular grant requires the recipient of the grant to match funds. But don't be discouraged by that requirement. Read on—because in this program, that is not a particularly burdensome technical requirement, since labor costs such as payroll could qualify as matching funds per the definition of the "Formula and Matching Requirements" in the program description. There is also a nonburdensome requirement to keep records for three years and file quarterly reports. Most recipients of grants have some sort of obligation to keep records or report on activities.

For more detailed help in writing the grant, a number of excellent guides to writing grant applications can be found on the Internet. One of the best is at www.walkablock.com/write.htm. One of the reasons it is a favorite is not just because of all the helpful advice; it is also free.

"Granted," the grant application process can be either relatively easy or a bit more complex. But when it comes to the process of obtaining this type of Other People's Money or using it, the advice from *Rich Dad Poor Dad* is undoubtedly appropriate: "You need to know what you're looking for and then go look for it!"

Chapter 16

Introducing the Securities Laws

In earlier chapters, we introduced you to some of the requirements and the limitations on your activities imposed by securities law. We revisit the subject head-on in this chapter. Understand, we are not attempting to turn you into a securities attorney or broker. The particular detailed ins and outs of the securities law are beyond the scope of this book. Our intent is that you come away with the ability to identify potentially significant securities law issues—which you can refer to a securities lawyer for resolution. We will start by running through the basic issues and the basics of securities law, then try to put things in perspective with a couple of hypotheticals.

The Basic Issues and Considerations

When you are planning to raise money for your business, there are initially three basic securities questions that must be answered:

First, will the transaction involve a security? If it will, there are rules relating to disclosure of information that must be observed, and unless the transaction falls within very specific exceptions, registration with the Security and Exchange Commission (SEC) is required. Second, assuming that the transaction involves a security, are you in a position to register the securities and "go public"? For example, you typically need at least two years of audited financials for registration.

And finally, do you want to go public even if you can? The cost of going public is often prohibitive for a small company, and there are no guarantees that the initial public offering making the securities available to the public will produce the amount that you expect. You must also be willing to accept additional administrative and accounting burdens, expanded potential liabilities, and the fact that the details of your business affairs will be made public.

Assuming that the transaction involves a security, and, for whatever reason, an IPO is not the answer, there is another question: Does the transaction qualify under one of the exemptions? If it does not, you will have to change your plans. We will discuss the various exemptions to the registration requirement in a moment.

In practice, you would examine your opportunities and weigh the respective pros and cons.

Why are you seeking OPM? Is it to facilitate growth of your business or to execute an exit/profit-taking strategy for you or other investors in your business? If your intent is to grow, you may want to explore alternatives to selling securities.

- Is there a potential strategic alliance that would provide you the resources that you need and otherwise let you meet your goals without implicating the securities laws?
- Is it possible to develop an outlicensing strategy to use your intellectual property assets to generate the capital that you need?
- Do you have a business that is amenable to franchising?
- Do you have assets that could be the basis for a sale/lease-back arrangement? (Although sale/lease-back arrangements can sometimes be considered a sale of securities.)
- How about a loan from a financial institution?

What Is a Security?

The securities law is amazingly pervasive. People often don't even realize that they are dealing with a "security." For example, it would not occur to most people that when they send an e-mail asking their cousin George for money to help fund their business, they are probably asking him to invest in a "security."

With few exceptions, anytime that you sell "stock" in your business or otherwise bring money into your business from an outside source and the money source does not (a) receive goods or services in return for the money or (b) take an active role in the management of your business, the transaction involves some form of security. The sale of stock or other equity shares in a company, one of the most popular ways businesses raise capital, almost invariably comes under the securities law. However, the definition of securities covers much, much more than just stock.

The definition of a security is very broad. Any sort of investment instrument is likely to be covered. That was certainly the government's intent. If you think something might be a security, it probably is. And even if you think that an investment may not be a security, it probably is. The federal statute was intended "to encompass virtually any instrument that might be sold as an investment"—essentially anything that involves using someone else's money based on "the promise of profits," prospects of a "return" from other than the investor's own efforts, or makes the money subject to the entrepreneurial or managerial efforts of others.

The statute specifically names stock as a security. Anything that is common stock in a business, as we would typically think of that term, is a security. The only time an issue arises as to whether stock is a security is when something is called "stock" when it really isn't.

Notes (loans) that reflect an "investment," as opposed to being in the normal course of business, are considered securities. As a rule of thumb, if your business takes a loan (or you take a loan for your business), other than (a) a loan from a bank, (b) a short-term loan, or (c) a mortgage on real property, you should assume that the loan will be considered a security. This is particularly true in any situation where you would tend to think of the source of the money as "an investor" rather than a lender. The analysis of "debt" to determine if it is likely to be considered a security is tricky, and frankly, something best left to your attorney.

The definition of securities also includes "investment contracts." Unfortunately, the statute does not provide a definition for investment contracts. If you want to be safe, you can assume that when people pay money to your business, their interests will be considered securities if (a) they expect (rightly or wrongly) to get a return on that money (i.e., to make a profit) and (b) they are not involved with the activity that generates the profit or in the management of your business.

This safety net may catch contracts that are not necessarily investment contracts (more in some jurisdictions than others, depending upon the specific interpretation of the law), but it will prevent you from inadvertently violating the securities laws.

Obviously, not every contract is a security. Many contracts are simply doing business, not investing in a business. A simple purchase of a product or a service that is not of the type expected to generate revenue for the purchaser is not an investment contract. On the other hand, if a group of people each put money into your business and do not receive a product or the direct benefit of services, but instead expect to share in profits of the business, their interests will be considered securities—if not loans or equity interests, then investment contracts. It gets hairy when an arrangement falls between those ends of the spectrum. If there is any issue of whether a transaction could be considered a security, you should consult your attorney.

The type of entity that you choose for your business and the manner in which your co-venturers participate in the business can determine whether or not securities are involved and if applicable, the requirements and burdens placed upon you by the securities law. If you are interested in learning more about these issues, you may want to visit my web

> Unless the transaction or the securities fall within very specific exemptions, it is considered a "public" offering—and the security or the transaction involving the sale of that security must be registered with the appropriate agency (the SEC and/or an analogous state agency).

site www.mlechter.com, as well as the Rich Dad organization web site www.richdad.com for future materials.

Consequences of Involving a Security

In essence, if your efforts to raise money involve the sale of securities, the federal law imposes a number of requirements and restrictions. For example, you must make "full disclosure" to the potential investor of all "material facts." Something is a "material fact" if it is something that investors would typically want to consider before making the decision to purchase the security.

Written information must be provided to the investor in a specific format (a prospectus in a prescribed form). The prospectus must be filed with the SEC as part of a registration statement before the securities are offered for sale, and the SEC must approve the registration statement (declare it "effective") before any sales are actually made. The registration process is sometimes referred to as "going public." The first time a security is offered to the public is referred to as an initial public offering (IPO).

If the security is registered, you are required to maintain certain internal audit controls and publicly disclose certain information relating to your business operations, financial conditions, and management.

It is extremely expensive to go public and comply with the reporting and disclosure requirements of being a public company.

An IPO is a costly undertaking; in a typical IPO, about 15 percent to 25 percent of the money raised goes to pay direct expenses. Even more resources are spent indirectly (e.g., management time, disruption of business). That, however, is just the beginning. Complying with the disclosure and internal audit control requirements for publicly traded companies can run tens if not hundreds of thousands of dollars. The average yearly cost of being a public company (including directors' fees, directors' and officers' liability insurance, audit and securities compliance related legal fees) has been reported in 2004 to be almost $2.5 million.[20]

In addition to the requirements imposed by federal law, most states have also enacted their own "blue sky" laws, applying to securities that are sold

---

20. Thomas Hartman, "The Cost of Being Public in the Era of Sarbanes-Oxley," 2004 National Directors Institute, Chicago, May 19, 2004.

strictly within that state. While most of the state laws track the federal securities laws, the blue sky laws tend to vary from state to state. Even where identical language is used in the statutes of different states, the agency responsible for securities in that state, and the state courts, may interpret the identical language differently from their counterparts in another state. In some instances, the states provide exemptions from state registration that have no counterpart in the federal law.

In general, however, the state blue sky laws require that securities offerings be registered with the state agency and that broker/dealers, individual stockbrokers, and investment advisors doing business (directly or indirectly) in the state be licensed and file periodic reports with the state. Generally, before any security can be sold in any state, that security must be registered pursuant to the blue sky laws unless the sale of the security falls within a specific exemption from the registration requirements under those laws.

Under the federal securities law, the SEC does not make an assessment as to whether the security represents a good or bad investment. It merely requires that all relevant information be disclosed, and the purchaser of the security can make his or her own assessment of that information. Under the blue sky laws of some states, however, the state agency conducts a "merit review"; and you are required to convince the state agency that the security represents a "good deal" before they will register the security.

The consequences of failing to comply with the securities laws can be severe—and then some. Penalties can include payment of substantial fines or even prison sentences. At a minimum, you would be vulnerable to the potentially significant claims of "aggrieved" investors as well as actions brought by interested state and federal agencies. Equity (stock) investors normally assume the risk that the business in which they invest might fail. However, if your business fails, even through no fault of your own, and you did not comply with the securities laws, you may be required to pay investors back their investment, as well as for other losses that they may have incurred. For that matter, even if your business does not fail, if you have not complied with the securities laws, you could still be required to return money to investors whose expectations were not met or who, for whatever reason, "want out."

Consider the situation where there is a change in the circumstances of one of your investors—say, a divorce or a lost job, or some other "deal" that went bad, or an opportunity to participate in a "better" deal. That investor might want to "cash out" of your business. If you did not comply with the securities laws, the investor may well be able to rescind, and put you in the position of having to come up with the money to pay back the investment. That sort of thing can play havoc with your business's cash flow and financial plan.

The Exceptions to the Registration Requirement

If you are "issuing" securities, the only way you can avoid the expense, administrative burden, disclosure and exposure of going public is by qualifying for one of the various exemptions to the registration requirements of the federal securities law. (And even then you must contend with the applicable state law.) So how do you qualify for an exemption? The first step is to determine which exemption to seek.

Different exemptions apply under different circumstances. Whether or not any particular exemption applies to your particular circumstances depends primarily on the amount of money you are seeking, the entities from whom you seek it, and the manner in which you seek it. The trick is to plan ahead, preferably with advice of counsel. Your money-raising activities need to be carefully

Disclaimer

The securities laws are extremely complex. Entire textbooks (for lawyers) have been written about the subjects that we are trying to cover here in a relatively few pages. This book is not a substitute for good legal counsel. It is not intended to provide legal advice. You should consult with an experienced securities lawyer to develop a financing plan that ensures compliance with the securities laws. In any event, if you plan to rely on an exemption, you should make sure beforehand that what you plan to do will qualify under your specific circumstances. If you proceed with fund-raising without consulting an experienced securities lawyer, you proceed at your own risk. As we say in legalese, the author and publisher specifically disclaim any liability from the use or application of the information contained in this book.

structured and controlled to make sure that you qualify for one of the exemptions.

Each exemption has different qualification criteria. The primary requirements for each of the individual federal exemptions that are most pertinent from the perspective of bringing OPM into a (nonpublic) business are provided in the tables at the end of this chapter. In general, the requirements of the respective exemptions tend to differ with respect to:

1. Limitations on the dollar amount of the offering (or other offerings within a predetermined time period)
2. Limitations on the number and nature of the entities to which the security can be offered
3. Restrictions on the types of entities offering the securities (issuers) to which the exemption is available
4. Whether or not the offering must be private—whether or not general solicitation or advertising is permitted
5. The nature of the disclosure that must be made and/or documents provided to the offerees
6. The nature of filing with the SEC
7. Restrictions on stock transfer
8. Whether or not the exemption provides any relief from (preempts) state registration requirements

You also need to keep in mind that you must comply with both federal and state laws. In general, you want to qualify not only for an exemption from federal registration but also for a separate exemption from state registration. Most states have exemptions that correspond to the federal exemptions. However, the conditions for qualifying for the state exemptions are not necessarily the same as those for the corresponding federal exemptions. And there are sometimes exemptions from state registration with no corresponding federal exemption. (We will get to hypotheticals in a moment that should help to put this into context.)

As the "issuer" of (i.e., the entity offering) a security, you have the burden of establishing that you fall within an exemption. There is little latitude; if there is any deviation from the significant requirements for an exemption, the exemption is lost. If you do not qualify for the exemption, you may be subject to potential civil and possibly criminal penalties and rescission of the transaction. Even if you are successful in avoiding liability, failure to comply with the statutes and regulations could still disqualify you from obtaining exemptions for later transactions.

The following hypotheticals may help put the concepts we just covered into perspective. My colleagues from Squire Sanders (Squire, Sanders & Dempsey, LLP) in the hypothetical (other than Newbie) are real people, and although the companies, other characters, and specific conversations are fictional, I tried to imagine the way the conversations would have gone if they had actually occurred (except that I took the liberty of omitting some of the expletives that might have crept into the conversations).

Hypothetical 1: Scope of the Securities Law

This first story is intended to illustrate how the securities law reaches into places you might not suspect. It also touches on the registration requirement and the exemptions to that requirement (which will be addressed again in the second hypothetical). Because the conversation is generally real to life, there is quite a bit of jargon thrown around. You may want to come back and reread this hypothetical after you have finished the rest of this chapter.

I was at my desk, reviewing the pro forma for a potential investment property, when the phone rang. I answered and heard the voice of Chris Johnson, my longtime friend and colleague from Squire Sanders.

"Mike, are we on for the game Sunday?" he asked. We both had season tickets to the Arizona Cardinals games. The pregame tailgate party was a decade-long ritual.

"Absolutely," I replied.

"Is there anything we can bring?" Chris asked.

"I think we have everything covered. You can bring the beverages if you like."

"Will do. By the way," he said, "I just got a call from Sam Yessman. He's going to the game today. He may stop by to say hello."

"Okay by me." Sam and a fellow named Louis Cannon (I called him Loose

Cannon) owned a company named Cosmo Corp. "I never could figure out how Sam could stand to work with Louis all those years. That guy is dangerous. You're not still doing work for those guys, are you?"

"No. I didn't have any more tolerance for Loose Cannon's abuse than you did."

"So how is Sam doing?"

"He's done better. He tells me that he and Louis have been sued for Securities Act violations."

"Really?"

I guess I was not really surprised to hear that. Louis was truly a loose cannon. I had encountered Cosmo Corp. a number of years earlier, while I was still practicing law full-time. Sam had come to my partner Chris with a draft of an agreement between Cosmo and an outfit called Smooth-Talk, LLC, for review. There were a number of intellectual property aspects to the agreement, and Chris had asked me to work with him on the matter.

According to Sam, the principals of Smooth-Talk were old friends of Louis's. Cosmo and Smooth-Talk were going to collaborate on producing a particular product, and Cosmo would get certain rights in the product. And, of course, time was of the essence. Sam explained that Louis was emphatic that there was only a narrow window of opportunity. They wanted overnight turnaround on the agreement, even though they had had the draft in-house for a number of weeks before they consulted us. As it happens, Louis was out of town, being wined and dined by his old friends at Smooth-Talk.

The agreement, as it was written, was rife with problems. It failed to give Cosmo the rights in the product that Sam said they were supposed to get. There were provisions that potentially foreclosed other business opportunities for Cosmo. That was the good part. There were other provisions in the agreement that put Cosmo's trademarks at risk and still others that obligated Cosmo to indemnify (hold harmless) Smooth-Talk for things totally under Smooth-Talk's control. If Smooth-Talk did something that got them sued, Cosmo would have had to pay Smooth-Talk's attorney's fees and any damages, even if Smooth-Talk was totally at fault or intentionally caused the problem. (That is a position that you never want to be in.) The agreement had all the earmarks of the opening salvo of an overly aggressive negotiator who took extreme positions with the expectation of being cut back.

Chris and I literally spent the night analyzing the agreement and met with Sam the next day to go through it. We pointed out the problem provisions, explained their ramifications, and suggested changes to the agreement that would fix the problems (meeting both parties' legitimate concerns). Sam faxed a copy of our marked-up version of the agreement to Louis, and we called him by telephone to discuss our advice.

Louis, however, did not want to hear about anything that could "queer the deal." His position was "they wouldn't do that" or "that's not our agreement" (even though the written agreement was explicit) and "I'm willing to take that risk." It was as if he was negotiating on Smooth-Talk's behalf. My take was that he was so enamored of the "deal" (as he understood it) that he had blinders on to reality. Beyond that, I don't think that he had the stomach for negotiation. He didn't want to hurt his old friends' feelings.

Understand—we were not trying to "kill the deal." We were trying to negotiate a deal that satisfied the goals of all parties but still protected Cosmo's interests.

Louis, of course, saw it differently. After we turned off the speakerphone and Sam picked up the handset, Louis said (loudly enough that both CJ and I could hear him), "I'm not going to let any #the@!#!! lawyers run my business." He signed the agreement as it was despite our advice.

You never know how those things will end up. Sometimes everything goes well with the deal, and nobody ever even looks at the written agreement. The problems arise when things go wrong and you have to look to the agreement to resolve the issues. With Loose Cannon, things tended to go wrong a lot. As it happened, that particular agreement with Smooth-Talk never went anywhere. Smooth-Talk never performed, there was never any product, and the agreement more or less died of its own accord. Cosmo was lucky: A shoddy agreement often leads to true disaster. In this case, Cosmo merely lost the time and money they invested in the project (they had no recourse against Smooth-Talk).

In any event, that was the first of a number of similar episodes with Cosmo and Louis Cannon. Louis would go forward with deals without counsel, or in spite of counsel. And we would have to clean up the mess. Louis never figured out how to use lawyers. From Louis's perspective, the lawyers just get in the way. Of course, Loose Cannon thought everyone who does anything but say "yes, sir" to him just gets in the way. This was a different world for me. I was used to clients who appreciated my advice—who went out of their way to solicit my advice. Anyway, I finally got sufficiently frustrated that I told Cosmo that I wouldn't work with them anymore. So that was why I was not surprised to hear that they had been charged with securities law violations.

"So what happened? Did they try to do a financing for Cosmo on their own? Or did Louis try his hand at going public" I asked sarcastically.

"No, they didn't do a financing . . . at least not directly. Louis apparently did the wrong deal," Chris replied.

"What do you mean?"

"He acquired a business from one of his old friends, Tyrone M'Bomb."

"Ty M'Bomb? The handyman? Wasn't Ty the handyman that Sam brought to our office a few years back, introducing him around?"

"It was more than a few years ago, but I think it's the same guy. Anyway, Ty went into home renovations. He started a rehab business . . . called it Fix & Flip."

"That makes sense—it leveraged his expertise as a handyman."

"Right. Anyway, Ty got himself a real estate agent's license and affiliated with one of those brokers that let agents operate under their brokerage license on a fee basis. You know . . . the agent pays a monthly fee, but otherwise does his own thing. Ty's idea was to identify run-down properties in nice neighborhoods through the MLS, purchase them, refurbish them, and flip 'em."

"Okay. Him and a zillion others. Some people do very well at it. Where did the securities law come in?"

"I'm getting to that. Apparently, he didn't have the funds to purchase the properties himself, so he went looking for investors. He set up a Web site. Every time he identified a target property he would post it on the Web site and solicit investors."

"Oh, boy, I think I see what's coming. Passive investors?" I asked. Most people don't realize it, but most passive investments (as opposed to those that involve active roles in business management) in businesses are considered securities. As a general proposition, you are not allowed to make general solicitations or advertise for investors. A Web site is considered to be a general solicitation or advertisement. You can sometimes use a Web site to raise capital for a business, but there are very specific rules that must be observed, or you quickly find yourself in violation of the securities law. You typically have to restrict access to the investment information—through, for example, passwords—to "qualified" investors. The criteria for being a qualified investor depend on the circumstances—and specific exemption from registration that you are seeking. For example, to be qualified, sometimes the potential investor must have a certain net worth and/or income level or reside in a specific state. Sometimes he or she has to be someone with whom you already have an existing relationship.

"You got it. Investment-contract-type securities. You ought to take a look at the Web site." Chris gave me the URL, and while we talked, I pulled it up on my computer. The home page came into focus on my screen. This is what I saw:

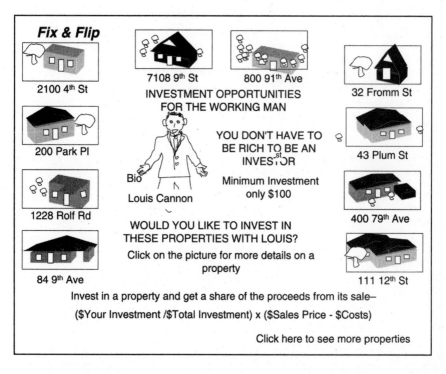

Chris told me that the home page originally showed Ty and linked to his biographical data, with an accurate description of his experience at buying and flipping residential properties. After Cosmo acquired Fix & Flip, the Web site was changed to feature Louis.

"So what happened to Ty?" I asked

"He's still around. Part of the deal was a five-year employment contract. Cosmo paid him top dollar for Fix & Flip and then paid him top dollar again to continue to do the actual work."

I clicked on one of the property pictures and was taken to a screen requiring me to enter my name, address, and e-mail address and to click a box confirming that I was over twenty-one years old. There was also an "opt out" box with respect to e-mail notices. That I definitely clicked—the last thing I needed was more spam. I made up a name and address and entered my e-mail as uce@ftc.gov (an e-mail account at the Federal Trade Commission to which you can forward spam).

"It's not password-protected," I commented as I hit enter, and was taken to the page associated with the property I had clicked. Here is what it looked like:

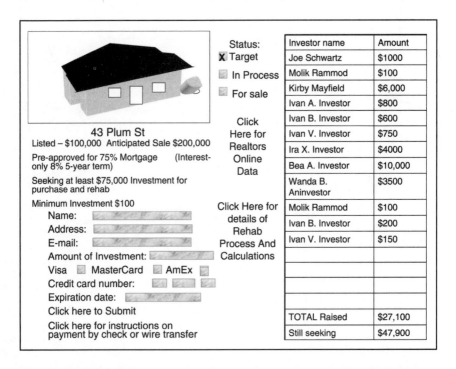

			Investor name	Amount
	Status:		Joe Schwartz	$1000
	X Target		Molik Rammod	$100
	In Process		Kirby Mayfield	$6,000
	For sale		Ivan A. Investor	$800
43 Plum St	Click		Ivan B. Investor	$600
Listed – $100,000 Anticipated Sale $200,000	Here for		Ivan V. Investor	$750
Pre-approved for 75% Mortgage (Interest-only 8% 5-year term)	Realtors Online		Ira X. Investor	$4000
Data			Bea A. Investor	$10,000
Seeking at least $75,000 Investment for purchase and rehab			Wanda B. Aninvestor	$3500
Minimum Investment $100	Click Here for		Molik Rammod	$100
Name:	details of		Ivan B. Investor	$200
Address:	Rehab		Ivan V. Investor	$150
E-mail:	Process And			
Amount of Investment:	Calculations			
Visa MasterCard AmEx				
Credit card number:				
Expiration date:				
Click here to Submit			TOTAL Raised	$27,100
Click here for instructions on payment by check or wire transfer			Still seeking	$47,900

"How did Ty get 75 percent loan to value mortgages on a rehab?" I asked. "It seems very high for a rehab."

"I'm not sure. I have to assume that he had other collateral to secure the loan—maybe his house. Or a cosigner. Or it may have been noninstitutional money. Individuals. Maybe even the seller of the property."

"I guess the system would have worked even if he had to put more money down on the properties. He would just have to set a higher number for the investment sought."

While Chris was talking, I clicked through to the "Rehab Process and Calculations" page. The page described the Fix & Flip business model and the particulars of the investment. Here's what I saw:

"Interesting," I commented. "What happens if the investor isn't interested in investing in a different property?"

F&F Rehab Process and Calculations

- We obtain pre-approval of a mortgage at the maximum loan to value ratio available and best terms (typically short-term, interest only).
- Once sufficient are funds are raised for a property, we will submit an offer for the property at list price (with inspection contingencies). We act as buying agent, and charge a realtors commission of 6% (typically shared with seller's agent).
- If we are not successful in our efforts to purchase the property you selected, we will transfer your investment to a different property and notify you by e-mail.
- F&F will act as general contractor for the refurbishing, and will hire subcontractors to the actual work. We charge a fee of 25% of monies paid to subcontractors (for labor and materials).
- When the refurbishing is complete, we will list the property on the MLS. We will determine the listing price, and whether or not to accept any offer. We charge a realtors commission of 6% (typically shared with buyers agent).
- When the property is sold, we will distribute the proceeds within 30 days of the closing. Each investor will receive a pro rata share of the "profits" in accordance with the formula
- ($Your Investment /$Total Investment) x ($Sales Price - $ Costs)
- Costs include:
  All closing costs, and mortgage service
  Any transaction fees paid for investments paid for by credit card
  The general contractor fees and realtors commissions paid to F & F

Chris laughed. "From what I understand, return of funds was never volunteered, but as a matter of policy, Ty would return funds immediately if an objection was raised in response to the e-mail. Apparently, once Cosmo took over, Louis changed the 'immediately' part of the policy. He was not so quick to return the funds—but he returned them if the investor was persistent."

Chris continued, "Ty apparently was very successful with this thing. He made his money by acting as general contractor for the rehab and as real estate agent on the purchase and sale of the property. He was actually doing rehabs on about three or four properties at a time. He figured out the timing so that he had the right number and mix of properties on the Web site to keep that number relatively constant. He would buy his typical property for around $100,000, put about $50,000 into the rehab, and then sell the updated property for around $200,000. He would look to the investors to put up the money for the down payment, the carrying costs, and the costs of rehab. So if he qualified for a 75 percent mortgage, he would put down $25,000 and raise an additional $50,000 for the rehab and carrying expenses. Sam said that Ty was averaging around $20,000 in fees per property and was moving three or four each quarter. So as a one-man show, he was making over $300,000 or so a year with this deal. Not bad when his initial investment was just the cost of putting up the Web site.

"And his investors were happy as clams. They were making around 25 to 30 percent cash on cash return, with each property flipping on average in six months. Annualized, that's a return of 100 to 120 percent."

"Too bad he was violating the Securities Act. I take it that nobody ever went after him?"

"Nope. He was lucky," Chris replied. "He apparently stayed under the SEC's radar. His investors were making money, so nobody was complaining. A classic example of the 'good deal defense'—no harm, no foul. But things changed after Cosmo acquired Fix & Flip—"

"What sort of entity was Fix & Flip?" I interrupted.

"An LLC. Cosmo acquired 100 percent ownership."

"With Louis, I assume that there were no warranties or indemnities," I said, rapid-fire. Sometimes I fall into cross-examination mode without realizing it.

"Sam didn't say, but I assume not—remember this was a Louis deal. Are you going to let me finish the story?"

"Sorry. So what happened?"

"Ty had apparently been making a killing with Fix & Flip, but as soon as Cosmo acquired Fix & Flip, they started running into problems. It turned out that one of the houses that they purchased had mold—it was unsellable. Apparently a Louis deal—they bought it 'as is' without even consulting Ty. They also underestimated the costs of renovating one of the other properties. It put the price of the refurbished house greatly in excess of neighborhood comparables—they weren't able to sell the house at a price where the investment could be recouped.

"Then the renovations of other houses took longer than expected, and others simply did not sell as quickly as budgeted. Apparently, Louis decided, this time over Ty's objection, that they could double the number of properties being refurbished at one time. Anyway, Cosmo still owned the houses when investment money for those properties was exhausted—and had to keep paying the mortgages. So they stopped making money for the investors, and I guess some of them sued to get their money back."

"Well, maybe this time Louis'll learn," I commented.

"It doesn't look like it. The Web site is still up. My other line's ringing, I've got to go. See you Sunday," Chris said, and hung up.

I hung up as well and got on with my day.

Sunday rolled around, and a group of us were tailgating in the stadium parking lot before the Cardinals game. It was a beautiful day. Chris had brought a portable TV, and we were watching the highlights from games being played on the East Coast. The folding tables and chairs were set up with tablecloths in place. The ladies were laying out a feast. My wife, Sharon, had prepared her signature shish kebabs and was tending the grill. Chris's wife, also named Chris, was laying out all of the munchies. If the Cardinals game play was as good as our pregame food, it would be a fantastic day.

I'd forgotten that Chris had mentioned that Sam Yessman might stop by, until Sam showed up. Chris introduced him to the group. We started out with small talk, proceeded to the Cardinals' prospects for today's game and the season, but the topic of conversation soon turned to Cosmo and the suit for securities law violations.

"I guess you heard that we were sued over Fix & Flip," Sam said to me.

"Chris mentioned it," I replied.

"Yeah, a whole group of customers brought suit asking for their money back. Claimed we were selling unregistered securities and that they were entitled to recession—"

"You mean rescission?"

Sam nodded affirmatively and continued without a pause. "Then, yesterday, the SEC got involved. They're asking for some sort of an injunction, and penalties—$500,000!"

"Five hundred thousand?" Chris exclaimed. "That means they consider this a third-tier violation. Fraud and significant risk of substantial losses to others."

"Or reckless disregard for regulatory requirement and risk of substantial loss," I commented. "That's the first you've heard from the SEC? I guess I'm a little curious as to—"

"Uh . . . they had sent us a letter or something telling us to shut down the site," Sam replied before I could finish my question. "Louis dealt with it. He called them and told them to stuff it—that we were not selling securities and were not doing anything wrong. Louis says that the suits are bogus—there's no way that we could be selling securities. We're not selling stock. The only thing we are guilty of is some bad business decisions."

Chris stifled a groan. "Sam, a lot of things are securities besides stock. You are selling investment interests in properties—investment contracts. Investment contracts are considered securities. When people invest money in a common enterprise, such as one of your rehab properties, and expect a profit based on your efforts—buying, refurbishing, and selling the property—that's an investment contract, a security.

"When securities are involved, there are both federal and state laws that apply. You either have to register the securities or make sure that you qualify for an exemption to registration. You have to do that at both the federal and state levels. You obviously have not registered the interests in the properties that you're selling. And as best I can tell without really getting into the issue, you don't qualify for any of the exemptions." Chris was being kind; there was no way what Fix & Flip was doing came under an exemption. "This is serious stuff. You violate the securities law, and not only can your investors get their money back, but you're facing potential civil penalties and possibly jail time."

"Sam," I asked, "have you talked to your attorney about this?" I suspect that my tone was a bit accusatory, but Sam didn't bat an eyelash.

"Not yet. We don't have to respond for another week. Louis wants to make sure that the attorney doesn't spend too much time preparing a—" I looked over at Chris. We both just shook our heads in disbelief. "I wish your attorney luck," I interrupted. "You guys are shooting yourself in the foot."

Sam shrugged. "I'm not sure it matters anyway. Fix & Flip is a separate LLC, and with the luck we've had recently, there's not much money left in it. Louis posted a number of new properties so that we could get in enough new money to cover the existing mortgages. But after using the new money to pay the mortgages on the old properties, we didn't have enough down payment to get mortgages on the new properties—and the dog properties still haven't sold."

Chris and I caught each other's eyes. That answered the question about why the SEC had gotten involved. When Louis began using money invested in new properties to pay the mortgages on the problem houses, he was committing a fraud. "Shades of Mr. Ponzi," I muttered.

Sam continued, "There are still a couple of mortgages that we had to guarantee, but the rest of them are in the name of the LLC, just secured by the properties. Louis is talking about just letting the banks foreclose and putting Fix & Flip in bankruptcy."

"Section 15—Controlling Persons Liability," I muttered, looking over at Chris and still shaking my head. I spoke up. "I've got bad news for you, Sam. When you're talking about securities law violations, management is not shielded by LLC status and the liability is not discharged by bankruptcy."

"Mike's right, Sam," Chris said. "The management is liable for violations of the securities law by the LLC unless they can show that they didn't know—that it was reasonable for them not to know—about the acts that constitute the violation. How involved were you with Fix & Flip?"

Sam shrugged.

Chris sighed. "You may want to have your own attorney on this one, Sam. Different from the attorney representing Louis. Anyway, good luck."

I glanced at my watch. "We better start packing up. Kickoff is in ten minutes." I looked over at Sam. "Good luck to you, Sam." I didn't say the next sentence out loud. "You're going to need it."

After the game, the chairs and tables were set up again, and we relaxed waiting for traffic to die down. I will leave you in suspense as to how the game went.

I turned to Chris. "You know, I've been wondering what Fix & Flip would have to do to make their system fly under the securities law."

"Good question. I'd have to think about that . . . Federal registration isn't the real issue. I think that it would be easy enough for them to keep the business and potential investors strictly intrastate. They are organized in Arizona, and all the business that they are doing—all of the properties—are within Arizona, so as long as it is made clear on the Web site that only people residing in Arizona can participate, it would be strictly intrastate. That would avoid the issue of federal registration. The question is what they would have to do to comply with state law."

"I was thinking that a home page that qualified as an announcement under the Arizona Qualified Purchaser Rule might work," I responded.

I was referring to an Arizona regulation (R14-4-139—and no, I did not remember the number off the top of my head) that permits what is in essence a limited public offering of up to $5 million of securities in a one-year period to "qualified purchasers" that meet certain net worth and income requirements. The rule permits an "announcement" that the investment is being offered, but specifically limits the type of information that can be included in the announcement. Things like contact information for the company offering the investment, a brief description of the business, a brief description of the security (investment), and a statement making it clear that the investment has not been registered or approved by the state, that the announcement is not the actual offer, and that the actual offer is limited to "qualified purchasers."

I went on with my musing. "They would have to make sure that they don't go over the $5 million in the twelve-month limit, and, in this case, the announcement would have to make it clear that the offer is limited to qualified purchasers that reside in Arizona to make sure that it stays intrastate. And I guess they would either have to also limit the offer to accredited investors—qualified purchasers that reside in Arizona and are also accredited investors—or beef up the content of the Web site, the interior pages with information on the actual investments."

There are specific requirements with respect to the type of information that must be provided to the investors and the form in which it must be presented—unless all of the investors qualify as "accredited" (some people would say "rich"). Accredited investors, in this context, are a subset of qualified purchasers, with considerably higher net worth and/or income requirements than the thresholds for qualified purchaser.

The Web site, as it is presently, would not comply with the form and content requirements of the regulations. So if the investments are available to nonaccredited investors, the Web site would have to be changed (beefed up) to comply with the regulations. If the offer is limited to accredited investors, however, the actual information on the investment provided becomes less critical. That is not to say, of course, that it can be inaccurate or misleading, but you get relief from the specific form and content requirements of the regulations.

I continued. "So a home page would have to meet the requirements for an 'announcement,' and potential investors would click through to a page that would require them to qualify—provide information showing that they meet the requirements—as accredited investor residing in Arizona." If they qualified as an accredited investor, they are necessarily a qualified purchaser under the Arizona law. "Once they qualify, you would assign them a password that gave them access to the specifics on the investments."

"You may need to somehow verify the information that they give you—make sure that they really are an accredited investor in Arizona," Chris commented.

"Chris, do you think that you could get away with having the photos of the properties on the home page and still meet the requirements for an 'announcement'?" I asked.

"I doubt it. The announcement has to be pretty vanilla. You'd probably pretty much have to start from scratch on the home page. But you could put something together and bounce it off of the Corporation Commission. Ask them for a letter approving whatever it is that you propose to use. Maybe someday someone will actually do the research and figure out how to do it right."

"You never know. It could be a fun project to take on."

"But not for Louis Cannon."

"No. Definitely not for Louis Cannon."

Hypothetical 2: Exemptions from Registration

This story relates to the registration requirement and the exemptions to that requirement, and how successive offerings can get you into trouble if you are not careful. Like the first hypothetical, the conversation (although fictional) is generally real to life, and there is quite a bit of jargon thrown around, particularly about specific federal and state exemptions. Even so, I think you will get the idea.

The speaker had been less than scintillating, and the dinner had definitely been of the rubber chicken variety. At least the company was good; I and a few of my longtime friends and colleagues from Squire Sanders, Chris Johnson and Greg Hall, both corporate finance and securities lawyers, Dave Rogers, one of the intellectual property attorneys, and Don Wall, one of the litigators, had retired to the lounge to watch the end of one of the basketball play-off games on the big screen. One of the brand-new associates, newly admitted to the bar, had joined us. They called her Newbie. I didn't catch her real name.

We were just starting to change the subject to the upcoming baseball season and the prospects for the Arizona Diamondbacks when John Pound-foolish walked over. John had been an employee of a company that we had represented in years past. He had ultimately left to start his own business. He had come to us to represent him, but because of potential conflicts, among other things, we had referred him to another firm in town. I had never worked with him directly, but I knew him fairly well on a social basis.

"Gentlemen!" He grinned as he pulled up a chair. He nodded at Newbie. "And lady. How are you doing this evening?"

"Doing just fine, John. What are you up to these days?" Chris replied.

"You know that I sold out of Spinoffco." Spinoffco was the name of the company that he had started when he left our client.

Greg nodded. "I heard that. Someone told me that you had gotten into the office furniture business."

"That's right. Knockoffco, Inc."

That rang a bell with me. "Didn't you have an issue with some design patents?"

John grimaced. "Don't remind me. I got sued for design patent infringement and trademark infringement. My primary product line. Ended up settling, but it set me back big-time. I had to redesign the whole product line. I had to bring in a bunch of new investors to fund it. Diluted my stock down to 60 percent. I raised a million five. Closed out the offering about five months ago"

"What did you do, some sort of Reg D offering?" Chris asked.

"No. Tom"—John could tell from the perplexed look on Newbie's face that she did not recognize the name—"my attorney said I didn't have to. Limited the offer to qualified investors here in Arizona. Since it was just Arizona investors, we didn't need to do anything with the Feds."

"Qualified investors?" Greg asked. "Are you talking about an Arizona Rule 139 Qualified Purchaser Public Offering Exemption? You published an announcement and all that?"

"You got it! Rule 139," John replied.

The new attorney raised her eyebrows and shrugged. She looked over to Greg for an explanation.

He grinned. "You know that when you sell securities, you are required to register the securities with the SEC or a state agency or both. Right?"

She nodded, and Greg continued.

"Here in Arizona that agency is the Corporation Commission.

"Anyway, registration is an expensive process and obligates you to make a lot of information public. So you want to avoid it if you can, unless you are out to raise the really big bucks. That is where the exemptions come in. The federal and state securities laws define a bunch of different exemptions to the registration requirements. If you can meet the criteria for an exemption, you don't have to register. The exemptions typically have different criteria to qualify. Sometimes there are restrictions on the location of the offerees—the folks that are given the opportunity to purchase the securities—whether they are located in state or out of state. There are often limits on the maximum amount of offering—how much money you can raise from selling securities—during a given period of time, typically six months or twelve months. And restrictions on who the securities can be offered to—how well-off they need to be, how sophisticated, whether or not they can afford to lose the money they invest." Greg paused for a moment and then asked, "Newbie, you know about 'accredited' and 'sophisticated' investors?"

She nodded. "'Accredited' basically means that the investor is rich—a millionaire—and 'sophisticated' means the investor has enough information and experience to understand the risks of the investment. Right?"

"Close enough," Greg replied. "Let's see. Where were we? Oh, yeah—typical requirements to qualify the exemptions. The exemptions will often

have restrictions on how many purchasers there can be, the type of information that has to be provided to the purchaser, and what you have to file
with the governmental agency."

Greg looked over at me. I think that he thought I was having too much
fun just listening. "Okay, professor." He laughed. "This is a test. What did I
leave out?"

I thought for a moment and then replied, "Limitations on the manner of
offering—public versus private."

"Right on! Give the man a cigar!" Greg exclaimed in a passable imitation
of W. C. Fields.

"Whether the offering can be public, or whether it has to stay private."

"Now, 'private' doesn't mean secret. Basically, it just means that there
can't be any offers to strangers or any type of advertising. To keep an offering private, you can only offer the securities to people you already know.
Most of the federal exemptions don't permit any sort of general solicitation
or advertising. There are only a couple of exceptions."

"Okay. Let's see if I remember," I interjected. At this point in the evening,
I wasn't sure how well my memory was functioning. "Intrastate offerings,
Reg A, Rule 504, based on state registrations or exceptions . . . and that's
about all I can think of. The rest of the federal exemptions require the offering to be private."

"That sounds right," Greg answered. "Although there are some restrictions on what you can do under Reg A.

"Anyway, at the federal level there are three basic groups of exemptions
that you tend to see a lot: the intrastate offering exemption, where the offering—all aspects of the offering—are entirely within a single state; the private
offering exemptions, where the offering is entirely private; the small issue exemptions, where the dollar amount of the offering is below certain levels.

"All of the exemptions have different qualification criteria, like I was talking
about before. The small issue exemptions are included in Regulation A and
Regulation D. Reg D actually includes a number of different exemptions—the
Rule 504, Rule 505, and Rule 506 exemptions. Rule 506 is actually one of the
private offering exemptions—it's not limited as to amount. There's also an exemption for small private offerings strictly to accredited investors. Anyway,

there are a bunch of other federal exemptions, but we don't need to go into them right now."

"So what is Rule 139?" Newbie asked.

"Greg, maybe you should run through the relationship between federal and state laws for Newbie before you get into that," I suggested.

"Did you want to explain it?"

"No, you go ahead." I was trying to both listen to Greg's explanation of the securities law to Newbie and follow a parallel conversation that Chris was having with Poundfoolish.

"Okay" Greg said. "What you have to understand is that you must have separate exemptions from both the federal and state registration requirements. Most of the time the states will have exemptions that correspond to the federal exemptions. However, the conditions for qualifying for the state exemptions are not necessarily the same as those for the corresponding federal exemptions. And there are sometimes exemptions from state registration with no corresponding federal exemption.

"Okay, so you have to have an exemption from federal registration and a separate exemption from state registration. Sometimes, meeting the requirements for a federal exemption is enough to qualify for an exemption from state registration. Sometimes it is not. In one case—that's the Rule 506 exemption—qualifying for the federal exemption preempts state registration requirements beyond filing a notice with the state. In other cases, at least for offerings up to $1 million, registering with the state or meeting the requirements for state exemptions can qualify you for a federal exemption that permits a public offering—permits advertising—at least to the extent that the state exemption permits it. Those are the Rule 504 exemptions that Mike mentioned." Greg paused to take a breath and then asked Newbie, "Following me so far?"

"I think so," she responded. "But you know that securities law is not a subject that they test you on in the bar exam."

"Or intellectual property law," Rogers piped in. He raised his glass in a mock toast. "To the specialists!" He laughed.

"This is true." Greg chuckled. "Should I go on?"

"Please. I take it that Rule 139 defines one of the exemptions to registration in Arizona."

"That's right. Rule 139 lets you make a limited public offering of restricted securities—up to $5 million—as long as it's restricted to qualified purchasers. 'Restricted' means that the securities can't be resold unless they are registered or exempted—legends have to be placed on the disclosure documents and certificates and so forth.

"A qualified purchaser is sort of a baby accredited investor under Arizona law," Greg explained. "There are certain minimum net worth and gross income requirements—at this point, net worth has to be more than $250,000 and annual income more than $100,000. And the investment can't exceed a certain percentage—10 percent—of the investor's net worth. An accredited investor always meets the criteria for qualified purchaser, but a qualified purchaser does not necessarily make the grade for either accredited investor or sophisticated investor under the federal law. Still with me?"

She nodded, and Greg continued.

"The thing that is particularly interesting about a Rule 139 offering is that you can do things to promote the offering that are considered to be general solicitation or advertising under the federal law. Under Rule 139, you can publish announcements of the offering as long as you comply with content requirements—restrictions actually—and make it clear in the announcement that the actual offer is limited to qualified purchasers. Of course, you still need an exemption from federal registration. If you announce the offering, that means that it's not private, and that limits your choices of federal exemptions. You will have to qualify as a purely intrastate offering, or for the exemption under federal Rule 504—but there is a $1-million limit for Rule 504 offerings. Or, depending on the type of promotional activities, Regulation A."

While Greg was talking to Newbie, Chris and Don continued the conversation with John Poundfoolish. John had just confirmed that his offering had been under Arizona Rule 139.

"You closed out the offering five months ago, and you still remember the rule number?" Don asked, clearly surprised. "What are you, a closet attorney?"

Poundfoolish laughed. "Well, actually, I reused the documents last month for a new offering. I had the opportunity to acquire an outfit in Utah.

Less than $5 million and I picked up a manufacturing facility three times the size of the one that I have in Arizona. And the distribution channels in Utah helped me increase sales by a factor of ten."

"How large was the offering?" Chris asked.

"Four and a half million," John replied.

"Let me make sure I have this straight. You raised a million and a half dollars five months ago, and now you are raising another four and a half million?" Chris inquired.

"That's right."

"And the four and a half million that you're raising now will be used to acquire facilities and distribution channels in Utah?"

"Yup."

"And that means that you will have larger facilities—more capacity—in Utah than in Arizona and will be doing more business in Utah than in Arizona?"

"That's right. Three times more manufacturing capacity and ten times the sales."

"You announced the second offering the same way that you did the first?"

"Exactly the same—except for the price of the securities."

I couldn't help myself and interrupted. "I take it that you didn't bother to talk to your attorney about this new offering."

"No, I didn't. I didn't need to. I had just spent good money for the first offering. No need to reinvent the wheel. I just used the same documents again—all I did was update the financials for the offering memorandum. There was no need to get the attorney involved again."

Chris shook his head. "Actually, you probably should have. I strongly suggest that you call your attorney and tell him about the second offering."

"What do you mean? You think that there's a problem?" Poundfoolish exclaimed. "You think my attorney gave me bad advice?"

I interjected. "Not at all. The problem wasn't the advice that you got. The problem was that you didn't bother to get advice on the second offering." Some people simply cannot conceive that they could be the source of a problem.

I guess the fact that I was losing patience with Poundfoolish was reflected in my tone; Chris touched me on the arm, signaling me to back off.

"John," Chris replied calmly. "I'm not going to go into it with you. Call your attorney. We've heard enough to think that there might be a problem, but we aren't in a position to examine all of the facts. And frankly, you shouldn't say anything more about this to us. We do not represent you, and we are not consulting with you with a view toward representing you. There is no attorney-client privilege here. You already have an attorney; you should go talk to him."

Poundfoolish mumbled something, then got up and stomped off.

Chris, Don, and I looked at each other and shook our heads. "Man," I quipped, "Poundfoolish really lives up to his name, doesn't he? Is he in as much of a box as I think he is?"

"Sounds like it," Chris answered.

Newbie looked perplexed, so I explained. "The first offering qualified under the 'intrastate' exemption to federal registration. The problem is that it doesn't look like Poundfoolish had a federal exemption for that second offering. That puts him in violation of the federal law. And on top of that, the first and second offerings were only five months apart. That means that they could be integrated—in effect, considered a single offering, for purposes of federal laws—so the first offering would also be in violation of the federal law. He may be in trouble in Arizona too. The second offering may have put him over the maximum dollar limit for Rule 139—you are limited to raising $5 million in any twelve-month period."

Chris took over. "I think that we can assume that they qualified under the Arizona rule for the state exemption for the first offering. And they were apparently relying on the 'intrastate offering' exemption to federal registration in the first offering. Based on what he said, he didn't get qualified for a Reg A offering—that's a relatively involved process—like a mini-registration. He would have remembered it if they had gone the Reg A route. The offering was for a million and a half dollars—over the limit for Rule 504—and the announcement knocks out pretty much everything else. The 'intrastate offering' exemption is pretty much all that was left available.

"When he did the first offering, at least as I understand it, Knockoffco had all of its facilities in Arizona and did most of its business in Arizona. I assume they are organized in Arizona. So limiting the offer to Arizona residents would be enough to qualify for the federal 'intrastate' exemption. The problem is that when Poundfoolish did the second offering, it didn't qualify for the 'intrastate' exemption. To qualify for the exemption, the issuer—Knockoffco—has to both be resident in the state and 'doing business' in the state. The money raised also has to be used for activities in the state. The money from the second offering is being used in Utah, not Arizona. And when the dust settles, Knockoffco will be bigger, and doing more business, in Utah than in Arizona. He doesn't even come close to making the safe harbor of Rule 147. I'm not sure that there's any way that second offering could possibly qualify for the 'intrastate offering' exemption."

"Safe harbor?" Newbie asked.

I laughed. "Complicated, huh? The problem is that the statutes don't define all of the terms and phrases that they use. That means that those terms can be interpreted many different ways. For example, the statute says that to qualify for the 'intrastate' exemption, a company has to be 'resident and doing business within' the state where the securities are sold. So what does that mean? If you are doing business in more than one state, can you still qualify? How much business do you need to be doing in the state in order to qualify? Sometimes, instead of trying to define terms, the SEC rules provide what they call 'safe harbors.' If you comply with the provisions of the safe harbor rules, you know that you qualify for the exemption. However, you might still qualify under the statutory exemption even if you don't strictly follow the safe harbor requirements. Of course, you have the burden of proving that you're entitled to the exemption."

"So what can Poundfoolish do at this point?" Dave Rogers asked. He had been so quiet I had almost forgotten that he was there.

"I'm really not sure," I replied. "Pray, I guess. Keep his investors happy and pray that no one ever contests the offering. Or maybe recall the offering, give everyone their money back, wait six months, and do it again the right way. Chris, Greg, Don, what do you think?"

They all shrugged, almost in unison. Chris replied, "That's Tom's—Poundfoolish's attorney's—problem."

Newbie's eyes were glazed over. "Boy, that's pretty complicated stuff."

We just laughed. But she was right.

If you are interested in learning more about whether or not the securities law applies to a transaction, the burdens and obligations imposed by the securities law (and the requirements for exemptions from certain of those obligations), and the pros and cons of going public, I invite you to visit my web site www.mlechter.com, as well as the Rich Dad organization web site *www.richdad.com* for further materials.

Closing

The intent of this book is to open your eyes to the endless possibilities for capital needs of your business. Don't let anyone tell you that "it takes money to make money." A million-dollar idea *always* has a shot at delivering a million-dollar return. You just need to know when and how to use Other People's Money and Resources. OPM and OPR are the stepping-stones of the path to riches.

In *Protecting Your #1 Asset*, my earlier contribution to the Rich Dad's Advisors series, we discussed intellectual property and how to turn an idea into an asset. Intellectual property—your ideas, the results of your creativity, your relationships, and your reputation—is clearly your business's most important asset. IP is the primary basis for sustainable competitive advantage. And when everything is boiled down to its essence, it is one of the primary attractions to sources of OPM. It is the tool that can provide you with maximum leverage.

We all have ideas. They become valuable assets when we protect them, define them, develop them, and leverage them. Some of the very best ideas, I'd venture, never see the light of day—let alone the true potential for million-dollar returns—because the individual who thought of them didn't know where to begin in terms of capitalizing upon them. They believed it when someone told them that it takes money to make money.

This book is content rich—and for good reason. A "good idea"—for a business, an invention, a process, or even an improvement—is really only as good as our ability to turn that concept into reality.

In writing this book, we took great pains to overview a wide variety of types and sources of OPM and OPR. But more than that, it was our goal to spur strategic thinking and analysis. A great idea is only the beginning. Understanding how you can bring it to life by securing the necessary funds or resources takes research, planning, strategic thinking, and creativity.

The questions posed throughout this book were created and positioned not only to underscore the scope and variety of sources of OPM and OPR but to help emphasize how that strategic thinking, timing, positioning, marketing, and creativity can play key roles. There is strategy involved in choosing the right type of OPM or OPR, finding the right source, and securing the funds or resources necessary to turn an idea into a viable business. This book is intended to help you see how planning and pacing—in your search and negotiation for OPM—can enable you to own and control a greater interest in the business venture you created.

You are not limited by your own wherewithal. Don't say, "I can't afford it." Or "I can't afford to hire the best team of advisors." Or "I can't afford to patent my idea." Or "I can't afford to launch this company." Or "I can't afford to grow this company." Or "I can't afford to take my idea big-time." Say, instead, "How can I afford it?" This question opens our minds to possibilities and opportunities that our eyes don't see. And one—though a many-faceted—answer to "how" is by use of Other People's Money and Resources. Do you still think you have to be rich to make money? The answer is in this book. It's up to you. Now take action!!

Appendix

Exemptions from Registration Requirements

Exemption	(§3b) **Regulation D. Rule 504 b(1)** (Seed Capital Rule) Limited offerings ≤ $1 million
Conditions required	Disclosure documents delivered before sale to all nonaccredited investors
Permitted offerees	No restrictions
$ limit on the offering	Aggregate offering price not to exceed $1 million during the 12 months before the start of and during the offering
General solicitation or advertising?	NOT permitted
SEC filing requirements	Five copies of notice on Form D within 15 days of first sale (Rule 503 (a))
Restrictions on stock transfer	Restricted
Limitations on issuer	1. Not subject to reporting requirements under 1934 exchange act 2. Not investment company 3. Must have specific business plan or purpose (other than merger with unidentified companies) (no shelf registration) 4. Not the subject of action for failing to file Rule 503 notice of offering with SEC (not "Rule 507 bad boy")
State registration preemption	NO preemption—subject to state registration
Disclosure information requirements (nonreporting issuer)	Not specified (Rule 502(b)(1))

Exemption	(§3b) **Regulation D. Rule 504 b(1)(i) and (ii)**
	Limited offerings ≤$1 million
	State registration exemption
Conditions required	Duly registered in all (at least one) states where the security is sold that have registration and disclosure requirements; and disclosure documents are delivered before sale to all purchasers (in all states, irrespective of state requirements)
Permitted offerees	No restrictions
$ limit on the offering	Aggregate offering price not to exceed $1 million during the 12 months before the start of and during the offering
General solicitation or advertising?	Permitted
SEC filing requirements	Five copies of notice on Form D within 15 days of first sale (Rule 503 (a))
Restrictions on stock transfer	None
Limitations on issuer	1. Not subject to reporting requirements under 1934 exchange act
	2. Not investment company
	3. Must have specific business plan or purpose (other than merger with unidentified companies) (no shelf registration)
	4. Not the subject of action for failing to file Rule 503 notice of offering with SEC (not "Rule 507 bad boy")
State registration preemption	NO preemption—subject to state registration
Disclosure information requirements (nonreporting issuer)	Not specified (Rule 502(b)(1)) (except to the extent that compliance with state law disclosure requirements is required for the exemption)

Exemption	(§3b) **Regulation D. Rule 504 b(1)(iii)** (Seed Capital Rule) Limited offerings ≤ $1 million State exemption/accredited investors exemption
Conditions required	Qualifies for exemptions permitting general advertising in all states where sold
Permitted offerees	Accredited investors only
$ limit on the offering	Aggregate offering price not to exceed $1 million during the 12 months before the start of and during the offering
General solicitation or advertising?	Permitted
SEC filing requirements	Five copies of notice on Form D within 15 days of first sale (Rule 503 (a))
Restrictions on stock transfer	None
Limitations on issuer	1. Not subject to reporting requirements under 1934 exchange act 2. Not investment company 3. Must have specific business plan or purpose (other than merger with unidentified companies) (no shelf registration) 4. Not the subject of action for failing to file Rule 503 notice of offering with SEC (not "Rule 507 bad boy")
State registration preemption	NO preemption—subject to state registration
Disclosure information requirements (nonreporting issuer)	Not specified (Rule 502(b)(1)) (except to the extent that compliance with state law is required for the exemption)

Exemption	(§3b) **Regulation D. Rule 505** Limited offerings ≤ $5 million
Conditions required	Disclosure documents delivered before sale to all nonaccredited investors
Permitted offerees	Unlimited number of accredited investors plus 35 additional persons
$ limit on the offering	Aggregate offering price not to exceed $5 million during the 12 months before the start of and during the offering
General solicitation or advertising?	NOT permitted
SEC filing requirements	Five copies of notice on Form D within 15 days of first sale (Rule 503 (a)). Notice must include undertaking (agreement) to provide disclosure materials upon request (Rule 503 (c))
Restrictions on stock transfer	Restricted. May not be resold without registration or other exemption
Limitations on issuer	1. Not "Rule 507 bad boy" 2. Not investment company
State registration preemption	NO preemption—subject to state registration
Disclosure information requirements (nonreporting issuer)	Rule 502(b) *If any nonaccredited investor—* Same type of narrative information required by Form 1-A plus *For offerings up to $2 million*: GAAP financial statements (per Item 310 of Form S-B). At least the balance sheet must be audited *For offerings up to $5 million*: The financial statement information required in Form SB-2. At least balance sheet must be audited. LPs can provide financials on the basis of federal income tax returns prepared by CPA

Exemption	§4(2) Transactions Not Involving Any Public Offering
	Regulation D. Rule 506 Safe Harbor
Conditions required	Disclosure documents delivered before sale to all nonaccredited investors
Permitted offerees	Unlimited number of accredited investors plus 35 sophisticated investors
$ limit on the offering	No limit
General solicitation or advertising?	NOT permitted
SEC filing requirements	Five copies of notice on Form D within 15 days of first sale (Rule 503 (a))
Restrictions on stock transfer	Restricted. May not be resold without registration or other exemption
Limitations on issuer	Not "Rule 507 bad boy"
State registration preemption	State registration preempted (except notice filing substantially similar to SEC requirements—Form D) (§18(b)(4)(D))
Disclosure information requirements (nonreporting issuer)	Rule 502(b) *If any nonaccredited investor—* Same type of narrative information required by Form 1-A plus
	For offerings up to $2 million: GAAP financial statements (per Item 310 of Form S-B). At least the balance sheet must be audited
	For offerings up to $7.5 million: The financial statement information required in Form SB-2. At least balance sheet must be audited. LPs can provide financials on the basis of federal income tax returns prepared by CPA
	For offerings over $7.5 million: The financial statement as would be required in a registration statement filed under the act on the form that the issuer would be entitled to use. At least balance sheet must be audited. LPs can provide financials on the basis of federal income tax returns prepared by CPA

Exemption	(§3b) **Regulation A** (17 CFR §§230.251–263)
Conditions required	Offering circular (Rule 253) must be provided before sale
Permitted offerees	No restrictions
$ limit on the offering	$5 million (with no more than $1.5 million attributable to secondary sales) during the 12 months before the start of and during the offering
General solicitation or advertising?	Limited. Permitted as long as it states where to obtain offering circular and contains only specified information (name of issuer, title of security, amount of offering and per-unit price, general type of business, general character and location of business properties)
SEC filing requirements	7 copies of Form 1-A within 15 days of first sale (Rule 251d, 252). 7 copies of sales materials five days before use (Rule 256). Form 2-A to report sales and use of proceeds every six months (Rule 257)
Restrictions on stock transfer	None
Limitations on issuer	1. U.S. and Canadian entities only 2. Not investment company 3. Not "Rule 262 bad boy"
State registration preemption	NO preemption
Disclosure information requirements (nonreporting issuer)	Rule 253 Offering circular—narrative and financial information required by Form 1-A including GAAP financial statements (audited statements not required unless otherwise available)

Exemption	**§4(6) Accredited Investor Exception**
Conditions required	None specified
Permitted offerees	Any number, but accredited investors only
$ limit on the offering	$5 million
General solicitation or advertising?	NOT permitted
SEC filing requirements	Form D (17 CFR §239.500)
Restrictions on stock transfer	Restricted
Limitations on issuer	None
State registration preemption	NO preemption
Disclosure information requirements (nonreporting issuer)	Not specified

Exemption	**§3(a)(11) Intrastate Offerings Rule 147** Safe Harbor
Conditions required	All offers and sales within the single state (subject to six-month integration rule)
Permitted offerees	Only residents of the issuer's "home" state
$ limit on the offering	Unlimited
General solicitation or advertising?	Not prohibited. Any offers must disclose, in writing, the limitations on resale and precautions against interstate offers and sales
SEC filing requirements	None
Restrictions on stock transfer	No resales to nonresidents for a period of nine months from completion of offering (restrictive legend required); only isolated sales to nonresidents thereafter (Rule 147(e))
Limitations on issuer	Issuer is resident of and doing business within the state in which all offers and sales are made (at least 80 percent of gross revenues from state; at least 80 percent of assets in state; at least 80 percent of offering intended to be used in state; and if limited liability entity, incorporated or organized within the state or partnership or individual, principal office in state) (Rule 147(c)(2))
State registration preemption	NO preemption
Disclosure information requirements (nonreporting issuer)	Not specified. All offers must disclose in writing the restriction on resale (Rule 147(f)(3))

Exemption	**Regulation S Offerings** Outside the U.S. (17 CFR §§901–905)
Conditions required	Offshore transactions only, no directed selling in U.S.
Permitted offerees	Non-U.S. residents only
$ limit on the offering	Unlimited
General solicitation or advertising?	Not prohibited
SEC filing requirements	None
Restrictions on stock transfer	Cannot be resold into U.S. for at least one year. Restricted (Rule 144)
Limitations on issuer	None
State registration preemption	NO preemption
Disclosure information requirements (nonreporting issuer)	Not specified

About the Author

Michael Lechter, Esq. is an attorney specializing in intellectual property law since the early 1970s. A Rich Dad's Advisor, author of *Protecting Your #1 Asset* and now *Other People's Money*, Michael teaches people how to turn ideas into income-generating assets and build businesses on behalf of his clients.

Michael A. Lechter is Counsel to the international law firm of Squire, Sanders & Dempsey L.L.P., and serves as an Adjunct Professor at Arizona State University. He is a patent attorney who has been admitted to practice in a number of states as well as to the Patent Bar. He is an internationally known expert in the field of intellectual property. Representation includes everything from authors and publishers, to breweries and professional sports teams to major medical device manufacturers. When asked what he does for a living, he typically replies, "I build forts and fight pirates."

He has been the architect of strategies for building businesses using both conventional and creative non-conventional forms and sources of "Other People's" money and resources. His experience in representing venture capitalists in evaluating potential investment companies, in the role of an angel investor, and representing start-up and emerging businesses permits him to bring a unique perspective to the subject of building a business using Other People's Money.

Michael is also the author of *The Intellectual Property Handbook*, coordinating editor of *Successful Patents* and *Patenting for Engineers and Scientists*, contributing author to the *Encyclopedia Of Electrical And Electronics Engineering*, and *The LESI Guide to Licensing Best Practices* . He has lectured extensively throughout the world on intellectual property law. Upon request of the House Judiciary Committee he has submitted testimony to the Congress of the United States, and has participated in various United Nations and foreign government proceedings on intellectual property law and technology transfer. He is also a former trustee of the Licensing Executives Society USA/Canada, and a delegate for LES USA/Canada to Licensing Executives Society International.

You can contact Michael Lechter at info@mlechter.com.

Intellectual Property Tools

Building Forts & Fighting Pirates®

In today's business environment it is imperative not only to be financially literate, but also to be knowledgeable with respect to intellectual property. My book *Protecting Your #1 Asset* will alert you to the pitfalls that can strip you of your rights or create liabilities. *Intellectual Property Tools* provides an additional set of documentary tools to aid you in turning your ideas into assets, protecting your intellectual property, and avoiding liability to third parties.

Identify potential intellectual property assets in your business. To capitalize on an idea or development, you must first recognize that you have something worth protecting. The second step is to then identify precisely what it is about it (specific aspects and features) that makes it worth protecting - those aspects that are "unique," "better," "different," or distinctive. To do that, you must dissect and examine all aspects of your business processes, products and services from a number of different perspectives to determine the specific aspects that:

· differentiate your business from your competitors.
· attract customers to you instead of the competition.
· give you a competitive advantage.
· others would pay to be able to use.

This is sometimes easier said than done. *Intellectual Property Tools* includes an *Intellectual Property Self-Audit Checklist* to help you perform this analysis (as well as to check to make sure that you have the right types of agreements in place).

Retain rights in your IP when dealing with others. After identifying a potential IP asset, you must establish your rights to the idea. This means you must memorialize the idea and create evidence of the creative process; make sure that you actually own and retain the rights to the idea; and take the steps to apply the applicable legal protection mechanisms. Protecting your rights in intellectual property involves not only internal procedures, but also establishing - through written agreements - the appropriate legal relationships with both employees and third parties. Unless the proper agreements are in place, trade secret/confidential status can be lost, patent bar "clocks" can be started, and you may find that you do not own everything that you would think you do. (Just because you pay for something does not mean that you will own the rights to it). The *Intellectual Property Self-Audit Checklist* helps you identify the agreements that you should have in place to avoid those nasty surprises.

The preparation of agreements can, of course, entail considerable attorney's fees. While all agreements should be reviewed by competent counsel to ensure that the agreement covers your particular circumstances, *Intellectual Property Tools* provides a variety of invaluable sample agreements to establish confidentiality and/or ownership of intellectual property under a variety of circumstances typically encountered in business. The agreements are listed (and hyperlinks provided) in the Table of Contents. Basic development agreements, confidentiality agreements and work for hire agreements are a few examples of the agreements included in *Intellectual Property Tools*.

A word of caution regarding the way that you use these agreements: the documents in this product are intended to be references, NOT Legal Advice, and they may not apply to, or adequately address, your particular circumstances. Different fact situations call for different provisions in agreements and the law can vary from jurisdiction to jurisdiction. I am sure you can appreciate that the IP Tools are not intended to be a substitute for the advice of a good intellectual property attorney. Before you use any agreement you should consult with a competent intellectual property attorney to make sure that it is applicable to, and addresses all of, your specific circumstances and needs. Of course, by presenting your attorney a draft agreement for review you will typically be able to greatly reduce legal fees.

Reducing the cost of patent preparation. There is no question that the preparation of a patent application is expensive. The application (in effect, a proposed patent) typically must include a written description of the invention (with a coordinated drawing) with enough detail that the typical person working in the relevant area of technology can actually make and use the invention, as well as a set of "claims" that define the inventor's rights. There are two primary factors affecting the cost of preparing a patent application: the complexity of the invention (both from a legal and technological perspective), and the materials available to the patent attorney from which to prepare the application. The more complete and organized the materials provided to the attorney, the less time required to prepare the application, and hence reduced expense. The *Patent Disclosure Form* will help you collect and organize the information in a way that will facilitate preparation of a patent application. In addition to soliciting information regarding inventorship, dates and evidence of invention, potential statutory bars to patentability, and the prior art, the *Patent Disclosure Form* attempts to direct you through the description of your invention, collecting and presenting the information in a format that is readily usable by the attorney in preparing the application, -- and therefore tends to make preparation of the application less costly.

While the *Intellectual Property Tools* will not take the place of advice from good intellectual property counsel, they can be of great assistance to you with respect to your intellectual property. For more information about these and other tools visit my web site at www.mlechter.com. I wish you great success in your business.

Michael A. Lechter

Building Forts & Fighting Pirates® to Protect Your Ideas

Michael A. Lechter, P.C.
6611 N. 64th Place · Paradise Valley, Arizona 85253 · USA
Phone: 480.607.1940 · Fax: 480.607.1923

- Coming Soon -

New Tools Available For Building Your Business!

Visit www.mlechter.com periodically for updates and new tools to help you build your business. Tools that can give you an edge in building your business such as an electronic addendum to Other People's Money which includes more material and information on securities laws issues and franchising.

Franchising represents one of the most pervasive uses of Other People's Money and Resources. Franchising is one of the more popular, and can be one of the most successful, methods to jumpstart a business. One of the great benefits of franchising is that you are using OPM regardless of which side of the franchise coin you are on. Read why franchising is a great source of OPM.

We would not try to turn you into a securities attorney or broker overnight. The area of securities law is extremely complicated and full of landmines. However, if you are interested in learning more about some of the common problems and pitfalls in the field, such as how to recognize a security, whether or not the securities laws apply to your business transactions, the burdens and obligations imposed by the securities laws (and the requirements for exemptions from certain obligations), and the pros and cons of going public, I invite you to visit my web site:

www.mlechter.com

as well as the Rich Dad organization web site:

www.richdad.com

Michael A. Lechter

Robert Kiyosaki's Edumercial
An Educational Commercial

The Three Incomes

In the world of accounting, there are three different types of income: earned, passive, and portfolio. When my real dad said to me, "Go to school, get good grades, and find a safe secure job," he was recommending I work for earned income. When my rich dad said, "The rich don't work for money, they have their money work for them," he was talking about passive income and portfolio income. Passive income, in most cases, is derived from real estate investments. Portfolio income is income derived from paper assets, such as stocks, bonds, and mutual funds.

Rich Dad used to say, "The key to becoming wealthy is the ability to convert earned income into passive income and/or portfolio income as quickly as possible." He would say, "The taxes are highest on earned income. The least taxed income is passive income. That is another reason why you want your money working hard for you. The government taxes the income you work hard for - more than the income your money works hard for."

The Key to Financial Freedom

The key to financial freedom and great wealth is a person's ability or skill to convert earned income into passive income and/or portfolio income. That is the skill that my rich dad spent a lot of time teaching Mike and me. Having that skill is the reason my wife Kim and I are financially free, never needing to work again. We continue to work because we choose to. Today we own a real estate investment company for passive income and participate in private placements and initial public offerings of stock for portfolio income.

Investing to become rich requires a different set of personal skills – skills essential for financial success as well as low-risk and high-investment returns. In other words, knowing how to create assets that buy other assets. The problem is that gaining the basic education and experience required is often time consuming, frightening, and expensive, especially when you make mistakes with your own money. That is why I created the patented educational board games trademarked as CASHFLOW®.

THE NEW YORK TIMES

writes:

"Move over, Monopoly®...
A new board game that
aims to teach people how
to get rich is gaining fans
the world over!"

MONOPOLY® is a trademark of Hasbro, Inc.

WHY PLAY GAMES?

Games are **powerful learning tools** because they enable people to experience 'hands-on' learning. As a **true reflection of behavior**, games are a **window to our attitudes**, our **abilities to see opportunities**, and **assess risk and rewards**.

Each of the CASHFLOW® games creates a forum in which to evaluate life decisions regarding money and finances and immediately see the results of your decisions.

Play often and learn what it takes to get out of the Rat Race- for good!

For more information go to:
www.richdad.com

TIRED OF THE SAME OLD FINANCIAL ADVICE?

Tired of hearing... "work hard, live frugally, cut up your credit cards, and get out of debt?"

READY TO HEAR WHY AND HOW THE RICH ARE GETTING RICHER?

The Rich Dad book series explains WHY and HOW in easy-to-understand terms so you can focus on and understand the keys to creating wealth and investment strategies of the rich. Each book will convey messages of hope and empowerment, enabling you to take control of your financial future.

"Never before has a single author or series of books – like Rich Dad – so dominated the best sellers lists. It's a feat unprecedented in the publishing arena."

- Larry Kirshbaum, Chairman *Time Warner Book Group*

YOU DON'T HAVE TO BE AN 'A' STUDENT...

BUT IT PAYS TO HAVE 'A' STUDENTS ON YOUR TEAM OF FINANCIAL ADVISORS

Rich Dad's Advisors are the 'A' students that advise Robert and his team - and who have played a key role in the Rich Dad success story.

Rich Dad's Advisors book series covers every key aspect of business and investing - from legal entities and intellectual property protection, accounting and tax strategies, sales and leadership skills to real estate investing and property management and investing in all asset classes.

RichKidSmartKid.com

Money is a life skill---but we don't teach our children about money in school. I am asking for your help in getting financial education into the hands of interested teachers and school administrators.

RichKidSmartKid.com was created as an innovative and interactive Web site designed to convey key concepts about money and finance in ways that are fun and challenging...and educational for young people in grades K through 12. It contains 4 mini-games that teach:

Assets vs. Liabilities
Good Debt vs. Bad Debt
Importance of Charity
Passive Income vs. Earned Income

AND, schools may also register at **www.richkidsmartkid.com** to receive a FREE download of our electronic version of CASHFLOW for Kids at School.

How You Can Make a Difference

Play CASHFLOW® for KIDS and CASHFLOW 101 with family and friends and share the richkidsmartkid.com Web site with your local teachers and school administrators.

Join me now in taking financial education to our schools and e-mail me of your interest at Iwill@richdad.com. Together we can better prepare our children for the financial world they will face.

Thank you!

DISCOVER THE POWER OF THESE RICH DAD PROGRAMS:

• *Rich Dad's You Can Choose to Be Rich*
• *Rich Dad's 6 Steps to Becoming a Successful Real Estate Investor*
• *Rich Dad's How to Increase the Income from Your Real Estate Investments*

Step-by-step guides with audio components and comprehensive workbooks ensure that you can take the knowledge you gain and apply it to increasing the value and profitability of your investment portfolio.

ARE YOU WINNING OR LOSING THE GAME OF MONEY?